[See p. 78

A MEMBER OF A GIRLS' GARDEN CLUB

THE WORK OF
THE RURAL SCHOOL

BY

J. D. EGGLESTON

PRESIDENT OF THE VIRGINIA POLY-
TECHNIC INSTITUTE, FORMERLY CHIEF
OF FIELD SERVICE IN RURAL EDUCA-
TION, U. S. BUREAU OF EDUCATION
AND STATE SUPERINTENDENT OF
PUBLIC INSTRUCTION IN VIRGINIA

AND

ROBERT W. BRUÈRE

ILLUSTRATED

HARPER & BROTHERS PUBLISHERS
NEW YORK AND LONDON
MCMXIII

I–N

TO
THE MEMORY OF
FRANCIS W. PARKER
AND
SEAMAN A. KNAPP
AND
TO
HOLLIS B. FRISSELL

CONTENTS

CONTENTS

CONTENTS

CHAPTER VIII

CONTENTS

ILLUSTRATIONS

THE WORK OF THE RURAL SCHOOL

THE WORK OF THE
RURAL SCHOOL

I

INTRODUCTION

DURING the past ten years the rural-school system of the United States has been in a condition of unprecedented ferment. Experiments looking to the fundamental reorganization of the rural-school program have been under way in practically all of the states. Modern school-buildings are springing up everywhere, transportation wagons by the thousands have been put in motion, and country roads are beginning to be improved to accommodate them. Normal schools, colleges and universities, educational associations, the United States Department of Agriculture, and the public press have been manifesting a fresh interest in the education of country children and the social and economic rehabilitation of rural communities. In 1912 a new division was created in the United States Bureau of Education for the specific purpose of advancing the interests of the rural school and country life. For the first time since our pioneer days, when the nation was predominantly agricultural and the little red schoolhouse was the favorite symbol of the democratic American spirit, the whole nation is turning with interested concern and constructive purpose to the rural school.

To what is this freshly awakened interest due? For an answer one must look to the facts of our agricultural development during the first decade of the twentieth century.

In the *Quarterly Journal of Economics* for November, 1912, Mr. J. L. Coulter, of the United States Bureau of the Census, epitomizes the findings of the Division of Agriculture of the Census of 1910. The census shows that during the ten years from 1899 to 1909 agricultural production in the United States increased only 10 per cent. as compared with the preceding decade, while the population—the number of mouths to be fed—increased 21 per cent! And this failure of the food-supply to keep pace with the population was most serious in those staples upon which the elemental life of the nation most directly depends. To meet an increase of 21 per cent. in the population the aggregate production of wheat increased only 3.8 per cent., of orchard fruits only 1.8 per cent., while the production of corn actually decreased 4.3 per cent. The facts here brought to light make it plain that it is the menace of hunger that is turning the nation to the rural school as the only instrument capable of averting wide-spread disaster.

"We have now reached a stage in the history of this country," says Mr. Coulter, "when farmers in average years do not produce much more of the raw materials used for food, forage, and clothing than is needed within the country. *In poor years the production may not in future equal the demands of the consumers.*"

Here we have one of the important causes of the increased cost of living, of the grinding economic pressure that during recent years has perplexed the spirit of the nation and hampered the free onward motion of our national progress. When the farmers stop producing an abundant surplus our growing millions face not only lowered standards of living, but in many cases actual want and starvation. When the harvests cease to be abundant the fires of our national life in country and city alike begin to burn low, the productive powers of the nation are checked—the entire economic and social organism suffers a kind of paralysis.

Confronted by this danger, the nation is turning to the rural school because, owing to the changes wrought by the last century in our economic and social life, and more especially in the economic and social conditions surrounding agricultural production, the rural school more than any other one instrument to-day controls the food-supply of the nation.

Not since the days when the one-room school followed the pioneer into the wilderness and through literacy kept open the channels of civilization, has so great a responsibility rested upon the rural school; never before have the workers in rural education faced such momentous opportunities for patriotic service.

And everywhere the rural-school workers are earnestly striving to meet this national crisis. The practical measures which they are adopting point in two principal directions, the one toward increased production through the diffusion of scientific knowledge, the other toward the socialization of rural life, in order that through economic coöperation and the development of a new social conscience the benefits of increased production may accrue not only to the nation at large, but to the local communities and the homes of the individual producers.

The need for development in both of these directions is revealed by the most cursory review of the history of agricultural lands and the evolution of social ideals in our rural communities.

There used to be a song, very popular in the days when the universal cry was "Go West, young man, go West," the burden of which, recurring at the end of every verse, was, "For Uncle Sam is rich enough to give us each a farm." At the time this pleasant family affluence did really exist in America. Uncle Sam did give us farms, hundreds and thousands of us, so that it is difficult for us to get out of our minds the fact that the days of his prodigality are over. But, alas, they are! The records of the Bureau of the Census show that "the area available for agricultural purposes was very largely occupied between 1800 and 1900." The essential meaning of this fact from the national point of view is that the future development of agricultural production must come through the application of science and modern methods of business management to the land already occupied. The apprentice system, the handing down of tradition from father to son, is inadequate to the new needs of agriculture as it has long since proved inadequate to the needs of large-scale machine production. The only effective way in which the rapidly growing science of cultivation, farm management, and marketing can be brought to bear upon agriculture is through the public school.

But the crudeness of inherited agricultural methods is not alone responsible for the failure of agricultural production to keep pace with our growth in population and our advancing standards of living. An equally important factor has been the lack of social ideals in rural life which has had a demoralizing effect upon the uses to which agricultural lands have been put. The mere increase in agricultural production will not solve the rural-life problem unless at the same time the workers in rural education can cure what a country clergyman has called "the tuberculosis of American farm life—individualism."

The spiritual evolution of the American country community has recently been traced in a delightful and scholarly book by Dr. Warren H. Wilson, Superintendent of the Department of Church and Country Life of the

INTRODUCTION

Presbyterian Board of Home Missions. Dr. Wilson divides the history of the American country community into four periods—the periods of the Pioneer, the Land Farmer, the Exploiter, and the Husbandman.

The Pioneer was a free-lance adventurer. He hunted and tanned, cleared the forest, plowed, harvested, and ground his grain—*alone*. "He placed his cabin without regard to social experience," for he had no social experience to regard. His conception of democracy was a state in which every man was free to go his own way without reference to the ways of other men. His ideals were ideals of stark self-reliance and a jealous primitive independence. "Self-preservation was the struggle of his life." He was a man without books, often without schools, usually without a consciousness of social obligation. By choice, he lived and died alone.

"The Land Farmer was the typical American countryman, who succeeded the Pioneer." He lived in a time of crude abundance. He swarmed across the country "seeking everywhere the first values of a virgin land." His thought for generations has been "to make his own farm prosperous, to raise some crop that others shall not raise, to have a harvest that other men have not, and to find a market that other men have not discovered, by which he and his farm and his family group may prosper. The Land Farmer has no idea of community prosperity."

The Exploiter is peculiarly the product of the last twenty years. He is the man who gets his money, not by tilling the soil, but by speculating in land. He is the ultimate product of that crass individualism which is "the tuberculosis of American farm life."

"The sign of exploitation is a rapid increase in the market value of farm lands, independent of any increase in essential value to the farmer, due to frequent sale and purchase." In his *Agrarian Changes in the Middle West*

Mr. J. B. Ross tells us that "farms which from the original entry until 1890 had been owned by one family, or which had changed owners but once or twice, and whose owners were proud to assert that their broad acres had never been encumbered with mortgages, since 1890 have been sold as often as ten times, in more numerous cases four or five times, and a large part of the purchase price is secured by encumbering the estates."

This exploitation of land is extending all over the country. In the Gulf States and the Carolinas, in Tennessee and Kentucky, prices of farm land have increased in the last five years from 25 to 100 per cent. "Even in the most conservative centers of Pennsylvania the prices of farm land have increased in the same period from 20 to 25 per cent." Everywhere the increase in the market value of farm lands is largely independent of the increase in essential value to the farmer. In Indiana a net increase of 5 per cent. in the farmers' income had been attended by an increase in land values of more than 100 per cent.

This rise in the market price of land no doubt received its first impulse from the preëmption of our free lands; but the Exploiter, taking advantage of normally rising values, has "bulled" the market, until the buying and selling of land has taken on an unwholesome speculative character. Men buy land, not to cultivate it in the interest of the community, but to sell it for an unearned profit.

What are the results of this exploitation from the point of view of rural life and national economy? They are expressed in the terms "absentee-landlordism" and tenant farming. Surveys made by the experts of the Presbyterian Board show that in an area covering 1,764 square miles of the best farm lands of Illinois 53 per cent. of the farmers are tenants, and similar surveys in Missouri show that "in many parts of this state more than half of the farmers are renters." These are typical examples of a national tendency whose gravity is indicated by the fact that the farm lease throughout the United States generally is for one year only. The owner wishes to be free to sell on a rising market. Consequently the tenant takes as much out of the land as possible and puts as little as possible back into its permanent improvement. Dean Charles F. Curtiss, of the State College of Iowa, declares that "the American system of farm tenantry is the worst of which I have knowledge in any country."

All these facts mean that vast tracts of land are being held out of cultivation, and that other vast tracts are being undercultivated and "skinned." The census of 1900 showed that 49.4 per cent., or slightly less than one-half of all the land in farms in the United States, was improved. In spite of the rise in the market value of farm products, which during the last census period amounted on the average to 66.6 per cent., the improved lands in 1910 had risen to only 54.4 per cent. of the total available for agricultural purposes. At a time when the nation's need of food is acute land is being held out of use for purely speculative purposes.

Now, ethically and spiritually considered, the salient characteristic of the Exploiter, as of the Pioneer and the Land Farmer, is the crass individualism that distinguished the *laissez faire* period of our political economy. The good of that economy has been accomplished. It rediscovered the world, opened up new continents, vastly increased the world's aggregate wealth, produced railroads, telegraph and telephone systems, created new standards of living and new desires and wants that have become new necessities. But to-day we face the evils of that economy—the concentration of wealth and power in too few hands, the pressure of high prices upon the mass of the people, a too rapidly declining birth-rate, the spread of poverty in country and city alike. And it is these evils that the rural-school workers are striving to meet through the development of a new spirit, a new vision, in rural communities.

The expression of this new vision—this new social conscience—on the economic side is *coöperation;* on the social side, the *new neighborliness*. It is this social conscience that has given the rural-school workers their new slogan, "We must hitch education up with life!" with which they are leading us into the period of the Husbandman—the man who is wedded to the soil, who is master of the science of agriculture, and who has the wisdom to see that his own best advantage and that of his household is ultimately wrapped up in the best advantage of the community and the nation. To the husbandman scientific agriculture is not scientific production only, but scientific business methods in the management of his farm and in the marketing of his crops. And the impulse toward economic coöperation, as toward the larger social life which is the new neighborliness, he is deriving principally from the men and women who are putting new life and new purpose into rural education.

For in spite of all the thoughtless criticism that has been visited upon our public schools the workers in public education have not been heedless to the new demands of the times. Considering the baffling speed with which the kaleidoscope of our modern life has rearranged the constituent parts of our social and economic organization, the schools have accomplished results in the adjustment of education to contemporary needs that call for unstinted praise. This is not to say, of course, that the schools have done all that they could or should. No teacher or principal or superintendent with living and growing ideals would claim that. But the extended use of the school plant in our cities and the far-reaching experiments in health conservation and vocational training show that the city schools have not been idle. And in the country the progress in the development and reorganiza-

8

tion of public education promises to bring about a complete and most satisfactory revolution. The vitalizing of elementary instruction, the multiplication of consolidated schools, the extension of demonstration work into the every-day life of boys and girls, men and women, the drawing together of all the forces of constructive righteousness into community associations for the promotion of the general welfare, are inspiring signs that the workers in our rural schools have not been sleeping, that they have eyes for their momentous opportunities, and spirits resolute to bear the new responsibilities our changing generation has laid upon them.

Already, in fact, the outlines of a reorganized rural-school system can be traced in the successful experiments that have been conducted in all corners of the United States. This book is an attempt to trace these outlines. The materials out of which it is built have been collected in the course of years from the experience and through the courtesy of hundreds of rural-school workers. It is a record of achievements and the statement of a program for future work based upon these achievements. No attempt has been made to give a comprehensive review of all that has been done. There is no better proof of the vitality of the new rural-school movement than the fact that statistics of achievement which are correct to-day are incorrect, because incomplete, to-morrow. Typical instances alone have been cited. But no statement is made that is not based upon proved experience. It is our hope that what we have set down here will serve as a bond of coöperation and helpfulness among the scattered thousands in the rural schools who are striving to relate their special local problems to the larger national movement that is receiving its impulse from the changing heart of the nation.

II

THE promise of our generation is in the growing faith that human life is sacred, and that the waste of life or of the things from which it draws its sustenance is the great transgression. For the first time in history we are beginning to see that this earth is not a dismal accident, that human life is not transitory. As science broadens our vision we begin to see that human life is the material God has given us to build a world with, that the civilization that each morning springs anew from the labor of our myriad hands is an integral part of the eternal process, that individually and collectively we who serve one another on farm and in factory, in the school and the varied activities of civic life, are co-workers with God in His creative purposes. Our business, we begin to understand, is not our individual salvation only, but the conservation and wise use of all life, the development through mutual aid of its worth and strength and beauty.

The opportunity of the rural school in the building of our civilization is summed up in the fact that it, more than any other one instrument, controls the food-supply of the nation—the foundation of our spiritual as well as of our physical life. From the point of view of the nation the work of the public school is to get a maximum product in efficient citizenship out of the community to which it is assigned, and the distinguishing mark of efficient citizenship in the rural community is skill in the production of food. From the point of view of the local community by which the individual school is maintained the work of the school is to organize the community life, to inspire it with national and social ideals, to increase its social and economic well-being, and to bring to the community the benefits of modern invention, the most recent achievements in science and art. From the point of view of the children the work of the school is to conserve their health, to lead them into an understanding of civilization, and so to train their faculties that they may advance their individual welfare through efficient work in the service of their homes, their community, and the nation. From whichever of these points of view the rural school approaches its problem, it cannot succeed without a thorough knowledge of the local community, its resources and possibilities, its deficiencies and needs. The foundation of an effective school program must be a community survey.

In the early days, when the work of the public school was confined to the three R's, when the actual education of the children, their real preparation for life, went on in the field, the threshing-room, the barn, the workshop, and the kitchen, all that was needed was an itinerant pedagogue, or a building where the children could be housed during certain hours of the day, with a teacher capable of giving them their letters and a modicum of geography and arithmetic. But all this has been changed by the industrial revolution that has dragged agriculture into the world economy and undermined the apprentice system. The isolated homes no longer give the children an adequate preparation for life. This task has been shifted to the school, and if the school is to meet the new needs of to-day even as well as the apprentice system met the old needs of an earlier generation it must understand the opportunities and problems of each individual home and of all the homes together in their community relationships.

Six years ago a young man was put in charge of a

country district in which there were three rural schools of the traditional cheese-box type. The community was a typical farming community. In spite of rich soils the value of agricultural production was not increasing so rapidly as the market value of land. Land speculation was rife, and tenant-farming was growing. In spite of the wealth of a certain number of individuals farm life had fallen into disrepute. Year by year an increasing number of the rising generation abandoned their ancestral farms for city life, selling outright or leasing their lands for short terms to immigrants. The social and spiritual life of the community was listless and anemic.

The problem that confronted this young man was precisely the problem which, in one form or another, confronts rural-school workers everywhere in the nation to-day. If he was to hold the children on the land he must make rural life economically, socially, and spiritually attractive to them. To make rural life attractive he must increase the general wealth of the community, and in order to increase the community's general wealth he must train the farmers and their children in modern methods of agriculture and business management, and in the principles of coöperative marketing—through the school.

How he solved his problem is recorded in a letter to a friend, which, because of its very informality, its straight-forward candor, its freedom from self-consciousness, has an illustrative value superior to that of the usually stilted official report.

X— [he wrote] is in the trucking section of the Atlantic seaboard. Its people must market their crops in two weeks' time because they supply the market between South Carolina and New Jersey. If they are too early they cause an over-supply at the Carolina time; if too late, at the New Jersey time.

Being in this fix, they feel they must force their crops and raise always from two to three crops a year. They, therefore, use immense quantities of commercial fertilizer. They regard their soil as a *place to transform commercial fertilizer into perishable produce*, and not as a source in itself of food elements. Their close cultivation destroys humus in the soil, lowers its water-holding capacity, destroys helpful organic life, fosters insect pests, and, in the absence of crop rotation, poisons their land even against their single crop.

Being "truck mad," they neglect general agricultural necessities such as corn for their stock or hay for their horses and mules, or hogs to feed their families. They import from one-third to one-half of their corn and hay from the West, two-thirds of their hog meat and lard from the packers, get seven-eighths of their milk from cans, four-fifths of their butter and all their cheese from the creameries.

Another thing: Our truckers are the greatest gamblers in the state. They depend too much on chance, the weather, an undersized measure, and the honesty of commission men. Take the small trucker, Mr. B. L. D.: a fair year means that he has sold during the year $17,500 worth of produce. But—

His fertilizer bill is	$ 6,000
His labor bill is	3,750
His packing bill is	3,450
His freight (railroad and water) bill is . . .	2,600
His commission bill is	1,700
Total	$17,500

What has he made? And in all probability he has been extravagant and gone in debt because handling so great a sum of money without proper bookkeeping has given him a false sense of financial security. There are dozens of his kind.

This, in part, was this young man's diagnosis of the unhealthy social and economic life of the community as the result of which the schools were down at the heel, the churches were without inspiration and influence, the boys and girls were emigrating as fast as they could. On the basis of this partial economic survey he sketched a community program which in turn determined the pro-gram of his public school:

THE WORK OF THE RURAL SCHOOL

So far, we of the school [he wrote] have attempted to interest our patrons in the following program:

1. A larger crop of corn, insisting upon the selection of proper seed and the adoption of shallow cultivation, and discarding the practice of cutting fodder and tops.

2. A larger hay crop by means of demonstration work.

3. The substitution of seed-potatoes grown in the mountains of our own state for imported potatoes, thus cheapening the cost of transportation and getting a seed more free from disease.

4. More green manure crops—after early potatoes, between corn rows, in strawberry patches and asparagus beds.

5. Introduction of cow-peas and soja beans (rare as diamonds in former times).

6. More hogs and better hogs. Securing at reasonable prices for our farmers pure-bred stock—Duroc Jersey, Berkshire, and Poland China.

7. More sheep. Inducing farmers to grow a few for wool, etc.

8 Securing earlier and more prolific varieties of cotton, so that this crop may mature earlier here, be more profitable and more available as a staple crop.

9. Starting, or rather arousing, interest in a farmers' coöperative company that will sell the perishable produce in this community directly to the large markets of the country instead of having the producers entirely at the mercy of the commission men whose honesty is the substance of things hoped for, the evidence of things not seen.

This company is to control the grading and packing of the stuff, the placing of it in market, and the fertilizer question.

10. The establishment of a thorough, practical county school of cooking, sewing, and economy for the girls. Why should not the girls use the favorite, long-treasured special recipes of mothers and grandmothers to make *for profit* wholesome, good, toothsome, appetizing, pure preserves for marketing in town to poor city people who now have to use canned stuff? Thus the girls will all know the special recipes of each family, know how to cook these things, and be the better home-makers, besides making money from their work.

We want to keep the boys and girls in the country and make them better farmers and farmers' wives than are their parents.

We want to have the parents learn from the children. We want to make every boy and girl within the reach of our influence a contributing influence to the community and the state.

But what have all these facts to do with the education of the children, which is, after all, the principal business of the public school? The answer is that without a community program based upon the facts of community life it would have been impossible so to reorganize the school program as to give the children a preparation for life, the lack of which was causing them to abandon their country homes as quickly as possible. This school-worker realized that an effective school program can be developed to-day only as an integral part of the community program, and that the efficient education of the children is contingent upon the organization and development of the entire community life. When he began his work a few of the farmers in his district were enjoying gamblers' profits; a few more were managing to make both ends meet; the majority were suffering the evil consequences of tradition-bound and unscientific agricultural and business methods. Because the majority were not prosperous there was no enthusiasm for a higher tax rate, no enthusiasm for better roads, no interest in spending money upon a school system that was not improving the conditions of life in the community. In order to win public support for the schools it was necessary to make the school serve the practical needs of the community; and how could this be done without a first-hand knowledge of the social and economic condition of the community as a whole and of the individual homes within its boundaries?

Sir Horace Plunkett, who has done so much for the regeneration of rural life in Ireland, says in his recent book, *The Rural Life Problem in the United States*, that in the organization of country life it is necessary to go into the very heart of the people's every-day experience. This wisdom was the inspiration of the rural-school worker whose community survey we are considering. Having surveyed his community, he approached his task of reorganization through the every-day experiences of his pupils.

Harold Calhoun came to the school, was induced to join the corn club, developed an unsuspected hankering for farming, borrowed two acres of land from his father, planted corn and potatoes, and by following proper methods of cultivation not only made the best potato crop ever grown on that farm, but increased the yield of corn per acre by one-half over his father's yield. The father got interested and has gone into partnership with his son. It had been Harold's idea to go to town and get a job with the street-car company. He now has hopes of helping his father lift the mortgage, and says he will live and die a farmer. He has a sensible father.

Patrick Fox wanted to enter the corn contest. Patrick's people were kind of down on the school, and Patrick senior considered himself the originator of the popular axiom that a "nigger and a mule can teach more agriculture than all the schools in the world," and was obnoxiously frank about it. So was the school. Our domestic-science teacher went to board at Patrick's home. She got a hearing for the work, and induced the father to give the boy one acre and the chance. Patrick won the first prize for the best ten ears and also for the best single ear. If he had been elected President his father couldn't be more proud!

Mrs. Raleigh Blake, the minister's wife, did not like domestic science. Make housemaids and cooks of her daughters! In fact, she and her girls and her girls' friends were belligerent in their outspoken opposition. We had to kidnap Mildred Blake off the public road and bring her to class one day. Mildred decided she would *not* study domestic science. The school decided otherwise! Finally her interest warmed; from motives of pride she entered for a prize at the school fair. Her blood was up. She won! To-day it would take more than all the king's men to drive her from the school.

The energy required to adjust this school program to the community life sometimes found violent expression before it was effective. But it was effective! At the end of five years a fresh survey of the community showed these facts:

The school has increased the production of corn in this locality by one-half, not only as a separate crop, but as a follow crop. Alfalfa has been profitably grown for the first time. Early maturing varieties of cotton have been introduced. We have shown to the satisfaction of our farmers that home-grown seed-potatoes are equal to the best imported. Through the help of the boys methods of truck-farming have been revolutionized. The school is frequently asked to give advice in regard to crop rotation, fruit-tree pruning, selection of pure seeds, preparation of seed-beds, method of cultivation, selection of plant-foods, pure-bred swine and farm animals proper for this locality.

The inoculation of hogs last year by a member of the school staff saved thousands of dollars to our farmers.

A number of the farmers have united with the school in buying fertilizer.

A coöperative farmers' exchange is now in operation.

The boys of this community have been organized into corn and trucking clubs, the girls into garden, canning, and poultry clubs.

The school has become a social center, and the anemia of the community's spiritual life is finding a rapid and permanent cure. The people are happy and prosperous. The cityward emigration has been checked.

Such work cannot be done without infinite tact, patience, enthusiasm, and understanding—an understanding which cannot be acquired without the help of a community survey. But once the school has won public confidence by a single practical service, the community will follow its leadership in many things. The three scattered schools in this community have been brought together into a thoroughly modern consolidated school. The school is the center of a health campaign which, on the basis of a sanitary survey, is reorganizing health conditions throughout the community. It is helping to introduce labor-saving devices for the women in the homes as well as improved machinery for the use of the men in the fields. By a card system of home record it is giving school credit for work done by the children at home and certified by the parents. Its agricultural director, acting as a demonstration agent for the United States Department of Agriculture, organizes the boys into corn and potato and trucking clubs, follows them to their homes and continues their education by instructing and guiding them in their every-day work. The head of its department of domestic science takes the same course with the girls. She follows them into their homes and gardens and coöperates with them and their mothers in working out their problems of domestic economy and household management. Through extension and demonstration work *the school has dovetailed the school program into the community program;* it has made itself the dynamic center of the community's entire social and economic life.

Now, what is remarkable about all this? First, its unusual common sense, its recognition of the fact that the children cannot be prepared for life in general, but must be prepared for the specific life of their particular environment; second, its fearless recognition of the fact that economic prosperity is at the basis of any healthy civilization, that a vigorous spiritual life cannot flourish in a community where any considerable number of individuals is starved and brutalized by physical destitution; and, third, its clear perception of the fact that the education of the children cannot be separated from the development of the community to which the children belong, just as the development of the community itself cannot be separated from the development of the state and nation.

Judging from the progress rural-school workers in all sections of the country have made in "hitching education up with life," surveys similar to the one here recorded must be far from uncommon. But in spite of their obviously fundamental importance to the formulation of intelligent and effective rural-school programs, they have remained practically unknown to educational literature. No doubt the men and women who have made them are too busy with the every-day task of reorganizing their schools and putting the findings of their surveys into practice to take time to write, and too modest to realize the importance of sharing their experience with their fellow-workers. The survey upon which this discussion is based—in many respects the best we have been able to find—came into our possession as a by-product of friendly discussion and private correspondence.

Among the best published examples of rural-community surveys made with specific reference to the formulation of community programs involving all phases of community life are those issued during the past three years by the Department of Church and Country Life of the Board of Home Missions of the Presbyterian Church in the United States. These surveys are particularly valuable because the problems of the rural church, upon which they are designed to throw light, have proved to be identical with the problems confronting the rural school, and because the solution of the problems they define concerns the rural school even more directly than it does the country church. "The first condition which affects the country churches," says Dr. Warren H. Wilson, under whose supervision the surveys were made, "is the change in the way the people in the country get their livelihood. So that the country churches, for their own salvation, need to preach the gospel of better farming." This is unquestionably true, and the recognition of this fact heralds a new day of inspiring service for the country church. But it is obvious that in a nation where the school is a public institution and the church is not, the work of improving agriculture, of rehabilitating country life and charging it with new ideals of social and patriotic service must be done principally by the public school. The country church will do its most effective work by seconding the rural school in its brave effort to meet the momentous responsibilities which the nation has laid upon it.

In scope and method these surveys of the Department of Church and Country Life of the Presbyterian Church are models for the men and women who have consecrated their lives to the development of the rural community through the rural school. Although they are primarily concerned with the future of the country church as the spiritual leader of the country community, they invariably begin with a study of economic conditions—acreage, crops, land values, ownership, and tenantry—and proceed from these economic conditions to the educational and religious conditions, the recreational activities of the people, and the existing provisions for recreation and social enjoyment. The facts they reveal, when contrasted with the prevailing popular opinions and impressions about the typical rural community in America, make it clear that the rural community is either a forgotten or a hitherto undiscovered country.

The survey in Illinois, for example, covered 1,764 square miles. It considered the *economic*, *sociological*, *educational*, and *religious* conditions of the communities in the given order. Among the noteworthy facts brought to light by the *economic* survey are such as these:

The average area of each of the forty-four communities surveyed is fifty-four square miles. The farm land in central Illinois, in the "corn belt" of the world, is for the most part a rich black loam. It is level prairie, except for a little way along the streams, where there is some rough land given over to forests and pastures. In only twelve of the communities is coal mined, either privately or by companies. The chief products of this region are corn, oats, hay, and wheat, in the order given. The average corn crop for last year was forty bushels per acre, or a little above the average for the state. The average size of farms is one hundred and forty-three acres, about the average for the entire United States. The smallest farms are of forty acres and the largest six hundred acres. In one-half the communities the tendency for the last ten years has been to enlarge the farms, while in about one-fifth of the communities the tendency seems to be to break up the farms into smaller ones. The very best of machinery is used on the farms, and the most modern, but in 20 per cent. of the communities it is poorly cared for.

There is no more than the beginning of improved scientific farming in this region. . . .

Sixty-three per cent. of the communities report a loss in fertility of the soil, all the way from 10 per cent. to "rapidly going down." *Only 23 per cent. of the places report an increase in production. . . .*

The greatest change in this region is in the status of the men who run the farms. Only a few years ago this region was entirely farmed by the owners themselves, but within the past few years many of the owners have moved to the cities and towns or sold their farms to speculators and large land-owners, until now *53 per cent. of the farms are run by tenants, and only 47 per cent. by the owners themselves. . . .*

In 58 per cent. of the communities there is absolutely nothing in the way of recreational life. . . . The places where people meet, in order of preference, are stores, restaurants, pool-rooms, saloons, elevators, and barber shops. . . .

In these forty-four communities there are two hundred and twenty-five churches of twenty denominations, only seventy-seven of which have grown any in the past ten years, forty-five are at a standstill, fifty-six have lost in membership, while forty-seven have been abandoned in the last ten years. . . .

The rural-school buildings are for the most part old and out of date, one-room, low ceilings, dingy and dark.

These facts are typical of the facts brought to light by the rural surveys in Indiana, Kentucky, Pennsylvania, Tennessee, Maryland, and Missouri. There is sufficient evidence to show that they are typical of rural conditions throughout the United States. Everywhere the condition of the country church, like that of the rural school, is found to be the counterpart and reflex of the economic and social conditions of the rural community; the progress of the rural school, like the salvation of the country church, is inseparably involved in the economic and social rehabilitation of rural-community life.

But how can this rehabilitation be effected in communities where no one knows what the actual facts are?

Before a school program is drafted, and where possible before the site is chosen, before the building or buildings are erected, before the school-plant is equipped, the school authorities should make a community survey to find out what the prevailing aspirations of the community are, to discover its economic and social resources and possibilities, its deficiencies and needs. Upon the facts brought to light by the survey, an economic and social program for the entire community should be based, and the school program must be developed as the central part of the community program.

No rigid rules can be laid down as to the manner in which a survey should be made. There will be as many different sets of conditions as there are communities. But whether the leading activity of the community is truck-farming, or fruit-growing, or the raising of corn or wheat or cattle or dairy products, the underlying purpose of the survey remains the same. Whatever the distinctive business of the community may be, it is the business of the teacher and the principal and the superintendent to understand that business and all the related factors that make for or against community happiness and prosperity. The extent of the general and school population, the sanitary conditions in the individual homes and the district, the prevailing methods of home and farm management, the facilities for intercommunication—roads, telephones, mail service, and the like—the ownership of the land, the extent of tenant-farming; in short, all the facts that have a vital bearing upon the community life are essential to the adjustment of the work of the school to the economic and spiritual needs of the community. Without such knowledge it is impossible to "hitch education up with life." And this remains true, let us repeat, whether the school is situated in the trucking section, or the corn belt, or in the states that specialize in fruits, or dairying, or cattle, or cotton, or wheat; it is as true of the economically prosperous as of the economically backward regions.

The first object of a community survey is to familiarize the school-workers with the way in which the people in their communities get their living and the conditions under which they live. Without this knowledge it must remain impossible to build the school program out of the activities of the community—impossible to "hitch education up with life." But of almost equal importance to the school is a survey of the recreations of the people and of the facilities for recreation. It is a common error to suppose that because country folk live close to nature they do not need the provisions for systematic recreation that are universally recognized as essential to the physical and moral well-being of city people. A survey of fifty-three rural communities in Pennsylvania, made by the agents of the Presbyterian Board, makes it very clear that country folk are not content with the poetic companionship of birds and flowers, green pastures and running streams. Like all healthy and civilized human beings, they crave human companionship, especially in their hours of leisure. Neither is it true that when they abandon the bucolic pastimes traditionally associated with life in the open country they drift into evil "city ways." But while this Pennsylvania survey shows that the pastimes of country people are generally of the most simple and wholesome nature, it also reveals the unfortunate fact that their leisure is an asset almost entirely neglected by both church and school. The following table is an interesting abstract of what the country people do with their leisure when they do anything at all:

Baseball	20 per cent.
Socials and picnics	18 " "
Pool and billiards	13 " "
Moving-picture shows	11 " "
Gymnasium athletics	5 " "
Concerts and lectures	3 " "
Skating	3 " "
Dancing	3 " "
Cards	3 " "
Basketball	3 " "
Football	3 " "
Tennis	3 " "
Bowling	2 " "
Golf	1 " "

But for the most part the social gatherings of country people in rural Pennsylvania, as elsewhere, are entirely unorganized and casual, and take place principally at the post-office, the village or cross-roads stores, poolrooms, and the railroad stations. "Add together the proportion of meetings in such places, and the total is 78 per cent. of the whole." At these casual meetings the energies are released which if intelligently organized could be converted into a social force of the highest advantage to the community. But, as the author of this survey says, "This is a field wholly uncultivated." The schools, like the churches, have not yet awakened to the fact that education is not a matter of childhood for childhood, but a matter of life for life, and that it is a cruel waste to attempt to cultivate the social and ethical instincts of the children during a few years and during a few hours of the day while these same instincts are permitted to run wild in the adult community—a cruel injustice to the children to pit their enthusiasms and plastic inexperience against the dull cynicism of a socially unaroused and torpid community. It is directly in the interest of the children that the school must become the social center for the entire community; and this it cannot become unless the school-workers know how the people spend their time, what their recreational facilities are, and what things they would enjoy if rightly organized and provided with adequate facilities. Time and time again it has been found that the easiest approach to the reorganization of a community's educational and economic life is through the social instincts and desires of the people.

Fortunately, the making of a community survey is neither costly nor excessively laborious. The surveys of the Presbyterian Board required the time sometimes of two, sometimes of only one investigator during a period of little more than two months. Possibly the most comprehensive survey of a rural community yet made is that recently published by the Bureau of Research in Agriculture of the Minnesota State University. This survey not only enters into all the essential facts of the present economic and social status of a typical rural county, but it reviews the history of the community's social and industrial institutions — its schools, homes, railroads, grain-elevators, stores, newspapers. And yet it was completed in the three summer months of 1912 by a single investigator.

In view of the fundamental importance of such a survey to the constructive development of a school program designed to prepare children for efficient citizenship, would it not richly repay the community to retain a teacher or supervising teacher or district or township or county superintendent during the summer months for the purpose of making one? If a survey is a justifiable part of the cost of building roads and houses and fences, why is it not equally justifiable in the building of an efficient citizenship? And what an education a community survey would be for the men and women who made it!

III

THE HEALTH OF THE CHILDREN

THE primary object of the community survey is to familiarize the school officials — trustees, principal, and teachers—with the community whose life it is the work of the school to organize, develop, and improve. But the foundation of the community life is in its children; the sacred material out of which the community of to-morrow must be built is principally in the plastic life of the oncoming generation.

It is often said that the child is the nation's greatest asset. This may or may not be true. The child is raw material; he is only a possible asset, a potentiality in citizenship. He becomes an asset when he has three qualifications—health, trained ability, and a living desire to serve the state.

Here is the immediate task of the school, the duty and privilege of the teacher—to conserve the health of the child, to train him for productive work, to imbue him with the spirit of civic service. To take the child and by neglect, indifference, or abuse to impair his health, or, receiving him with his health impaired, to fail to make him whole, is sacrilege. To keep the child from infancy through adolescence and then to send him forth untrained for useful work is to despise the gift of God. To accept the task of public education from the state and not to imbue him with a living desire to serve the state is treason. For the state can justify the levy of taxes for public education only on the ground that it has ideals to serve, and that the intelligent preparation of the child for productive citizenship is essential to the attainment of those ideals.

When the children come to the public school they come not as the property of the individual homes that send them—often under compulsion; they come as consecrated material to be transformed into efficient citizens. And health, which includes a knowledge of the rules of public as well as of personal hygiene, is at the foundation of the possibility of efficient citizenship.

Clearly, when the state compels children to assemble in the public school it commits a crime when it exposes them to the possibility of infection. In the days when we were ignorant of the communicable nature of bacterial disease there may have been some excuse for carelessness in this matter. There is no excuse to-day. Happily, this truism is receiving general recognition by the common sense of the people.

Medical inspection was introduced into the public schools to protect the children and the community from the menace of epidemics. In the beginning, when children were discovered with communicable diseases they were merely sent home and quarantined. There was originally no intention of invading the home's authority over the physical welfare of the children. But the inspection for communicable diseases quickly revealed the fact that the homes were neglecting the care of the children's bodies— not through malice or indifference, but through ignorance. An astonishing number of children were found to have bad teeth, imperfect eyesight, adenoids, spinal curvature, and other defects, that not only interfered with their educational progress, but, uncorrected, were certain to impair their civic efficiency throughout their days. Medical inspection began to open the eyes of the school to its responsibility for the backwardness of many of the children in school and for their later careers as criminals, bums, or vagrants. As a result medical inspection is everywhere being extended to cover physical defects. Sometimes the school limits its initiative to examining the children and notifying the parents of the existence of defects. Sometimes the school exercises compulsion by excluding the child until the defect or defects have been corrected. And in some communities the school supervises the correction of the defects, either through the family physician or through special school clinics provided by the community. More and more the school is assuming large jurisdiction over the health of the children, which until a few years ago was, like the labor of children and their discipline—even when this extended to cruelty—considered the exclusive prerogative of the parents. Increasingly the state is placing the school and its coworker, the children's court, *in loco parentis.*

The point of view toward medical inspection which is rapidly coming to prevail has recently been expressed by Dr. F. B. Dresslar in a bulletin published by the United States Bureau of Education. Dr. Dresslar justifies public action in conserving the health of school-children on broad grounds of public policy. Has not the community, he asks, as much right to demand good health in its citizens and future citizens as it has to demand literacy?

And nowhere is the gospel of physical vigor, the sanctity of personal purity, and the godliness of right living more needed than in the rural school, because, owing to the peculiar handicaps in the way of a health program in the scattered country communities, the health of the country children has not received so much attention as the health of city children. Dr. L. J. Cooke, gymnasium director in the University of Minnesota, has recently published the results of a protracted investigation showing that the physique of city boys who enter that university is better than that of boys from the farms. The physical defects that especially afflict country boys are flabby muscles, hump shoulders, curved spines, low right shoulders, muscular weakness of heart action, small chest expansion, and small lung capacity.

In the boys from the farm [he says] the muscles of the arms and shoulders are usually well developed, while nearly every other part of the physical organism falls below the general average. The city youth, who usually has had more or less physical training, possesses a much better physique.

The Rev. Claire S. Adams, in a rural survey made in Illinois for the Presbyterian Board of Home Missions, points out that there is nothing in good air and hard work that will fortify a man or woman against a continued neglect of the elemental principles of health.

Country people [he says] are constantly suffering from sickness, small and great, against which they feel themselves helpless. The spirit of rebellion against sickness is general in cities and towns. People there expect to be well. But *in the country they expect to be sick*. On the farm the mother of the house is the health department. She has to know for the farm group all that the departments of health, police, and schools in the cities need to know about sanitation. The lack of this knowledge among farm women is the cause of the retarded sanitary development of the country. The cities, for all their great difficulties, are surpassing the country in their sanitary reform. The death rate is controlled in the city. In the country it is still increasing. The time will come, if present processes are permitted to go on, when people will flee to the city for good health in fear of the unrestrained diseases of the country. That time will not come if the farm mother can be taught sanitation, if the country children can be taught the elemental principles and practices of personal and public hygiene.

What a challenge these facts throw to the workers in our rural schools! For everywhere in our most enlightened communities the center of the new health movement

—as contrasted with the old anti-disease movement—has come to be the public school.

The technique of medical inspection has made immense strides in the past five or six years, especially in our metropolitan centers, and this technique is applicable, in the main, to all communities, whether urban or rural.

What are the practical steps in medical inspection as they present themselves to the rural school; what is their relative importance from the point of view of health and educational progress; and what is the simplest and most effective way in which these steps can be taken?

The most immediate step is the detection and exclusion of children with infectious and communicable diseases. To compel the children to gather in the school-building and not to protect them and the community from infection is nothing short of a crime. Clearly, however, the problem of detecting the presence of a contagious disease is beyond the ability of any one but a skilled physician. At the outset, therefore, the school authorities are confronted by the necessity of providing a medical officer whose duty it must be to visit the schools at short and regular intervals and to examine all children who have colds, coughs, and any other symptoms of indisposition.

There is no doubt [says Dr. Walter S. Cornell, Director of Medical Inspection of Public Schools in Philadelphia, in his book *Health and Medical Inspection of School Children*] that in the ideal system the medical inspector visits his school daily at approximately the same hour. A rigid system and a daily call for patients waken the teachers to their responsibility, and this daily search by the teachers for causes of physical defect, skin-disease, or sore throat soon increases their power of observation to a wonderful degree. Any working plan in a large city not entailing these daily visits can be justified only on the ground of economy.

If this is the best system in the city, why should the country children and their homes not enjoy an equally thorough protection? The cost of preventing the development and spread of disease, however high, is always cheaper in the end than indifference or neglect.

But there are considerations that may justify a less rigid system in suburban, village, and country districts.

Realizing [Dr. Cornell goes on] that the indorsement of infrequent visits may do harm to the cause of medical inspection by reason of misunderstanding, I nevertheless feel it necessary to state in justice to the public treasury that daily visits to *very small* suburban (village and country) schools are a non-justifiable expense. It is true that a case of scarlet fever or some minor contagious disease may develop in one day as well as another, but experience has shown that such cases are rare in these schools, and that a daily incidental visit by the medical inspector is usually a fruitless errand.

Visits at intervals of three or four days are in these cases sufficient.

Any system of medical inspection which provides for the visiting of large city schools [and is this not equally true of large country schools?] less frequently than on alternate days should be condemned.

As applied to the country school this authoritative declaration of principle will undoubtedly seem startling, almost revolutionary. But the questions that the rural-school worker—whether teacher, principal, superintendent, or trustee—must always ask are these: Have not the rural-school children, have not the country communities as much right as the cities to the best protection from communicable disease that modern science can give? Has not the discrimination against the health of the rural child and the country community gone on long enough?

Protection against communicable disease is undoubtedly the first necessity, but it is not more imperative, nor in the long run more profitable, than protection against the non-communicable physical defects that make the lives of the children miserable, retard their educational progress, and permanently undermine their physical stamina. A man's body is the tool with which he works, and when that tool is permitted to deteriorate, to rust or chip, to get out of order generally, he becomes a candidate for the human scrap-heap. Thousands of our vagrants, delinquents, and criminals have gone to the bad simply because their bodies were neglected in youth. To scatter physically or mentally defective children over the country is a greater evil than selling or sowing defective seed.

How can the work of keeping the children in sound physical condition be done with greatest efficiency and the least expenditure of brain, muscle, and money?

Says Dr. Cornell:

Taking the five primary physical defects—poor vision, nose and throat obstruction, deafness, decayed teeth, and poor nutrition—it seems to me that the examination of each child every two years is sufficient, *provided the school record of defective children is gone over each September and an endeavor made to secure the treatment previously recommended if this has not previously been obtained.* In this way the known defectives receive an *annual* examination.

An experienced examiner will require four or five minutes for each child. It is the custom in our large cities for the medical inspector to visit each school on his list for the examination of miscellaneous cases (referred to him by the teacher), and at the last school visited to make a systematic examination of from twenty to thirty children. By this method, if the proper number of school-children be assigned to his care, each child is systematically examined and the results recorded on his registration card every two years.

No system looking to the systematic examination of more than thirty children in one day is feasible. The eye-strain attendant on vision-testing, the amount of vitiated air inhaled during throat examinations, and the general activity required impose a limit on the examiner at this point.

The details of medical inspection must be left to the medical officer, whether he is employed directly by the school authorities or by the health authorities coöperating with the school. It is, however, the business of the school authorities to see that the medical examinations are made and that the discovered defects are corrected.

Why does this responsibility rest upon the school authorities? First, because good health is essential to efficient citizenship, and the school is directly responsible to the home and the nation for the efficiency of our future citizens. But there is another and more immediately pressing reason. Physical defects retard the educational progress of the children, and this not only means that the children must spend an undue amount of time in each grade—entailing a double or treble cost per child upon the public treasury—but also that they leave school without the minimum educational equipment that is essential to their future efficiency.

Poor vision means eye strain, which means headaches and general nervous derangement. A child that cannot see well cannot be a good pupil.

Nose and throat obstruction, whether because of adenoids or other abnormality, means mouth-breathing, sleeplessness, mental sluggishness, unhappiness, and subnormal vitality. A child that cannot breathe well cannot be a good pupil.

Deafness means lack of attention and inability to receive instruction. Moreover, deafness and earache are usually symptoms of serious disorders which, undiscovered and uncorrected, may mean early death. A child that cannot hear well cannot be a good pupil.

Decayed or defective teeth mean constant suffering, poor mastication, digestive derangements, impaired health. Decayed teeth not only poison the breath of the children, they infect all the food that passes into their stomachs. A child whose system is continually poisoned at the source of nutrition by decaying teeth cannot be a good pupil.

Poor nutrition is at once the result and a contributing cause of all other physical defects. Bad eyes, bad ears, bad teeth, obstructed breathing-passages all interfere with the normal processes of digestion. At the same time an improperly nourished child is like an underfed engine or one whose fire-box is full of clinkers. His stomach is not turning into his blood and body the materials needed for the growth and repair of tissues, and this means that all the organs are underfed. Besides, an undernourished child lacks resistance to disease and is the readiest prey to tuberculosis, pneumonia, and the like. Malnutrition, whether from insufficient food or improper food, means general debility, listlessness, inability to do the work of the school. A child with poor nutrition cannot be a good pupil.

From the point of view of educational progress, therefore, as well as from the point of view of the nation with its interest in physical efficiency, the school authorities must see to it that these defects are discovered and corrected. This task requires a maximum of patience and tact. It cannot be accomplished unless the school has the full confidence of the community and has won the interested and cordial coöperation of the parents. Parents are likely at the outset to resent being told that the physical condition of their children is not all that it should be; unless the educational authorities are careful and considerate, the examination of the children for physical defects may result in discord and bad feeling. On the other hand, the examination of the children and the notification of the parents when defects are discovered, if tactfully done, almost invariably proves a strong bond of sympathy and coöperation. When a defect is discovered a written notice should be sent to the parents stating the specific nature of the defect and urging a consultation with the family doctor. A general notice that does not name the specific defect or defects is pretty certain to be disregarded. And if the defect remains uncorrected even after the attention of the parents has been specifically called to it, a representative of the school should visit the home and explain to the parents the importance of correction. When reasoning and persuasion fail, the child should be excluded as rigorously as in the case of a contagious or communicable disease.

The defects enumerated above are the ones that will require the most active attention from the school authorities. But hardly less common are the orthopedic defects—flat foot, bow-leg, and the like—and the nervous derangements that may be due to some organic abnormality, or to the physical changes that play so large and important a part in the lives of growing children. The nervous derangements attendant upon the development of the sex organs need the most scrupulous attention. The instruction of the boys and girls in the simple and fundamental facts of sex and sex hygiene is imperative. Of course, there is always danger in intrusting this task to inexperienced or immature doctors or teachers; harm may result from the morbid exaggeration of facts that should be handled in a wholesome-minded, direct, and simply scientific fashion. But what man or woman whose education in the fundamental facts of sex and sex hygiene was neglected in youth will not agree that the omission of proper instruction is fraught with tragedy? Where there is any question as to the ability of the teacher or principal to impart the necessary minimum of instruction either through courses in elementary biology or through individual conferences with the pupils, or both, or where there is any reason to believe that the community is not prepared for the introduction of such instruction into the course of study, the desired results will be obtained by securing the services of a physician of high standing to address a series of parents' meetings and then leaving the matter of sex instruction to the parents.

Fortunately for the future health and vigor of the race, prudishness has had its day; sanity and healthy-mindedness are everywhere beginning to prevail. And the progress in the application of scientific knowledge that is protecting increasing numbers of children from nervous disorders and sex derangements is reaching out a hand of wisdom and kindness to the mentally abnormal, defective, and atypical children.

How many thousands have not suffered from our careless and heartless grouping of children into the totally inadequate categories of good and bad, bright and dull! In the vast majority of the cases the good child and good pupil is merely the normal and healthy child; the bad child and bad pupil is merely the child harassed by some physical or mental defect or abnormality.

The entire subject of the mentally atypical, abnormal, or defective child carries the school authorities into delicate ground. The parents who resent having their attention called to their children's defective eyes, ears, teeth, rebel against the marking of their children as mentally abnormal. And yet the failure on the part of the school to segregate such children, to give them special physical and mental care, means sorrow to the children, their degeneracy, and the decadence of the race. Furthermore, the presence in the school of a mentally abnormal child whose abnormality is undetected and for whom no special educational provision is made interferes with the normal progress of all the children. We punish the children and ourselves when we fail to heed the fact that abnormal or defective brains are no more monstrous, no more to be ashamed of than abnormal or defective eyes, or ears, or teeth.

Nowhere is prejudice and ignorance fraught with greater menace to the child, the school, and the community than in this matter of the examination and care of children who are mentally deficient. It is interesting, therefore, to have so great an authority as Dr. Cornell call attention to the fact that "Hawthorne, Leigh Hunt, Sir Isaac Newton, Darwin, Froebel, Linnaeus, Clive, and Wellington were reputed to be dull boys in school." And he goes on to state his opinion that the most successful men are seldom the brightest boys in school.

Dullness in itself is not necessarily a proof of mental deficiency, just as precocity is not necessarily a sign of genius; but, while not a proof of mental deficiency, dullness is an index pointing either to mental deficiency, to improper physical condition, or to something wrong in the children's school or home environment. In any case, it is a signal to warn the teacher that the child requires special attention. In most cases dull children, like feeble-minded children, require medical attention and special instruction, if not institutional care, but there are cases in which the correction of the child's school or home environment is all that is needed. Dr. Cornell cites the case of a boy who had remained in the fifth grade through five half-year terms under five different teachers, and who had come to be known among the teachers by the name of "Shiftless." When, however, he was promoted to the sixth grade at a venture his mind seemed to waken, he showed remarkable improvement, and at the end of forty days he ranked among the best scholars, with a rating of excellent in spelling, good in arithmetic, language, and history, and fair in geography and physiology. Such cases are not infrequent, and suggest the importance of periodic mental tests with a view to determining whether the so-called dull children are properly graded or whether the work which is being assigned them is the work best adapted to call out their latent powers. Such tests adapted to the use of the teacher without special training in psychiatrics has been devised by Professor Binet, of the University of Paris, France, and can be had upon application to almost any state department of education or to the Bureau of Education in Washington.

Once the health of the children has been accepted by the rural school as a normal part of its social and educational responsibility, medical inspection loses its mystery and most of its difficulties. How shall the country children be given equal protection with the children in the most advanced municipalities?

Common sense offers the simplest and best solution. Let the country school turn to the country doctor for his service and coöperation. The country doctor is one of the noblest figures in our national life; he is distinguished above most men for his unselfish interest in the health of his neighbors and for his readiness to make large personal sacrifice in behalf of the public welfare. The country districts that cannot command the public-spirited coöperation of an able country doctor will be found in the very small minority.

Undoubtedly, however, the experience of the cities will hold with equal force in the country; it is not safe to abuse the generosity of the doctor any more than it is safe to abuse the generosity of the merchant, or the civil engineer, or the banker, or the farmer. It will not do to forget that the doctor and his family need money to live on as much as other people. For this reason it is well to provide for the fair compensation of the country doctor who is willing to serve as medical inspector for the schools of the district.

In answer to the inquiry as to the proper salary for a medical inspector in the country who gives only a part of his time to the work, Dr. Cornell suggests that the inspector should be paid for the hours actually spent in the schools and for the time consumed in going from one school to another. If the doctor lives in a reasonable location, but all the schools are distant from his residence, he should be given credit for an extra half-hour for each school. If the schools are widely separated and the transportation facilities are bad the inspector should receive one hundred dollars a year for the keep of a conveyance, in which case the credit for a half-hour to and between schools should be omitted.

By way of illustrating the basis of remuneration Dr. Cornell takes an exceptionally large country district with ten schools and two thousand children; smaller districts will find no difficulty, however, in reducing his figures to scale.

Suppose [he says, by way of example] the borough of Northampton institutes medical inspection. There are two thousand children in ten different schools, and the total distance between schools is twelve miles. The population is scattered, and therefore contagious diseases, except long-apart epidemics of measles and chicken-pox, practically do not exist. Under such conditions the inspector can examine all the children in twelve thousand minutes (two hundred hours), inspect all their vaccination marks in ten hours or less, and make a sanitary inspection of each of the ten buildings three times a year, allowing thirty minutes to each inspection, making fifteen hours more. The children sent to him on each visit by the teachers would not average more than three children, each of whom would require five additional minutes. And if by the official regulation he visits each school twice a week for forty weeks, this would add two hundred hours more to his work.

All this would total four hundred and twenty-five hours. With ten months to do this work (except for the stated short visits already mentioned), he would thus average about forty hours a month, each month consisting of twenty school-days. Under such conditions a physician could almost arrange his own time to make his systematic examinations, even allowing that an hour will be consumed in going to and between schools. Two dollars per hour would therefore be good compensation, and would equal $850 for the year, to which should be added credit for a half-hour's time on each working-day (probably about a hundred and fifty in the year), equaling $75, or if the inspector must use a conveyance, $100. This would make a total salary of $950.

THE WORK OF THE RURAL SCHOOL

In cities $1,200 net a year is the standard allowance for part-time work for each medical inspector.

Is this too much to pay for the protection of the children and the entire community against the menace of epidemics and for the discovery and correction of the defects of teeth, eyes, ears, nose, throat, spine, etc., which hinder the children's school progress and when uncorrected impair their physical efficiency all their days? Let parents in the rural districts consider the cost of disease and epidemics among their cattle, trees, and grains, to say nothing of unchecked erosion in their fields, improper cultivation, and the like, and they will hardly hesitate to demand from the school authorities the expenditure of a few hundred dollars to protect their children and their homes!

Of course, the difficulty of the semi-volunteer, part-time service here described is that even the best of doctors is likely to consider a surgical operation or a visit to a patient more important, because usually more remunerative, than the same time spent in school. This tempts him to slight his public work and so reduces his efficiency as a medical inspector of school-children. The frequency with which this difficulty arises has developed a tendency in the cities to employ a limited number of physicians for their full time and to underpin their work with the work of trained nurses who do nothing but look after school-children at school and in their homes. Already the county authorities in most states pay a county health officer to take care of those who have become criminals or paupers, or to fight disease after it has become epidemic. Why should not these health officers be employed, like teachers and principals, for their full time to prevent disease, to correct defects, and to promote individual, domestic, and community hygiene? Some day our growing perception of the dollar-and-cent value of having our children properly cared for and properly instructed will lead to the development of a health service that will be coördinate with our present educational service.

But we cannot afford to wait for an ideal arrangement. We must use the facilities now at hand. And if the rural-school authorities do the best they can immediately, the future will undoubtedly take good care of itself.

IV

THE school program that omits to take the actual child as it finds him and to provide for a careful survey of his physical condition, with the purpose of having any defects corrected or diseases cured and promoting his normal physical development, fails to lay the solid foundation upon which alone an efficient citizenship can be built. To say to the children through word of mouth or through a text-book that they should keep themselves healthy and then to fail to make it possible for them to follow the advice is manifestly absurd. To say to a boy "You must breathe through your nose!" when an adenoid growth, about which he and his parents know nothing, makes it impossible for him to obey is nearer to the senile folly of blind custom than to the wisdom of living experience. To say to him "Sit up straight and stop leaning over your desk!" when he has a spinal curvature is a tragic farce. To tell the children that tooth-brushes will keep their teeth clean and sound when, unknown to themselves or their parents, ninety in a hundred of them already have decayed teeth that need immediate dental treatment is cruel mockery. To say to the children that it will injure their eyes to read facing the light when twenty in a hundred of them already have defective vision demanding glasses or medical care is to be guilty of inexcusable neglect. Contrary to the prevailing superstition, the cost of medical inspection, when provided by the public-school or health

authorities acting in coöperation, is very small. But
even if it were high it would be folly not to provide
it. And the proved fact of its low cost leaves the rural
community without its one seemingly valid excuse for
delay. If one-half the money that is put into hospitals,
sanitariums, and asylums for the cure or detention of
those who through neglect have become dangerously sick
or mentally incapacitated were devoted to the prevention
of disease and defectiveness in school-children, our national
efficiency would be immeasurably increased.

Following the survey of the health of the children
there should come a survey of their mental powers,
abilities, and experiences to discover in what particulars
they are strong or weak and in what direction each of
them individually needs special development. The
usual examination based on memory is entirely indequate.
An intelligent grouping of the children requires a careful
study of their powers of initiative, their powers of memory,
their imaginations, their ability to reason, their control
of their motor activities. Some children are "long" on
imagination and "short" on memory. Some reason
slowly, some quickly. Some have a "turn" for making
things with their hands; their fingers work deftly and
accurately—they need guidance and encouragement.
Some are unable to do things readily with their hands;
their fingers and bodies work awkwardly—they need patient and intelligent teaching. Some children express
themselves best through music, some through the spoken
word, some through writing, some through drawing, some
through making things. A rigid and stereotyped program will injure more latent abilities than it can
mend.

A little five-year-old boy while roaming around at
lunch-time saw a ground-squirrel. Instantly he was all
attention. Watching the little wild thing, he forgot school
and recess and failed to hear the bell. When he came to

himself he ran to the school, only to find that the door was shut and that he was ten minutes late.

"Why didn't you come when the bell rang?" the teacher asked.

"I didn't hear it," he said.

"What were you doing?"

"I was watching a ground-squirrel."

His ears were soundly boxed, and he was sent to his desk in tears and humiliation and was kept in after school.

A beautiful opportunity and a wicked betrayal of it!

A nine-year-old boy came into the schoolroom ten minutes late.

"Why are you late, Sammie?"

"I saw a water-dog in the branch as I came along and I wanted to catch him and bring him with me!"

"Did you catch him?"

"Yes, ma'am," he replied with shining eyes, "and here he is!"

In a moment the school was grouped around Sammie, and all the children were watching the water-dog. The program was changed that day, as it often was in that school. But there were some interesting things well said and well written; there were some related facts brought out. A beautiful opportunity and a quick appreciation of it.

What children need is expression; what they too often get is suppression, repression, oppression.

A careful survey is needed of the children's social attitude. Close observation will show that some children are egotistic and anti-social; that others merely lack good judgment and social perspective. All of them need careful guidance; their eyes need to be opened to the position of the individual in a democratic community.

Mere guesswork will not supply the basis for an intelligent school program. All teachers make some kind of survey of the children's mental and physical faculties even if it amounts to nothing more than seeing that some children are deaf, some pale, some "bad," and some "good." A few observe closely and make an honest effort to know each child well. And a few—a very few as yet—do not rest until they understand each child and his individual needs thoroughly—the state of his health, of his mental powers, his motor activities, his outlook upon the world of men and things about him. Has not the time come when what is true of this small minority should be true of all teachers whatsoever?

The spirit of the community survey and the health survey of the children is happily being adopted by the best schools everywhere as the controlling spirit in the government of the school and the discipline of the children. The education of the children cannot be effective unless it includes an adjustment between them and their community environment. Either the school program must be modified to suit the actual life of the community, or the life of the community, where that is backward, must be modified in such a way as to enable the children to put their school training into effective practice. Everywhere the ablest teachers are developing the school program and the community program as one.

Oddly enough, however, the adjustment of the school program to the community life has made least progress in the field of government where the adjustment would seem to be easiest and most natural. All of our political units, from the nation at large to the states, the counties, and districts, are under a democratic form of government, whereas the government of the public school remains for the most part autocratic and arbitrary.

According to the traditional practice, the school authorities make certain rules and the principal and teachers add certain others. Sometimes the rules are good and wholesome in themselves; often they are harsh and ill-advised. In either case, however, the children have no part in them but to obey. Their point of view is not considered, the wisdom and fairness of the rules are not discussed with them. Under these fixed and arbitrary methods is it to be expected that the children will learn to respect law and order? Is it to be expected that they will learn the reasonableness and the necessity for law unless they have had training in the making of law and have learned the value of law from their own experience? Is taking law on faith good preparation for citizenship in a democracy?

What is disorder or lawlessness in the accepted school-room sense? Any violation of the rules, however arbitrary and unreasonable the rules may be. One teacher forbids all talking; to talk or whisper during school-hours is, accordingly, to disobey the law. A child, utterly weary of sitting in a stuffy room, and not infrequently suffering because he doesn't fit his desk, slips down in his chair and sticks his feet out into the aisle; if this is against the rules, he has disobeyed the law. Another teacher lays down the rule that no child shall leave the room more than once during the session and that he will be kept after school for the second "offense." Accordingly the children refrain from going out a second time—often a crime against their health and morals—or they go and take their punishment. Do such rules foster respect for law?

The imposition of arbitrary authority breeds lawlessness. How commonly the children make a hero of the boy who does some outrageous or daredevil thing in violation of the rules! They respect the miscreant and take joy in seeing the authorities baffled. What is the reason for this rebellious attitude? Why is the "tell-tale" despised? It is because our entire democratic civilization is founded in a spirit of revolt against the arbitrary Old World laws like those of the royal forest, that saved a rabbit though a child starved, that held a peasant's life cheaper than a deer's, and that imposed taxation without representation. And yet the tradition of autocratic authority versus the common man is by no means dead, and has survived especially in the government of our schools. And the children instinctively feel that they are obeying the best spirit of their fathers in making common cause against the oppressor.

But this rebellious spirit does not prevail in children's clubs, in their athletic teams, or in the associations formed and governed by themselves. The honor system is a democratic system; public opinion controls, for the opinions of all in regard to the law have been consulted and the rules have been made by those who both obey and enforce obedience. A school in which the children share in making the laws is pretty certain to be a school in which good order exists, in which honor prevails, in which the best progress is made.

Experience has shown that when the children are consulted in making the rules for the orderly government of the school they are very quick to grasp the essentials of good order, and show keen discrimination in distinguishing between the less and the weightier matters that go to make up a disciplinary program. Being very sensitive to injustice, they are very much alive to what is right. A little round table at the opening of the school and from time to time throughout the year will win their instant attention and interest. They will discuss searchingly and skilfully the reasons for this law or rule; the reasons why this or that rule should have certain exceptions; the proper corrective for this or that violation. They take pride in being permitted to enact the laws for their own government, and they are rarely willing to see their own handiwork dishonored by any of their own number.

Obviously, the first step in the creation of a disciplinary program is to have the children imbued with the idea that the school was built for them and is maintained for them; that it is their duty and privilege to take care of and cherish this temple of childhood built and maintained for them at the expense of the community and the state. If tactfully guided and rightfully inspired, they will keep good order on the grounds and in the rooms; they will take care of the walls and desks, keep the closets in good shape and prevent defacements. Under a democratic system of government they will conduct themselves with a keen sense of social responsibility and do the numberless little necessary things that the most argus-eyed teacher cannot successfully manage in the cat-and-mouse atmosphere of school autocracy.

When the children help to make and enforce their own laws what will happen to their sense of civic ethics and their growth in efficient citizenship? When they have in their turn become a community of lawmakers, what will be the effect of self-government in school upon their respect for law, its reasonableness and necessity? Will it not then be natural for them to enter into the spirit of the law, to see that the laws entered upon the statutes are fair and just, and to regard a violator of the law with indignation? Is not an understanding of the spirit of the law essential to the healthy continuance of our democracy? And when shall the children acquire this understanding if not in the public schools where the twenty million children of to-day are being shaped into the citizens of to-morrow? If the school is a miniature community, and not merely an assemblage of isolated units, should it not be organized and developed as a community? If the children are capable of self-government in play, why not in work? Why should a child be subjected to autocratic discipline until he is twenty-one years old, and then be handed a ballot, certifying in effect that he is a graduate in democratic self-discipline? Experience has abundantly shown that the cure for the essential evils of lawlessness and misgovernment in a democratic community lies in the honor system and self-government in the public schools.

Despite the autocratic tradition the steady drift toward a more democratic management of the schools is freeing school discipline from much of its harshness and many of its unreasonable restrictions, and good order in the schools has increased in proportion. Very much to the astonishment of the prophets of evil, and very much to the delight of those who were apparently bent on turning the school world upside down, the more the children have been trusted, the more they have proved worthy of trust; the more responsibilities have been placed upon them, the more they have shown an appreciation of these responsibilities and the ability to meet them.

The foundation of good order in the school, as in the nation, is the common law—the *lex non scripta*—that grows out of the customs and usages of the members of a community in the course of their normal daily activities. It is obvious, therefore, that the rules of conduct in a school where the democratic spirit prevails must grow out of the activities of the children in their pursuit of the course of study. The rules made by the children are likely to be quite as arbitrary and unreasonable as those laid down by the school authorities unless they grow out of their actual daily experience. The problem of school discipline is therefore fundamentally a problem in the formulation of the course of study. The great opportunity of the elders—the trustees, the principal, and the teachers—to shape the children for efficient citizenship in the democracy arises in the determination of the general policy of the school.

It is often said that children are essentially barbarians, and that if they are not held strictly within the bounds of arbitrary authority they will quickly revert to the conduct of primitive man. This might be true if the children were segregated on a wild island entirely removed from the institutions of civilization. The trouble with the statement is that the conditions that would make it true never arise. The fact is that the children are members of a highly developed community, that from the days of early infancy and the nursery they have been living in an atmosphere of law and order, and that their domestic and community relationships do not cease when they go to school. The greatest asset which the educational authorities have in their work of developing a school program is precisely the experience which the children have shared as members of civilized homes and communities. So far from disregarding this fact, the wisest teachers and the best schools are basing their entire discipline and instruction upon the unformulated social wisdom which the children bring with them to the school.

Such names as those of Froebel and Pestalozzi and Francis Parker and John Dewey are prominently associated with this point of view, which is being applied more or less consciously by so many excellent teachers in so many parts of the country that it may seem invidious to select any one example of its practical application. And yet there is probably no place in the country where, in its application to the rural school, it is receiving so thoroughgoing a test as at the Experimental Rural School at Rock Hill, South Carolina.

The course of study and the government of the children at Rock Hill are based upon the theory that the business of the teacher is not so much to "hear" lessons as it is to organize, guide, and interpret the activities that are normal to the children as members of the community. Approaching the school in the early morning, you see across the privet hedge that surrounds the yard groups of children of all ages from six to sixteen at work in the ample school-garden. Some of the children are laying out seed-beds, some are hoeing, some are cutting flowers for the school-rooms, and still others are gathering lettuce for the midday meal. In an hour the children have worked off their superfluous energy and fidgetiness, they have accumulated experience which is to serve as the basis for the day's indoor work, and they are ready to go inside. First, however, they go to the pump in one of the porches of the schoolhouse and wash the soil from their hands and the sweat from their brows at this temporary substitute for the shower-baths that are soon to be installed. If it is wise to provide shower-baths and dressing-rooms for athletic teams, why is it not equally wise to provide them for the garden teams? Moreover, there are great educational advantages in such an equipment; for just as it is easy to impress upon the members of an athletic team the importance of personal hygiene as a condition of "fitness," so it is easy to bring the same lesson home to the children who take their exercise with spade and hoe and plow and who are quick to appreciate the delight of open pores and clean, glowing muscles.

But washing is a doubtful satisfaction without towels, and towels do not grow on trees. If each child is to make his or her own set of towels the questions immediately arise: What kind of material is needed? How long and wide should the towels be? How much material must be bought? What will the material cost?

Under the guidance of the teacher the number, size, and cost of the towels is discussed. Tape-measure in hand, the children consider various lengths, and finally decide on towels two feet long. The older pupils then use their arithmetic to find out how much toweling will be needed to supply the school. After the cloth is bought each child measures off his or her towels, the size of the hem is determined, and the work of basting begins. The teacher explains why the damask hem is best for the purpose in hand and shows the children how to make it. When the towels are finished the children find that the hem has reduced their length to twenty-two inches.

They have had an invaluable lesson in number, and understand its meaning as they could not have done had they spent the same time in solving book problems unrelated to their experience.

While they were in the garden the children had laid out some rows for beans. Several days before, a number of boxes had been made for testing the seed-beans, and the night before a handful of beans had been placed in water to soak. The teacher begins the lesson on beans with an informal discussion of the various varieties, of the regions to which the various varieties are best adapted. The children compare the size of the soaked beans with those that are not soaked. They are shown how to distinguish between sound seed and bad. They tear off the seed-coat of the swollen beans and remark its toughness. Then the teacher discusses with them the value of the bean as a food. After the discussion has been carried on as long as possible without fatiguing the children's attention they go into a room, and one of the older children puts on the board a number of new words arranged in three columns—name-words, descriptive words, and action-words. The words are spelled and their meanings explained. In the course of days the children follow the development of the beans and make blue-prints of them in their various stages of growth. From these words and these prints they make a Bean Book on wide, strong paper, the contents of which is indicated by the following stereotyped reproduction of the graceful, free-hand original:

Preparation of Soil

Cotton grew on the ground last year. We sowed crimson clover. We plowed it under in the spring. We broke up the ground. We broke the clods with a harrow. We laid off the rows three feet apart. We drilled the beans and covered them with three inches of dirt. We put some fertilizer on them June 15th. We worked them three times.

Blue-Print of Germinating Bean
First Stage

The bean has
      burst its seed-coat.
The roots have
      come out.

roots	fine	come
plant	tender	burst
ground		hold
food		get

Blue-Print of Germinating Bean
Second Stage

We can see the stem
      of the bean.

stem	long	grown
	curved	holds
	longer	
	upright	

Blue-Print of Germinating Bean
Third Stage

The stem has grown longer.

plumule	two	peeps
leaves	little	open
	thin	

BLUE-PRINT OF GERMINATING BEAN
Fourth Stage

The plumule
    has grown longer.
It has turned green.
The stem is green.

rain	larger	growing
sunshine	green	get
		catch
		wash
		breathe
		folded

BLUE-PRINT OF GERMINATING BEAN
Fifth Stage, with young leaves

The plumule has
    unfolded.
We can see the two
    green leaves.

bud	heart-shaped	shrinking
veins		shrunk
		unfolded
	smaller	gone

Why we Cultivate our Beans

We cultivate our beans to make them grow. It makes the soil soft. The roots can get food and water. It lets the plant have air. It forms a dust mulch. The dust mulch keeps the water in the ground. We kill the weeds and grass.

Weeds

Weeds and grass harm our beans. They take the food from them. They choke the beans. They keep the sun off of them. We can get rid of them by pulling them and digging them up. Sometimes we chop them off with the hoe. This is not a good way. It leaves the roots in the ground, and they come up again. Weeds do some good. They make lazy people cultivate their gardens.

A sequel to the Bean Book is a volume on Some Weeds from Our Bean Plot, illustrated with blue-prints of the broad-leaf plantain, the narrow-leaf plantain, the long-leaf plaintain, the smart-weed, the horse-nettle, and the like.

Here are lessons in hygiene, biology, agriculture, spelling, reading, arithmetic, drawing, grammar, geography, all growing out of a single morning's work. And of course the materials for the days to come are as varied and inexhaustible as nature herself.

About eleven o'clock preparations for the midday meal begin. The children are scattered over the building and the grounds—some of them in the workshop, some of them playing games, others busy at book-making or entertaining one another with stories. Lettuce is to be a part of the menu to-day, and the teacher calls for volunteers to prepare the fresh green heads. Several girls offer to do the work. The teacher turns to the blackboard, writes the word *lettuce* on the blackboard, and to the right of *lettuce* the names of the two girls who are to do the work of picking the leaves, selecting the good ones, washing and drying them leaf by leaf. The children spell the word and the two girls go to the kitchen. Volunteers are then called for to prepare the dressing for the lettuce.

Again a dozen hands go up. The word *dressing* is written on the blackboard, with the names of the children who are given the assignment. The word is spelled, and the next two go to the kitchen. Other children go to the porch and begin making the table ready. Immediately they are confronted by a nice problem in arithmetic. The table is eighteen feet long, there are three guests, thirty-two pupils, and the teacher. After placing a chair at each end of the table the question is, how many chairs must be placed on each side? The table is laid, and in a few minutes luncheon is served.

I think [writes a visitor] that they were the happiest, jolliest group I ever saw. Riddles were propounded, stories were told, short poems recited, and in it all and through it all there was perfect freedom and naturalness. At the conclusion of the meal volunteers were called into service. A number of girls washed and put up the dishes, others brushed the crumbs from the table and pulled the chairs back, while the boys swept the floor and drew the water. I have been permitted to attend a good many functions where the menu was somewhat more elaborate; but in all my life I have never found so much good cheer, so much unaffected simplicity and politeness, as I found in this little Carolina school where the teacher was hostess and where the children were models of good behavior. As we were gathered about the board the mocking-bird was singing in a near-by apple tree and the thrush was calling to his mate in a neighboring hedge, while a cat-bird was making his midday meal on a big fat caterpillar that he had found on a peach tree whose branches touched the porch on which we sat. Ten minutes after dinner I made a note of the following groups: Using the same table that had been used for luncheon, a group of girls were sewing— making laundry - bags, handkerchiefs, etc.; just inside the room the teacher was conducting a history recitation; not more than six feet away a group of boys were planning a net with which they hoped to capture a bumblebee that was needed for the museum; out on the grass a little girl was reading *Robinson Crusoe* to a group of children; down at the end of the porch a boy was doing some problems in arithmetic. Thus the work went on for the three hours that we stayed there—all busy, all happy.

Why is it that we have been so long in discovering the educational value of the school luncheon? For even to-day in the ordinary rural school the lunch hour is not only a wasted opportunity, but the parent of disorder, indigestion, and general discomfort. The children bring their luncheons in paper packages and tin or cardboard boxes. At noon they sit down on the wood-box, the school steps, at their desks, or in the yard, gulp down their cold victuals, scatter fragments about, and generally disregard their own or their comrades' comfort and health. They all act as if they were ashamed of eating, as if it were a bestial and unseemly necessity. None of the ordinary activities of the usual school program does so much to injure the manners, health, and morals of the children as the usual way of taking food, which should be an occasion for the practice of good breeding and the delights of human companionship.

But, now that the meal is over, there is work to be done in the kitchen and for the kitchen. On the walls of the cookroom at Rock Hill there is a schedule for the day's duties something like this:

SCHEDULE

Cups	Rose and Nell
Plates	Joe and Fred
Knives and Forks	Rose and Martha
Dust	Mary
Kettles	Lawrence and Charles
Water	Arthur and Conlie
Towels	Maggie and Estelle
Line	John
Carpenter's shop	Ann
Museum	Nellie and Bess
Flowers	Wilma and Johnnie

Some things in this schedule are a bit puzzling. "Why," you ask John, "is your name put down after line?" To your barbaric mind "Line . . . John" suggests ominous possibilities. But John explains that, "Yesterday the line on which we hang our towels and dish-cloths fell, and I had to fix it up this morning."

From the kitchen to the workshop, where only useful things are made; from the workshop to the museum with its collection of plants and patterns and insects; from the museum back to the front porch, the children go without confusion or noise because all their activity is purposeful and natural. They do not need *don'ts* or *thou shalt nots*. They are living the law. For what is good order, after all, but the order that results from the purposeful expression of energy?

There are days when the entire school goes out into the woods and fields to gather specimens for the museum and to observe wild nature; days when similar excursions are made to see what rivers are, and lakes and hills and valleys, or to study the relics of local history.

The course of study for these children at Rock Hill is built out of the normal activities of the community, organized, simplified, and interpreted. The teacher is not the taskmaster or the jailer, but the guide and philosopher to the children. And their government is not a set of abstract aud uncomprehended rules, imposed from above, but the common law, the *lex non scripta* which evolves naturally and inevitably for the necessity of living and doing things together. With them coöperation is not a theory; it is the living spirit of activities that cannot be successfully carried out except through mutual aid.

There are two sets of activities in this description of a day at Rock Hill—the activities such as washing the hands and preparing the meal that result from universal necessity, and the activities like hoeing and spading that are peculiar to the agricultural environment. But the spirit of the school—its government and course of study—is capable of application in any community whatsoever, city or country, north or south, east or west. What can be done with beans can be done equally well with corn or wheat, or in making chairs and tables in the workshop.

It may be objected that so informal a course of study as that described will make grading difficult or impossible, that it must ultimately undermine the children's sense of discipline, and that in any case it places an undue tax upon the attention, energy, and resources of the teacher. On the contrary, Mrs. Hetty S. Browne, the teacher in charge of the school, declares that the children who have made practical use of their arithmetic are quicker at the solution of original problems than children of the same age who have been held too close to the text-book; that by judicious assignment of tasks appropriate to the ages and abilities of the children they progress more rapidly and show a more rounded development than children who are restrained in the Procrustean bed of rigid and arbitrary grades; and that the interested expenditure of their energies upon the materials of their actual experience results in good order in the midst of the greatest liberty and in an admirable spirit of self-reliance and neighborly consideration. No doubt it is true that so informal a course of study demands for its successful leadership a vital personality, a well-trained mind, and a resourceful imagination. But on the other hand, the very demands which it makes tend to develop these qualities as they never can be developed where the personality of the teacher is subordinated to the routine of a text-book course and the daily program runs in cast-iron grooves. Text-books are of superlative value when they are used for reference and as tools; the more good books the teacher and children have at their command, the better. But when the text-book is permitted to supersede the living personality of an alert teacher and to chain the free, normal activities of the children, it defeats the ends of true education and becomes an instrument of torture and bondage.

We teach the more formal subjects [writes Mrs. Browne, in an article published in the *Atlantic Educational Journal* for December, 1912] such as reading, spelling, writing, arithmetic, drawing, language, as far as possible, in connection with our work in cooking, housekeeping, manual training, agriculture, sewing, etc. Some work has to be done in books, but this, as far as possible, is connected vitally with the work in which the child is interested.

The children work in groups. An older pupil works with several younger ones. He not only does his work in such a manner that the younger ones may use it for a model, but he helps them to do theirs. In this way he gets a double benefit from the lesson.

All of the pupils are engaged in the same line of work—boys and girls, and from the youngest to the oldest. The older pupils go into more elaborate detail than the younger ones do. I can explain my meaning better by taking some concrete examples:

1. In drawing the plan of the garden: Each child draws a plan of his own garden. The youngest draw simple rectangles; the older ones draw their plan to a scale, and the oldest draw theirs to a scale, and, in addition, indicate the directions on their plan.

2. In the cooking lessons: All cook the same thing. The younger ones do what they can; the older ones do the rest. Those who can write copy the recipe in a permanent notebook; the older ones, in addition to copying the recipe, describe the process of combining the materials. They also write simple compositions on subjects connected with their cooking, such as "How to Scour Knives," "The Different Kinds of Fruit," "How to Can Fruit for the Winter," "How to Preserve Fruit," "How to Keep Foods for the Winter."

3. In sewing: All work on the same problem. The older ones draft the patterns for the younger. The younger ones cut the garment by the pattern and make it, using simpler stitches than the older ones use.

4. In history: In this subject the older ones have a book which they read and study. They use the sand-table to make models. At the social period they take turns in telling the younger children stories they have read in history, referring to the sand-table for illustration. They tell the story not as a child reciting a lesson to a teacher, but as one person telling another a beautiful story or a thrilling adventure.

To go more into detail I shall take the simple boiling of the potato. The children have had a lesson in the boiling of water. Each child has a potato. On the table there are knives, water, glasses, cheesecloth, grater, bowls, and iodine. The children describe the potato, and as they do so the words developed are written on the blackboard in three columns. Not a word is said to the younger ones about the parts of speech, but the older ones understand. The describing of the potato is made a sense-perception lesson. The following words are developed:

Potato, skin, tuber, bud, stem, flesh; long, round, rough, thin, indented, underground, brown, whitish, firm, white; grows, sprouts, matures.

Later in the day this forms a language lesson and a spelling lesson for the advanced pupils. The various tests for starch are tried. The advanced pupils write on blackboard in complete sentences a description of the test and the conclusion reached. They write in a column these words:

Water, starch, woody fiber.

Directions for boiling the potato are written on blackboard. All who can do so read them. Potatoes are put on to boil. One child is appointed time-keeper.

All of the children turn their attention to the work they can do in connection with the potato. The more advanced ones, under the teacher's direction, learn something of the history of the potato from books. The youngest pupils model the potato with clay. All make a drawing of the potato. The youngest draw only the outline, while the more advanced make a study of the potato. In this lesson the pupil is studying reading, spelling, grammar, composition, history, geography, a little arithmetic, drawing, and clay modeling.

No doubt a "model school" has appeared to the minds of the readers of this description of the school at Rock

Hill. They see a specially trained teacher working with a carefully prepared "course of study"; children from "refined" homes; single, adjustable desks; a schoolhouse built in accordance with the latest plans for ventilation, lighting, and sanitation. Fortunately or unfortunately, the picture does not correspond with the facts. The teacher is just a healthy, vigorous woman without a trace of mannerism or of "pedagese" about her—without a suggestion of the didactic in attitude or voice. The children come principally from the homes of tenant farmers. There is not a patent desk in the house. The building was a modest residence that has been turned over to the school authorities. It is surrounded by porches, and on those porches, as in each of the several rooms, we found groups of busy children. At a particular moment we observed a group of girls busy in the kitchen; a group of boys doing some woodwork in the bench-room; several girls sewing together on one of the porches; four boys sitting about a stove and studying together; the teacher and seven children on the back porch reading an absorbing story. And not a desk! Just chairs and tables as at home.

One boy wished to "go out." He didn't ask permission; he just went, and in a few minutes he was back again at his work.

A little six-year-old walked up to the teacher and said: "I don't know how to work this next stitch."

"I haven't time to show you now," said the teacher; "go over there and ask Carrie to show you."

The child got a chair, took it over near the end of the porch, and in a moment Carrie, who was perhaps ten years old, was showing her how to work the stitch.

About half past ten a teacher came from the normal school near by and taught music to the whole school on the large side porch. After the lesson the children again went about their work. There wasn't any "marching."

The children walked naturally — they did everything naturally without boisterousness and equally without unnatural quiet.

Indeed, the most wonderful thing about the school was the pervasive air of perfect simplicity, perfect sincerity, perfect naturalness. In all the day's work we did not hear a *don't* or a pious platitude. And there was no sign of "busy work," that device of the devil to wheedle the children into contentment with a lifeless "program." Why should there have been? Every moment of the day was filled with the rich materials of normal, useful experience through which the children were learning how to read and write and think and work *together*. This is the only "busy work" that is worth while, because it needs doing wherever human beings move and live. And a course of study that arouses and holds the living interest of the children automatically solves the problem of democratic self-discipline. The best-governed school, like the best-governed community, is one in which the citizens live the law.

V

THE WIDENING OUTLOOK OF THE RURAL SCHOOL

THE solution of the problem of the course of study in the elementary grades is comparatively simple once it is agreed that it must be developed out of the normal activities of the children, concentrated on the materials of community life. The principle adopted at Rock Hill is equally applicable to city and rural schools, although the rural school has the great advantage of space, elbow-room, easier access to abundant materials. The satisfactory development of the methods so successfully followed at Rock Hill will require a much larger expenditure in the cities where land is dear and where the nearness of the homes to the school plant interferes with the complete control of the children even during school hours.

But heretofore the cities, in spite of their handicaps, have done more than the rural districts to liberalize the course of study through the development of the kindergarten, courses in domestic science and manual training, and the extension of the spirit of the kindergarten through the elementary grades by means of school-gardens, play-grounds, and workshops. Splendid efforts have been made in this direction; but the physical limitations of the city schools have tended to narrow the application of this liberal spirit by forcing the city teachers to invent materials to take the place of the natural materials that are so abundant in the country, with the result that even kindergarten, domestic-science, and manual-training practices have shown a tendency to fall into conventional and academic grooves. The rural school-teachers are comparatively free from these limitations, and there is every reason to expect that if they will take advantage of their more fortunate situation they will soon win a position of leadership in the adjustment of the course of study to the living needs of the children in the elementary grades.

The moment we leave the early elementary grades, however, and come to deal with the problems of the course of study for the children who have arrived at an age when it is necessary for them to consider the occupation through which they must earn a living, difficulties multiply. There are wide differences of opinion as to the age at which the training of the children should be definitely specialized. Here again, however, the rural school has a distinct advantage over the city school because of the vastly superior simplicity of the country-life problem. There are scores of practical vocations in all our industrial centers, whereas the dominant vocation in the country is agriculture.

The problem of industrial training for city children has been partially solved in Cincinnati, Ohio, and in Fitchburg, Massachusetts, by an open alliance between certain groups of manufacturers and the educational authorities. In 1909 the members of the Metal Trades Association of Cincinnati agreed that if the school authorities would furnish teachers, building, and ordinary school equipment, they would supply at least one hundred and fifty boys out of the ranks of their apprentices for four hours each week without docking their wages. As a result the city operates a continuation-school four and a half days a week during forty-eight weeks in the year. Several hundred apprentices are in attendance four hours a week, and receive their usual wage for attendance. Two half-days the instructors spend visiting the boys in their workshops, counseling with their foremen, and getting vital material for classroom use. The coöperating manufacturers are enthusiastic; they have found that the four hours a week spent by the boys in school, so far from decreasing their output, actually increases it. This result is in part accounted for by the systematic technical training of the boys, but in part also by the fact that the instructors furnished by the city, being men of special ability and experience, are frequently able to solve shop problems that are too stiff for the ordinary foremen. In 1911 an additional continuation-school was opened in Cincinnati for the apprentices in the eleven trades classed as the Allied Printing Trades; and a similar arrangement has been entered into by a small group of manufacturers in Fitchburg, Massachusetts, with the educational authorities of that city, for the special training of apprentices in the machinist's, patternmaker's, and saw-making trades.

Where such an alliance is effected the scheme works well for the small number of boys involved. In Rochester, where the attempt has been made to train a larger number of boys for specific vocations before the boys have gone to work, it has been found that only a small percentage of the boys enter or remain in the vocations for which the schools have especially trained them. The fullest and apparently the most successful effort to hitch up city schools with the actual industrial life of the city community has been made in Munich, Germany.

In Munich compulsory attendance upon the elementary schools is followed by compulsory attendance upon vocational continuation-schools for all boys and girls who do not elect the higher academic courses. Boys must attend until they are eighteen; girls for three years after they have completed the elementary grades. Side by side with the compulsory continuation-schools are voluntary continuation-schools for students who prefer vocational training to academic work, but who are not under the necessity of entering the trades.

Of the total school population of somewhat more than
100,000 children about 20,000 are in these industrial con-
tinuation - schools — 9,400 boys and 7,500 girls under
compulsion, and 3,700 girls as volunteers. The 9,400
boys are distributed into fifty-two trade and twelve
general industrial schools. Every trade having as many
as twenty-five apprentices has a school of its own. The
twelve general schools are attended by about 1,100 un-
skilled workmen—day-laborers, barrow-men, errand-boys,
servants. The 7,500 girls in the compulsory classes are
distributed into forty schools. All of these girls are
taught the principles of home-making in addition to the
technique of their chosen trades. There are several
voluntary continuation-schools for advanced apprentices
who are ready to become full-fledged journeymen and
masters. One of these is devoted to commercial apprentices, a second to painters, a third to the building trades,
another to the printers, locksmiths, and the like, a fifth
to the wood-workers. The butchers' trade - school is
operated in connection with the municipal slaughter-
house. In short, the continuation-schools of Munich are
woven into the very texture of the city's industrial life.

In describing these schools Dr. Georg Kerschensteiner,
Director of Education in Munich, says that attendance
was made compulsory on broad grounds of public policy,
because "the youthful worker has more and more become
an object of cheap labor," and cheap and ill-educated
labor is an unsatisfactory foundation for national efficiency.
So the children are forced to attend, although attendance
usually costs them a deduction in wages. Furthermore,
"as long as the continuation-school remains optional,
thousands of employers will prevent their youthful
workmen from making use of its opportunities, except at
the end of the day's work, when mind and body are
fatigued; and even in cases where some reasonable employers would be willing to grant their boys time for

study they would probably do it only if the training in question were principally in the interest of their own trade."

And besides, Dr. Kerschensteiner goes on to insist, it is a narrow view that sees in the competent workmen the exclusive aim of the industrial school; industrial education must regard "technical training only as a means for mental and moral training"; its object must be the enlightened citizen of an industrial democracy who has a living joy in his work, and who "not only seeks to advance his own welfare through his work, but also consciously places his labor in the service of the community." Accordingly, the student in the Munich continuation-schools is "instructed in the historical development of the trade to which he belongs; he is shown in the struggles of his fellow-workers the continually growing interdependence of interests among all citizens of a community; concrete examples of devotion to a common cause are placed before him; and so by degrees he is led to recognize how the problems arose which occupy town and nation to-day, and to understand the duties and rights of the individual within the state."

But in spite of the apparent success of the Munich plan in Munich the question as to whether it is applicable to American cities is still in debate. And there is a strong feeling that the experience of Rochester justifies the contention that the education of the children who are to enter industry should not be specialized during their public-school career, that specialization should be left to the industry itself and to the higher technical schools. For it must be remembered that the object of industrial training in the schools is not the enslavement of the children to any vocation, but the highest development of their capacities through "typical and continuous lines of activity which are of social value to everybody."

This is not the place for a detailed discussion of the

problem of industrial training as it appears in our industrial centers. The point is that here again the city problem is infinitely more complex and difficult than the analogous problem in the country. For it is a safe assumption that if rural life can be made socially and economically attractive the great majority of the children in the open country will look to the land and the profession of agriculture for a living.

The inauguration by the national government of the agricultural and mechanical colleges was the beginning of a great movement for scientific agriculture. Necessarily placed at the start largely in the hands of those whose training had been academic rather than scientific, these institutions have been gradually freeing themselves from the academic outlook, and have long since become an indispensable asset of our civilization. But the hope that a sufficient number of students would attend the agricultural colleges to transform agriculture did not materialize; and so in recent years the effort of these colleges, in addition to educating students in scientific agriculture, has been largely directed to the dissemination of information to adult farmers through bulletins and circulars based on the work of experiment stations and experiment farms, and in this the United States Department of Agriculture has also taken a very active and effective part. Millions of bulletins and circulars have been distributed, many of which have proved of great value in improving the methods of those who work on the land. The states, too, through their departments of agriculture, have helped in this phase of agricultural extension. One state college announces on its bulletin, "If you can't come to the college, the college will come to you." Another sends out a monthly *Annunciator*, dealing with problems of immediate concern to the farmers.

But, notwithstanding the great amount of good done by this extension work, it has been found that a very large proportion of the farmers do not send for the literature on agricultural subjects, and that of those who do, a very large proportion are unable to follow printed directions. In addition, therefore, to issuing bulletins, farmers' institutes and demonstration trains have been started by the agricultural colleges and the state agricultural departments, with the hearty coöperation of the United States Department of Agriculture. This method has also been a means of spreading information. Excellent exhibits of products and of labor-saving devices have been studied by the hundreds and thousands of men and women who have come to the stations to attend these institutes and to hear the talks made by the men and women having the exhibits in charge. Other thousands have been reached by the "movable school"—a school of a few days' duration held in the country districts for the benefit of farm men and women at a distance from the railroads. And in recent years many agricultural colleges have offered short winter and summer courses for the accommodation of those who are able to leave the farm only during the intervals of planting and harvesting. All these activities have been supplemental to the state farmers' institutes, which, with their local branches, have not only helped to spread knowledge, but have done much to secure legislation favorable to the development of agriculture and farm life. But the United States Department of Agriculture estimates that with all this effort not one farmer in a hundred is effectively reached.

The important result of all this activity has been its broadening influence on the popular conception of the function of public education. Courses in agriculture are now offered in the high schools and even the elementary schools of many states, and a demand has arisen for schools of agriculture and domestic science to reach the large number of country boys and girls who cannot attend college, and who, if they could do so, need an earlier and more elementary preparation than the colleges give. It has been widely recognized that to deny these students such training is to banish them forever from legitimate opportunity. The attempts to meet this demand have resulted in various types of schools—the county agricultural school, in which the teaching of agriculture and domestic science is placed in the curriculum with the usual academic studies; the congressional district schools, some of which have none of the so-called "cultural" studies, and others of which teach both the farm-life subjects and also the academic 'subjects; the county farm-life schools, which teach agriculture and domestic science together with the elementary subjects leading to these; and the agricultural high schools of the Minnesota type.

All of these schools are still in the experimental stage. They have been worth every dollar spent on them because they are helping to show the ways to go and the ways not to go. The criticism that, because some agricultural schools or farm-life schools have not met expectations, the whole plan of agricultural training is a failure and should be abolished is short-sighted on the part of those who are impatient for results and foolish on the part of those who still cling to the superstition that the best training in agriculture is a training in the purely academic subjects, and that our "culture" is in danger when it comes into contact with the soil.

It is not a waste of time or money to try experiments. All the money ever spent in the United States on agricultural colleges, agricultural schools, and agricultural experiments would not amount to the returns that the country has secured, for example, from the work of Babcock, of the agricultural department of the University of Wisconsin. No one contends that Thomas A. Edison was foolish because he spent one million dollars in cash and five years of time and performed over fifty thousand experiments before he succeeded in producing the proper filler for a little cylinder the size of one's finger which was needed to make his electric battery a commercial success. Some one is said to have asked Edison, after he had performed over nine hundred experiments with no apparent results, if he didn't think he was wasting his time.

"No," was his prompt reply; "I have found out over nine hundred ways not to do it!"

So the experimenters in agricultural instruction are clearing the way for proper methods of teaching agriculture and domestic science to boys and girls, men and women, and the best ways to carry the fruits of agricultural knowledge to the largest number of people.

Those who believe or hope that the whole industrial movement will be swept out of the schools and that the people of this country will confine their children to the three R's of the old curriculum—the reading, writing, and arithmetic of the elementary school, and the Latin, Greek, and higher mathematics of the high schools and colleges—delude themselves. It is perfectly evident that nothing can stop this movement, which will not only have those things taught which can be related to every-day life, but will insist that they shall be so related. A "culture" which is afraid of the soil is not even skin-deep. A course of study that permits its recipient to go out into the world imbued with the idea of easy self-aggrandizement, even if it is saturated with classical studies, is a refined hedonism that will not stand the acid test of modern requirements of citizenship in a democracy. It springs from the ancient idea that some work is degrading, while other work is not. Salary gives itself airs and makes faces at Wages. It is forgotten by some, and studiously overlooked by others, that the only thing degrading about any work is the motive behind it and the manner of its doing.

The traditional course of study offered by the classical colleges and the dominating influence of these institutions of higher learning have made a difficult situation for the

SCHOOL-BUILDING AND HOUSE FOR TEACHERS AND FOR DOMESTIC-
SCIENCE CLASSES

SCHOOL - BUILDING, TEACHERS' RESIDENCE, HORSE - SHEDS FOR THE
NEIGHBORS

TWO OHIO COMMUNITY CENTERS

elementary schools that have desired to widen their outlook and modernize their courses. A friction has resulted which has often proved irritating to both parties, but which has been of great value in forcing a renewed study of the content of the courses of study in their relation to contemporary life. The difficulty has arisen from a purblind attempt to force the children's activities to fit a medieval tradition instead of permitting the course of study to evolve naturally out of the normal life of living communities. Some of the colleges and universities, impressed with the irrepressible insistence of the new democratic spirit, are reorganizing and readjusting their entrance requirements and their courses of study. It is a slow and painful process. Any serious modification of a program that has been static for generations is necessarily slow and painful. But that there has been the courage to make the attempt is in itself a hopeful sign, and the approval that has instantly come to the pioneers in this democratic movement has given notice to the laggards that they must take a similar course or drop out altogether. The more numerous the colleges and universities that adopt a democratic program and outlook, the easier will it be for the elementary and high schools to develop an effective program. And the more the elementary and high schools insist upon a vital program, the more necessary will it become for the state and private institutions of higher learning to meet the situation by adjustment instead of by continued resistance.

Along with the attempt through agricultural and domestic-science schools to reach more boys and girls than the agricultural colleges can ever hope to reach, and to give those who plan to attend these colleges a more thorough preparation, has come a wide-spread movement, which, reaching down through the high schools to the elementary schools, has aroused enormous interest. This is the extension work by means of boys' corn and pig clubs, boys' and girls' garden clubs, and sewing and cooking clubs among the girls. It has sprung up "over night," as it were, and has naturally taken many forms. Hundreds of thousands of children in all parts of the United States have joined these clubs, and the exhibits of their handiwork at annual state fairs, at county fairs, and at school fairs have captured the popular imagination. It is significant that state departments of agriculture and education, agricultural colleges, universities, normal schools, and the United States Department of Agriculture have all joined in fostering this movement, though some of them have been swept forward by the tide rather than by their own free will. Rural-school work has been greatly quickened by this splendid next-step in the nation-wide democratization of public education which is doing so much to conserve and develop the latent boy-power and girl-power upon which the conservation and development of all else in the nation depends. In a majority of the states men and women are now employed whose whole time is given to organizing this extension work. The materials which they are carrying into the schoolrooms out of the living activities of the children are making it much easier than it formerly was for the teacher to free the course of study from formalism and to "hitch education up with life."

Probably the first form of extension work was that done in the school-garden, and it is safe to say that nothing has added more to the health, the happiness, and the education of the children, especially in the cities and towns. Wherever it has been intelligently used the school-garden has helped to free the children and the curriculum from bookishness. It has given the children a chance to come into intimate and joyous contact with earth and nature. It has given them an outlet for their energies and kept them from drifting into mischief. And it has given opportunities to the teachers to gather rich material for courses of study that were suffering woefully from a lack of fresh air.

The school-garden has not been used in the rural districts as freely as in the cities and towns because the country is slower to adopt new ideas; because it has been thought that children could get all the gardening they needed at home; because school-gardening has been considered a fad by those who could not see what it had to do with "education"; and because in vacation there are often not enough children near the school to look after the growing plants.

As a part of the school program—as a part of the "course of study," to use the usual term—the school-garden is, nevertheless, indispensable to the rural school.

Many vegetables can be raised during the fall and spring, while the school is in session. As a relaxation from the indoor studies it is of essential value; the daily use of the school-garden causes the children to advance more rapidly in their formal studies. It provides material for excellent lessons in botany, language, arithmetic, physics, biology, spelling, and reading. Many of the vegetables can be sold; many can be used in the cooking-classes, and can be served at the daily school lunches. The school-garden is a sign-board that says to the children, "Come and Do!" and is in striking contrast to the usual one that says, "Don't!" Children who have flowers and vegetables of their own expend their pent-up energies in orderly, and not in disorderly, activities. They learn the use of the best tools; how to cultivate and fertilize the soil; how to follow up one crop with another, so as to keep the land "busy"; all this makes for good citizenship.

The size of the garden will depend, of course, on the number of children who are to work in it. It should be used mainly by the little children if the school is one of several rooms. The larger children, as will be shown later, will have their gardens and agricultural plots at home. Whether the garden should be in separate plots for each child or should be worked in common by all the workers can probably best be answered by carrying on both plans together—the separate plots for the children to "own" individually, and to receive each one the fruits of his and her labor; and a "common" garden for the school, worked in coöperation by all, the proceeds to belong to the school community and to be used to purchase books, pictures, etc., for the common delight.

If there is a sufficient number of children in the immediate neighborhood to cultivate the garden during vacation, it should be kept going all summer. Where the school cottage is, as it should be, a part of the school equipment, the garden can be utilized the year round to supply the cottage on whatever fair and equitable terms may be decided upon, provided always that there shall be no exploitation of any one by any one else. The school-garden, to be of educative value, must be coöperative.

Here is an account of how a school-garden was started at a school situated on several acres of land on the edge of a farming village of about five hundred people who had never heard of school-gardening. The teacher who started the garden work had nothing but determination and tact. She had never attempted to teach gardening before. She began by securing the promise of the trustees that they would support her in her effort.

The patrons [she says, in describing the beginnings of the work] were nearly all opposed to it—to the formal garden work and the actual labor attached to it. Some said:

"My boys have farm work enough to do at home, and they don't have long in school no way. They've been doing that kind of work ever since they was born; 'tain't nothin' for them to learn. This here farming out of books I don't think much of."

Many requests came for boys to be excused from garden work. Mothers wrote notes, came to the school-doors and

IN THE GARDEN

CONSULTING THE TEACHER

AT THE ROCK HILL EXPERIMENTAL SCHOOL, S. C.

pleaded for their "sickly" little lean girl to be excused, or their overgrown fat girl that had never been allowed to over-exert herself, to be excused. They said that their daughters weren't allowed to use hoes and rakes at home; that it was foolish for people in the country to have to learn to farm. It was good enough for poor little city children, but country people knew all about it—"and too much, too." Some patrons even decided to employ a private teacher. One patron sent her daughter to the rural school three miles away for two or three weeks, but then applied to know if she would be allowed to return. The answer was, "She may if she will take gardening."

The principal said, "We must make this work elective. I believe in it, but I don't believe it should be compulsory. It is going to break up our school and ruin everything." I tried to make him see that he was unduly excited, that the patrons knew nothing about curriculums, and I was not going to give up; that I didn't believe the state should spend from one thousand to two thousand dollars per year to give training to two or three, when there were one hundred and fifty to be trained. The daily average attendance dropped about 5 per cent. for about one week and then all (except two) were back in place ready to do as they were bidden. In about three months every patron but two was helping us on our way. The principal was himself a genuine convert in a few weeks. The patrons who did not wholly believe in it viewed it with a question-mark until they themselves believed in it. A few openly and on all occasions spoke in favor of it, and said, "It is a good thing."

To overcome the indifference I did all possible to show the good in the work, to apply it to life, to get the pupils interested; and as soon as the child was won I had the patron. I visited some parents and explained to them what it all meant, and as soon as they understood, the indifference melted into warmth and coöperation. The same method was used with opposition, except that a compulsory order from the trustees was issued that no pupil could be excused from garden work without a certificate from a physician requesting it on health conditions.

The ground at the school was so rough that a man had to be employed to break it and get it into shape for the children. The school-board was persuaded to buy the following equipment:

One dozen large spading-forks (for boys).
One dozen small spading-forks (for girls).
Two dozen onion-hoes.
One dozen large scuffle-hoes (for boys).
One dozen small scuffle-hoes (for girls).
Two dozen trowels.
One ax.
One mattox.
One rat-proof seed-box.
About five dollars ($5) in seed.
One garden plow.
One dozen large rakes.
One dozen small rakes.
Perhaps a few other articles.
One garden line and reel.

All kinds of difficulties in regard to soil problems confronted us, and it was the 17th of July before our first real work with the pupils began.

The plots were laid off 14 x 16 feet, leaving a path two feet wide all around the plot. The plots were staked and numbered, and each pupil assigned one plot by number. To get the pupils to work during the summer I visited every home, explained the work, its object, its educational value, its commercial value, its health value, its moral value, and asked for volunteers. There were thirty-three (33) boys and girls from seven to sixteen years of age who promised to come every morning at six o'clock (I allowed them to vote on the hour), and work for two hours, and, if necessary, three hours, in these little gardens. The first morning the thirty-three happy children were there, and I had to study out the management of tools, not having enough of one kind to go around, and in some cases I allowed boys to bring tools from their homes. We could not afford any more then. (Those already bought were on ten months' time.)

The 17th of July was just in time to plant gardens for a production of fall vegetables. The pupils were promised all the money they could make on these plots. They averaged (with that late garden and in its beginnings) four dollars ($4) per plot per pupil (they gathered their products and sold them). The girls seemed to think the work a little heavy at first, but the boys watched the girls closely and offered to spade for them, to carry their tools to the toolhouse, to put them in place. I smiled approvingly at the boys for this, and gave them side-talks about good garden manners; and the very first teasing that started I talked to the girls alone, and then to the boys, showing them the immorality of teasing, and seldom ever again saw any inclination to tease. The ethical side of life showed more sweetly and prominently in the garden than elsewhere.

Three times a week these little gardeners came, and roses showed in faces in which I had never before seen them. Several girls and boys improved physically. Their interest in plant life seemed to give them an interest in all life. It was the most wide-awake work I ever did. It was as great a study in human life as in plant life, as great a study in brain soil as in earth soil; and I learned there as never before that there was as much difference in brain soil as in earth soil; that it produces as many and as great variety of products and permitted of as many varieties of cultivation, and that they all changed for the better under proper culture, and the culture of each one was as different from the culture of another as the culture of different plants.

The second session, 1909 and 1910, there was not one note of complaint or opposition, and every one seemed interested. I felt that I had the coöperation of patrons and pupils.

The pupils had not worked long before they hailed with delight every feature of the garden work, and when the bell rang for the work to stop and for all to line up and put tools in place they frequently asked to be allowed to work longer. During the school session some would ask to come on Saturday to work in their gardens.

The general improvement in home-yards and home-gardens gratified me quite as much as anything.

I secured many government seeds and distributed them among pupils to give away or to use at home. Many women and some men came for advice regarding their gardens; and some told me of what they had learned through their children, and how hard it had been to get them interested in home affairs before the school had a garden, and now how much they talked about the home-garden and planned for it.

During the winter months, when we had a very few lessons

outdoors, we studied the theory and then applied it during the spring and summer.

I did not accomplish there one-fourth of what was in my mind, but I enjoyed what was done and felt that it did some good.

The garden work was often used as the basis for number, language, and nature study in my regular class work.

I did this garden work in addition to my regular work without any additional salary.

Extending the school-garden to the home, but keeping it in close connection with the school program, has been a logical and beautiful evolution. Many of the children live too far from the school to utilize the school-garden except during school-hours. The home-garden not only meets this difficulty, but establishes an important connecting-link between the school and the home which cannot be formed with the school-garden alone.

A principal of a state normal school, who has done notable work in school-gardening, says: "I had long ago come to the conclusion that home-gardens were the solution of this question in nine cases out of ten. The difficulty of maintaining the school-garden during the summer months is insurmountable except in rare instances." And the influence of the home-garden reaches beyond the children to the homes themselves. "I cannot begin to tell you," says one writer, "of the improved appearance of the whole town, including the farmhouses on the outskirts. The cleaning and yard-decoration fever seem to be very contagious, spreading rapidly."

In the fall of 1911 the agricultural extension department of a western state university began organizing gardening clubs. By spring there were five thousand boys and girls actively at work, and 60 per cent. of them were working at home. The method of procedure is to send to any interested teacher enrolment-blanks and a constitution. When the enrolment-blanks are returned the boys and girls are given certain privileges provided by the constitution and by-laws, such as the following: The local club may receive from the division of agricultural education of the university, (1) the bi-weekly issued for the gardeners, (2) a club pin or button, (3) seeds, (4) permission to enter "growing" contests, etc. Each club has a supervisor, president, vice-president, secretary, and treasurer, the teacher in every club being the supervisor, the children holding the other offices. Reports of the work of the club are sent to the director of extension work at the university. Wherever practicable, a "garden city" is organized on a self-government basis. The director states that in many instances the gardens are quite ambitious affairs, some of them furnishing all of the vegetables for the home table, besides netting a small income to the grower.

The evolution of the course of study from such work as this is inevitable; lessons in botany, geography, reading, writing, arithmetic, oral and written expression, spelling, and drawing spring from it in abundance. Here are two examples in botany, spelling, writing, and language.

From a little girl:

Our teacher is having us write about our gardens. I have planted a garden at home that is doing better than the one at school. In my home-garden I have planted lettuce and radishes that are coming up, and carrots, onions, and spinach that haven't yet come up. For flowers I have planted sweet-peas, poppies, and pansies.

From a fifth-grade boy:

When I came into the room I found a lima bean, on my desk. It had been soaked for three days. How did the water enter the seed? It entered through the microphyle, a tiny hole. When the water entered, this caused action in the seed and made sugar. The water was next drawn through the coat of the seed by osmosis.

We then opened the seed-coat. We saw the embryo, which

is the baby plant, and the cotyledons, which are the two fat seed-leaves, or food-leaves.

This girl and boy seem to be able to express themselves with a reasonable degree of lucidity. The boy appears to know the meaning of the words *microphyle*, *osmosis*, *embryo*, and *cotyledon*. One is reminded of the distinguished clergyman who said before a school that a boy who expected to study electricity should know Greek, because without it he could not understand the meaning of the word *electricity* or know that it came from the Greek word *electron*. Meanwhile one little fellow, altogether innocent of his sad plight, had made an entirely workable outfit for wireless telegraphy.

Like the school-garden, the school-farm is necessary to the completely developed school program because it supplies in convenient form and at the school center some of the essential materials of community life through which the older children especially may apply and test their classroom information; because it can be made a place for experimentation in community problems, such as determining whether other crops than those commonly raised in the neighborhood can be made profitable, and whether larger yields of the usual crops can be obtained, and, if so, at what profit and in what way. Such experimentation calls for a study of soils and fertilizers, of seed and seed-selection; it demands a careful accounting of time, labor, machinery, and supplies; and, if it is to be of the fullest practical value, it will involve a study of marketing and a consideration of the value of the product both as food for home consumption and as a money crop.

The school-farm, then, should aim to reproduce in miniature the agricultural activities of the community. It need not, and should not, be of extended acreage; neither should the crops produced upon it be on a large area. Its primary purpose is not to supply crops for market, but to

provide the opportunity to raise enough crops of each
kind to demonstrate their value to the community and to
give the boys and girls at least an elementary training
in farm-accounting and management, and in the fundamental principles of coöperative marketing. A large
farm with elaborate equipment is not only unnecessary,
but of extremely problematic value.

The only essential difference between the educational
uses of the school-garden and the school-farm is that the
one is suitable for the small children and looks to the improvement of the home-garden, while the other is suitable
for the older boys and girls and looks to the improvement of
the home-farm. To make the entire community the school-
yard; to base the course of study upon the every-day
activities of the community and the normal experiences of
the children; to make the educative processes work
through the processes of every-day life; to untether the
children; to keep reaching out until every child feels the
guiding touch of a living, sympathetic hand—this is the
problem, this the tendency.

It is this tendency that has produced not only the
school-garden and school-farm, but also the agricultural
high schools and the farm-schools that are striving to
carry opportunities for practical training to the children
who are isolated. These schools have assumed various
forms and are variously known as congressional-district,
county, and township agricultural schools. In some of
them agriculture and domestic science are taught exclu-
sively; in some, agriculture and domestic science hardly
escape the academic atmosphere of the cultural tradition.
But most of them are alike in one essential thing—the
majority of the children who attend them must leave home
and board at or near the school in order to get the benefit
of their training, unless, indeed, the entire family, as not
infrequently happens, abandons the farm for the sake
of the children's education. The question accordingly

arises: Do these schools meet the demand for training in agriculture and domestic science? Do they reach and train all the children who need training?

In certain localities it may be necessary to establish farm boarding-schools for the older boys and girls, and to have a large acreage, not only for all-around practice, but also to enable those who need to do so to work their way through school. There are some boys and girls who will have no other place in which to get a training in farm and household management. In some localities such schools have already been established, and many of them are proving extremely useful because they are offering the only opportunities for practical training available to their students. Certainly, however, it is not best to adopt a general policy that will require any large numbers of boys and girls from ten to sixteen years of age to go off to a boarding-school in order to get even an elementary training in practical gardening, horticulture, dairying, sewing, cooking, and general agriculture. There are vast numbers of children who need this training and who cannot leave home, and vast numbers who should not leave home. To leave them out of the school program is to leave the school program incomplete. They must be considered. To wait for time to cure the trouble does not cure it for the boys and girls who need the training *now*. They cannot wait. Their opportunity is now or never. A policy of waiting is fatal to efficient citizenship. How can these children be reached? In answering this question it is necessary to consider the most recent step in the development of agricultural education—the Farmers' Coöperative Demonstration Work.

The complete school program must not only provide an educational scheme that will concentrate the children's activities upon the materials of community life, but it must also see that this educational scheme enables the rural children, as citizens in the making, to realize through their own efforts, properly directed, the economic value of one important phase of their efficient citizenship—namely, their efficiency as producers on a commercial basis.

It should go further than this: it should shape its educational scheme so that it can and will, either through its own resources or in coöperation with other forces, show the adults of the community how they may become more efficient producers. For education should reach the entire community, and it is even truer of the adults than of the children that a vast number of them cannot leave home; that a vast number of them will not leave; and that a vast number of them should not leave home to get needed instruction. Education is a matter of life for life, not a matter of childhood for childhood. And it is only a tradition that leaves the adult out of consideration in the school program. How can the adults be reached? As has already been pointed out, notwithstanding the agricultural colleges and their bulletins, circulars, demonstration-trains, movable schools, and other indispensable devices; notwithstanding the agricultural high schools and the farm-schools; notwithstanding the departments of agriculture and experiment stations, only a fraction of those who are already farming go away from home to learn better farming, or read the bulletins, or attend the institutes and movable schools, while only an infinitesimal fraction of the children who are to be farmers go away from home to learn agriculture.

One of the unpalatable and discouraging facts of life is that very few people know how to follow directions given through formal talks or through print. Very few teachers realize how seriously true this statement is. Another equally discouraging fact is that very few people know how to give directions; the tendency is to make them too general to be of practical value.

One trouble in giving directions is that it is impossible

to go into necessary details before a large group. Moreover, the farmers who know least about farming are, as a rule, very backward about asking questions in a crowd. There is no more sensitive class of people in the world than those who live and work in the country. Their isolation accentuates their shyness. If present, they may listen; and if some one happens to ask a question they are puzzled about they may be helped. But the important question is rarely asked; every one in the meeting usually keeps quiet. Teachers who have "mixed" with country people know this; they know, too, that oftentimes it is some seemingly insignificant point in a problem about farming that puzzles a large number of those who need help most. And in this one problem there may be six different things seemingly insignificant to the instructor that are puzzling six different men.

Take, for example, the question of good seed. Not one farmer in ten can tell good seed from poor, unless the contrast is glaring. And "telling" him the difference helps very little. He must be shown individually and made to take seed and test it in the presence of his instructor. Otherwise he takes seed on faith, as probably 90 per cent. of the farmers do. Under our present industrial system this is not "good business"—for the purchaser.

It is too often overlooked that adults who have done a certain thing a certain way for a long time have much more difficulty in changing that way than children would have. Why is this? The answer of course is that the adult has acquired a habit. "It is hard to teach an old dog new tricks." It is much easier to bend a young sapling than an old tree; it is much easier to shape a child than an old person. After a certain age the faculties of body and mind become static. There results what may be called the "fixed type."

It was a recognition of the fact that the large majority of farmers do not attend an agricultural college or school;

that a large majority of them do not read bulletins and circulars, and do not follow them when read; that a large majority do not attend institutes and movable schools; that a large majority of people, even if willing, do not know how to follow instructions at a distance; that there are about as many puzzles in one problem as there are minds working on it; that it is an exceedingly difficult thing to persuade a man that his way of doing a thing is wrong, and that even if convinced he is always helpless to change without the personal, present help of his instructor; that often he will keep silent to his own hurt—it was a recognition of these facts that led a few men some years ago to launch in a large way through the United States Department of Agriculture the plan known as the Farmers' Coöperative Demonstration Work for teaching adults and boys and girls how to farm satisfactorily and how to manage their farms, their homes, and their gardens to their own greater advantage and the greater advantage of the nation.

VI

COÖPERATIVE DEMONSTRATION WORK

THE thing had been done thousands of times. When Neighbor Brown, having "learned a thing or two," told Neighbor Jones that his way of working corn wouldn't bring the best crop there was quite a discussion. But finally when Brown's crop beat Jones's, Jones began to think. The next year Jones asked Brown a good many questions, and concluded to try Brown's plan. But habit was strong in Jones—habits in farmers are as hard and strong as their muscles—and in several little particulars Jones varied from Brown's directions, forgetting that it was the little foxes that spoiled the vines. And the crop didn't "pan out." Jones "knew that thing was all non-sense, anyhow"; he "had heard that college feller talk that way at the institute," and had forgotten all that was said before he got home. But when Brown went over and looked at Jones's crop he put his finger on the "little particulars" in which Jones had followed habit instead of following directions. Jones wondered how Brown knew.

The next year Brown went over at Jones's invitation and showed Jones how to plow. Jones had thought up to that time that anybody could plow. Brown made Jones go over his land with harrow and drag until Jones swore the whole six acres would blow away the first time a stiff wind came along. Then Brown looked at Jones's seed-corn. "This corn won't do for planting!" Jones

thought Brown must be crazy, but he only asked, "Why?"
"It's rat-eaten, and it is not prolific, anyway." And
Brown explained, "Don't you know there are 'runty'
seed and 'blooded' seed?" Brown went to the corn-
house with Jones and did the best he could in the pile.
And as the crop progressed Brown made Jones go over
it and keep the land finely mulched. Jones had his
doubts still, but, anxious as he was to say "I told you so,"
his pocket nerve had twinges and made him prefer the
prospect of a good stiff crop to the vindication of a stiff
pride. Jones made twice the crop that year that he had
ever made before, and it was an average year. Having
found out that a thirst for good crops must be translated
into a thirst for knowledge, Jones soon discovered that
what he thought was worn-out land on his farm was
really worn-out ideas in his head. So he made Brown
come over and show him about each crop, until he got the
"hang" of it. And that was "demonstration work."

Then a newspaper man came along and "wrote up
Jones"; fifty thousand people read the head-lines, and of
that number twenty thousand read the article. Ten
thousand of these forgot it; seven thousand didn't
believe it at all; twenty-five hundred thought it might be
so on Jones's land, but that "it wouldn't work on theirs."
Four hundred discussed it with their neighbors, and so
many opinions were offered, different from the article,
that they gave up the idea of trying. Ninety-five tried
the plan, with "variations," and made very little improvement, and at once declared the whole thing a fake. Five
of the readers, in five counties, followed directions accurately and succeeded.

In 1906 the "coöperative demonstration work" was
begun in a small way in Mississippi. Experience had
shown that the only sure method of getting Jones to
follow Brown was to send a Brown to work with every
Jones in Jones's own field. Through an agreement

reached between the United States Secretary of Agriculture and the General Education Board of New York City Dr. Seaman A. Knapp, who had spent most of his life in Iowa, and who was at that time in the United States Department of Agriculture, was detailed to take charge of the Browns. Dr. Knapp, during many years devoted to farming in Louisiana, had been the Brown to the Joneses of his community, and had shown them how by simple methods they might get the maximum of production for the time, money, and energy they put into their work. He now had his opportunity to make the entire South his community—and he did so. He multiplied himself by employing demonstration agents in the counties of the South to offer to "show" any farmer that wished to be shown. In 1908 the work had spread to seven states. It is now going on in fourteen states, with approximately nine hundred demonstration agents and one hundred and ten thousand demonstrators, or Browns, working under directions laid down by Dr. Knapp.

These demonstration agents try to visit the farmers on an average of once a month. They go upon the farms of those desiring advice and show them how to raise corn, grass, and cotton; how to plow and subsoil; how to harrow and drag; how to clean the land; how to fertilize with crops and other good fertilizers; how to select seed; how to rotate; how to make the most of what they have; how to start in such a small way, if necessary, that the farmer with no horse, or with only one horse or mule or ox, and a small run-down farm can get on his feet by his own efforts if he carefully follows directions.

The strength of the demonstration work as conducted under Dr. Knapp's instructions lies in his recognition of the absolute necessity of Brown going on Jones's farm at regular intervals to advise Jones and to show Jones, if Jones shows any desire to have Brown come; in his insistence that Brown is a very busy man, with many to advise and show, and that unless Jones agrees to follow directions implicitly he need not apply; on his insistence that Brown should start with Jones exactly where Jones is, and not where Jones ought to be—in other words, if Jones has a four-room cabin, one wife and nine children, one twenty-two-year-old-mule, one plow, one wagon, ten acres of rented land, one large unpaid bill at the store, one heart full of despair, one set of harness consisting of three parts leather, two parts strings, and one part cotton rope, then Brown is not to tell Jones how well Jones could do if only Jones had an automobile income, but he is to show Jones how, with Jones's present assets at home and liability at the store, he, Jones, can make from 50 to 200 per cent. larger crop.

Hundreds of thousands of acres of land have been transformed from barrenness to fertility; land that had been thought capable of bringing, and was bringing, only one-quarter to one-half bale of cotton to the acre is now bringing two bales; a ten, fifteen, twenty, and forty bushel crop of corn to the acre has jumped to thirty, fifty, sixty, eighty, a hundred and twenty-five, and even a hundred and fifty bushel crop; one-half-ton-to-the-acre grass has jumped to four, five, and six tons to the acre; land thought incapable of bringing alfalfa now brings four, five, and six tons per acre. The whole movement sounds unbelievable; it has come so suddenly, it is so full of possibilities, and yet so simple, that only those who have seen the transformation following in its wake can grasp the full significance of it. Hope has sprung up in the place of despair, poverty in many cases has come to independence, a hand-to-mouth existence to comfort, comfort to riches.

And with rare wisdom Dr. Knapp instilled into the hearts and heads of the demonstration agents that they must encourage the raising at home of more vegetables, more poultry and eggs, more meat, and better stock, and that they must show how these things can be gradually acquired. "Tell a farmer he needs better fencing and a better house," he once said, "and he will probably resent it. But show him first how to make bigger crops, and after that he will adopt almost any suggestion you make."

A few illustrations will in some measure indicate the transformation that is following the demonstration work.

A recent report shows that in one state where the average yield of corn per acre was 18 bushels, 1,600 farmers under the demonstration method averaged 46.9 bushels per acre. Twenty-two negroes in one county in another state averaged 64.8 bushels, where the state average was 19 bushels. With a state average of 609 pounds of seed-cotton per acre 60 negro farmers in one state produced 1,856.5 pounds per acre. In another state, where the state average was 732 pounds of seed-cotton per acre, the average for all the farmers working under demonstration methods was 1,510 pounds. In yet another, where the average was 861 pounds of seed-cotton per acre, 131 farmers guided by demonstration agents averaged 2,100 pounds. The results of Brown's work with Jones on Jones's farm are strikingly shown by contrasting the average yield of corn per acre for the state and the average yield for all the demonstration farmers in the same state.

	Average for State	Average for Demonstration Farmers
One state	16	39.2
Another state	18	46.3
" "	18.2	39.2
" "	18.4	42.6
" "	24	41.9

The spirit and method of the demonstration agents—which is increasingly the spirit and method of the most successful teachers in the rural school—is delightfully revealed in a letter written by Mr. B——, a demonstration agent in a Southern state. The letter in part runs as follows:

You ask for information with reference to the demonstration work in P—— County, the names of a few farmers who have signally prospered thereby, their financial status caused by following such work, etc.

To begin with, I would call your attention to Mr. J. T——, of ——, R. F. D., No. 7, a man with whom I became acquainted in this work in the fall of 1909, something like a year after this work was assigned me. I was traveling along the road, and while meditating over the vast possibilities of the work my eyes suddenly fell upon an old man working in a field which skirted the road. He, two sons, and a daughter were picking cotton in a worn-out field. Stopping and inquiring with reference to his yield per acre, I ascertained it to have been one-quarter bale of cotton. I asked the older son, who approached my buggy, thinking I was a book or medicine agent, if his father would like to make larger yields and more profit on his farm. He said, "We would like to make more, but our land is so poor that we have to plant and cultivate many acres even for a small crop." I informed him that I was the government demonstration agent, and would call on them later and get them to do demonstration work for the year 1910. Giving me a dry smile indicative of doubt, and peering at me as though he considered me a fit subject for an insane asylum, he managed to bid me good day. Several weeks later I called again and found the old gentleman in the back of his field clearing land, which he considered necessary year after year in order to have a few fresh acres that would produce sufficiently to supply his family with food and clothing. After giving him my name and passing some compliments on the good work he and the boys were doing, I told him I had come to see if he would let me help him produce more on the land he claimed to be worn out. His answer was that he was growing all the land would produce, that he had heard that I was making big crops on my place, but that his land was poor and would not make big crops. He said he would show me some of his best land, and if I thought I could select an acre or two that would make anything worth while he would try it, provided it would not cost him anything for my services. I informed him that I was employed and paid by the government and was not permitted to charge for my services, and that the cost would be nothing. It being late in the afternoon, he asked me to spend the night with him, which invitation I readily accepted, as I was seventeen miles from home.

We reached his quiet home, which was located about two hundred yards from the public road. After he had fed his stock, which, by the way, consisted of two small, goatlike mules, on corn and fodder which were grown on his impoverished farm from a poorly selected variety of seed, we repaired to the house. All the while I had been telling him how he could improve his corn by getting tested seed, and keeping it selected year after year at gathering-time. I asked him if he had a number of blooded hogs and cows from which to obtain meat, lard, milk, and butter for his family. He told me that he had no hogs, that the cholera had killed them; that those which he had owned were not thoroughbred, and he had only one cow, and that she gave very little milk.

The family consisted of the old gentleman, his wife, three sons, two daughters, and a maiden sister to his wife. Each face beamed with honesty. As I saw it and felt it, only one thing was lacking to make them as happy as people may hope to be.

We talked freely of the work I had done on my farm along improved lines, and I assured Mr. —— that he could do equally as well as I had done; that my farm was as poor as his when I began the work; and that the past year others had gotten wonderful results and derived inestimable benefits by closely following the teachings of the demonstration work. During the conversation I realized that the whole family, especially the boys, were intensely interested. We arose early the following morning, partook of a good breakfast, after which we walked over his lands. I found that he had no fences, and that his ground and everything connected therewith was in a rather poor condition to make much show in demonstration work. Finally he pointed out a splendid spot of fresh land which he considered suitable for making a good yield of corn. I told him that it was especially needful that he begin to improve his old, poor land in order that he might make profitable crops thereon. Eventually he agreed to my selecting the place for demonstration. I selected a two-acre plot between the road and his home. He told me that he had tried to build up that land with cotton-seed and manure, and that he had not been able to gather more than one-quarter of a bale of cotton or eight or ten bushels of corn per acre, and that he had seen it planted to corn and cultivated well, and it made absolutely nothing. "If that is the chance to do demonstration work I'd rather not go into it, for it will turn out a complete failure," he said. I told him that all I would ask of him would be to prepare, fertilize, and cultivate as I would instruct, and if he did not get satisfactory results he might charge the failure to me. So, taking my selection of ground, he took up the demonstration work. Instructions in regard to preparation of ground were given and received with interest, and soon I was driving away to return the next month.

On returning one month later, Mr. —— informed me that the plot had been broken according to instructions.

As I had told him he could raise thoroughbred hogs and cattle at approximately the same cost that he could razor-back or scrub stock, he lost no time in securing some Berkshire hogs and Jersey cows. At the present time he has all of his farm, with the exception of four acres, fenced with hog or woven wire.

Commencing the first year, I visited him to plant peanuts, cow-peas, velvet-beans, sweet-potatoes, and sugar-cane; he has had plenty for home use, with many things for the market. He has sold many pairs of fine pigs, besides meat, peanuts, sweet-potatoes, syrup, and other things raised on his farm.

I continued to visit this demonstrator once a month; he and his sons, especially the younger one, a boy of unusual intelligence, receiving instructions with much eagerness. The old gentleman, knowing that the young man saw no future for himself on this impoverished land, and having spoken of getting him a position in some town or on a railroad, told him he might have the demonstration corn, and that he wanted him to pay close attention to Mr. B—— and see if he could not learn to farm as he did. The corn was cultivated strictly according to instructions, sprouted well, and grew vigorously. When gathering-time came Mr. —— called in his neighbors to see it, every one being eager to know just what the yield would be. He arranged to make an accurate measurement both of the land and corn, and it was found that his yield was fifty-two and one-half bushels per acre. Each one present was surprised to see so much corn gathered from land of this character at such little cost, which was twenty-eight cents per bushel—land rent, fertilizer, and labor considered—and compared the cost of producing corn by the demonstration method with the old method, and after doing so found that the old way of producing corn on the same kind of land had cost one dollar and forty cents per bushel. Every one present was convinced that he himself had not only lost money on his present crop, but had been losing year after year for many years.

The following year the same acre was taken in preparation for cotton as had been taken for corn the previous year. All of his corn-land was prepared and worked on demonstration methods. This being a dry year, and not so good for corn, the yield over the entire field was forty bushels per acre at a very slight increase in cost. The cotton was carefully weighed, and his yield was sixteen hundred pounds seed-cotton per acre, where he had gathered only four hundred pounds per acre as he had been farming.

Everything was changed from dull prospects, with no hope for the future, to a future of glorious promise. While these demonstrations were going on Mr. —— made as much improvement on other lines of farming. His older son has purchased land, horse and buggy, and is doing splendid demonstration work on his farm. The old gentleman has bought two large mules, and the younger son has a new buggy in which to glide about over our good roads, and is satisfied with farming and farm life. The young ladies no longer work in the fields; instead, they are putting their hands to duties around the home, making flowers grow and otherwise beautifying and making pleasant the place where they live and sleep, and the young children have now what may be termed their true school-days.

On one of my visits, finding Mr. —— feeling good over a bright future which stretched before him on account of the valuable lessons learned from the demonstration agent, he said: "Mr. B——, I will tell you now what I thought, and told the boys when you first came around to get us to try your method of farming. I knew we had worked our crops good, and that I got better crops some years than we did others on account of seasons, so I told my boys that you did not know anything about our land, and knew you would make a failure on our farm, but I would do as you said just to show you that I knew all about my farm. I did not doubt your making big crops on your farm, but I thought I knew you would fail on mine. I was of good mind not to have anything to do with it when you came and told me that you would take that old land out there on the road for a demonstration plot. But I thought I would not be curious, as you had been kind enough to come away over here to see me. We laughed about how you would fail on that poor old field. I told my son I wanted him to work it just like you said, so that you could attach no blame to us for the failure that was certain. I had seen it manured better than you advised, and it made hardly ten bushels per acre, and when you said we ought to produce forty or fifty bushels we knew you would be disappointed. But I see now that we were the ones who were fooled. If I had known this years ago, how much better off I could have been! I have worked long and hard, and my family has labored with me, and I have just learned the first principles of farming."

A wonderful improvement is seen along all lines—better schools, a veritable network of telephones, graded roads, better hogs and stock. There are about one hundred and forty demonstration farms in P—— County, all of which furnish examples similar to that set forth above. Volumes might be written to exemplify the efficacy of the work, and it is growing day by day, those testing it feeling that they have received a new lease on life. There are hundreds of farmers who have not directly taken up the work with the agent, yet the success of their neighbors has constrained them to follow the method, and the result is wonderful. The rural districts may be said to be " blossoming as the rose."

But if the United States Department of Agriculture, coöperating with certain states and with certain counties in those states, appoints demonstration agents to teach agriculture to the adults on their farms, why cannot this be made a part of the school program and the work be done through one or more central schools? Why one teacher of agriculture in the schools for boys and another teacher of agriculture for men outside the school and no connection between the two?

After starting with the adult farmers and getting the demonstration work under way for them, Dr. Knapp encouraged the plan of organizing boys' corn clubs. He said that the attention of the boys was being directed away from the farm. His plan was to have each boy in the clubs take one acre and, under plain, simply told directions sent out from Washington and followed up by the demonstration agents, prepare it, plant it to corn, and cultivate the crop. Boys ten years old and up were eligible. The acre was to be on the parents' farm, and the crop was to belong to the boy. The boy was to agree to follow directions, and the father was to agree not to interfere at any time with these directions.

The movement swept the South. Over seventy-five thousand boys are in these clubs. In addition to corn, they have become interested in garden work, cotton, grass, pigs, poultry, and dairy products. The school-fairs in the South are the annual features of the counties. Jerry Moore, of South Carolina, who raised two hundred and twenty-eight bushels of corn on his acre, has become so famous that a boy in the Sunday-school, the son of a Baptist minister, when asked a question about Jeremiah, said he knew very little about Jeremiah, but he knew all about Jerry Moore! Thousands of corn-boys in the South have started bank-accounts; many are helping their fathers and mothers out of debt; and the work, so far from interfering with their studies, has given them more interest in these by showing them the practical application of school training.

On farms where both the fathers and sons have taken the demonstration work the boys have made a better showing than their fathers because they follow directions more closely. And thousands of fathers have been converted to the new methods by the success of their boys. In cases where the fathers have sneered at the "book-farming," or the new methods pursued by the boys, the glaring contrast between the old-method father and the new-method son has been a sufficient object-lesson. In 1910 the 100 boys making the highest yields totaled 13,370 bushels on their 100 acres. In 1911 the 100 boys making the highest yields totaled 13,748 on their 100 acres. In 1910 one boy exceeded 200 bushels on his acre; in 1911 seven boys exceeded this production.

In one state 52 boys got over 100 bushels each at a cost of 30 cents a bushel; and 21 boys got 126 bushels each at a cost of 23 cents a bushel. In another state 25 boys averaged 111.6 bushels at 19.7 cents; the average for all farmers in the state was 18 bushels. In another state 65 boys averaged 109.9 bushels at 25 cents; the average in the state was 19 bushels. In another state 20 boys averaged 140.6 bushels at 23 cents; the average in the state was 19 bushels. In another state 15 boys averaged 127.6 bushels at 28 cents; the average in the state was 26.8 bushels.

Another state averaged 24 bushels: the adult demonstrators averaged 41.9; the boys averaged 61.2 bushels. In one county where a local organization employed a demonstration agent one boy raised 88 bushels of potatoes on a quarter of an acre, where his father got 58 bushels. At Appomattox Court House, Virginia, 18 boys, attending a school situated one mile from where Lee surrendered to Grant, averaged 84 bushels of corn per 'acre, one boy making 134 bushels. Truly, peace hath its victories no less renowned than war!

One of the discoveries made by the demonstration agents was the meanest man thus far recorded in American history. He refused to let his son have an acre of his land, but finally told him he could have an acre if he would grub it. The little fellow grubbed the acre, but his father then informed him that he would have to grub another, as he needed the first acre himself. The little fellow then grubbed another, and then plowed it. The demonstration agent had told the boy exactly how to plow it, but he had never seen any plowing done that way. The agent brought his own team ten miles and helped the boy plow the acre just right. Then, as the father refused to let the boy have any manure for the acre, the agent "went good" for the price. The father averaged 10 bushels per acre on his corn that year, and the boy made 80 bushels on his acre.

After the adult demonstration work and the boys' demonstration work got under way, the girls' garden work was started. The great desire of the girls to have a chance like their brothers brought a prompt response from them when it was decided to teach them how to raise and can vegetables at home. The work started in 1910. In 1911 there were 3,000 members, and in 1912 there were 25,000 members in the girls' garden and canning clubs. Dr. Knapp decided to have each member work one-tenth of an acre at home, with tomatoes as the principal crop at first.

The girls' clubs have been officially called "Canning and Poultry Clubs," because it is the intention to add the raising of poultry to the work of the clubs. The girls' garden work is done mainly through women demonstration agents. Portable canning outfits, convenient in size, are provided, varying in price from $6.50 to $12. All canning is done under the direction of the agent, and most of it is done out-of-doors in the most thorough and up-to-date manner. The goods rank very high on the market in every way. One girl on one-tenth of an acre, at a cost of $41.10, put up 950 cans of tomatoes, besides furnishing to the home $21.50 worth of raw tomatoes and selling $2.50 worth. Another girl put up 1,008 cans at a cost of $33.07, and sold the output for $110.80, making a net profit of $77.73. Another cleared $60.51, and another $55.55. Another girl put up 1,023 cans, part of which helped the family through the winter, and sold all the rest. In one state 37 girls averaged $25.42 net; in another 19 girls averaged $17.60 net; in another 28 girls averaged $22.90 net.

One farmer advised his little daughter not to stake up her tomatoes, as he had always gotten a good crop without it. She took the advice of the agent and raised three times as many as her father. Another little girl said, "I enrolled as a club member because I wanted to do something by myself and have some money of my own."

And how easy it is to evolve a course of study from such activities. Here is an example:

The fifth-grade girls have done some preserving for Mrs. Ferguson. She bought ⅔ bu. of peaches at $1.20 per bu., 12 lbs. sugar at $.07½ per lb., and $.05 worth of cloves. The labor was valued at $1.50. Eight quarts of preserves were made. The preserves are worth $.60 per qt. Did Mrs. Ferguson gain or lose in having the peaches preserved?

$1.20 cost of 1 bu. of peaches
⅔ bu. = what was bought
⅔ of $1.20 = $.80 = cost of ⅔ bu.
1 lb. of sugar cost $.07½
12 lbs. cost 12 × $.07½ = $.90

$ .80 cost of peaches	$ .60 value of 1 qt. of preserves
.90 " " sugar	8
.05 " " cloves	
1.50 for labor	$4.80 " " 8 qts. " "

$3.25 total expenses

$4.80 value of preserves
3.25 cost of making them

$1.55 gain

Already this next step in the reconstruction of rural life has attracted not only national but international attention. Bills are pending in Congress to introduce coöperative demonstration work into every state in the Union. The unique value of the demonstration method lies in the fact that it aims not so much to do something for the farmer, but to show him on his own farm how he may do something for himself. The psychology of the demonstration method is sound because it takes the farmer with all his whims, his prejudices, his fixed habits and suspicions —takes him just as he is and leads him by example rather than by precept. If he gets out of a rut he must do his own climbing; but he is shown how to climb. The ideal demonstration agent is the man who knows rural human nature and the fundamental principles and practices of good farming.

From the beginning of the coöperative demonstration work those who have been intrusted with its direction have very properly emphasized the need and possibilities of increased production. Dr. Seaman A. Knapp, who had come from New York State and who had later done pioneer work at the Iowa State College of Agriculture, was doing demonstration on his own account in his adopted home in Louisiana at the time when his example contributed to the establishment of the new division in the United States Department of Agriculture, of which he was the first head. For this and other reasons the beginnings of demonstration work on a large scale were made in the South, and in that section of our common country the pressing need was for increased production. That the need for increased production is not confined to the South, however, is strikingly shown by the agricultural statistics of the last census and by the significant fact that many of the most prosperous sections of our foremost agricultural states, such as Iowa and Missouri and Illinois, are calling for demonstration agents to help them to increase the production on their farms. Nowhere in the United States has production reached even an approximate maximum. At the same time there are many millions among our working population who are not securing enough of the necessaries of life to keep them either in efficiency or health. For many years to come it will be necessary to continue the emphasis upon increased production.

And yet, even at the beginning of this great movement to increase production through a more efficient education, the question is being asked: Will not increased production ultimately work to the injury of the producers by over-supplying the market and so breaking down prices? This same question has been raised for decades and centuries, whenever improved methods have increased the supply of any commodity. Fortunately, time has established the soundness of the obvious answer: The danger is not in oversupply, but in underconsumption. The development of higher standards of living, which is civilization, demands not only increased production, but more adequate methods of distribution. We have seen fruit rotting in heaps on the ground while in a neighboring city, hardly fourteen miles away, hundreds and thousands of families were unable to pay the price of single pieces of the same fruit. The farmer to-day receives much less than half of the price paid by the ultimate consumer. The financial distance—not the geographical distance—between producer and consumer is too great. Middlemen are of course necessary, but at present there are too many middlemen. And the crude methods of transportation, the even cruder methods of preparing the produce for market, and the almost complete lack of coöperation among producers in almost all sections of the country enable the middlemen to take profits not only from the middle, but from both ends. Only business coöperation, which means organization on scientific business lines by producers for the common benefit, will remedy the evils of crude, unscientific, and wasteful methods of distribution. One of the great problems confronting the workers in rural education is that of teaching the farmers how to increase their incomes while increasing and improving their product. Under present conditions the unorganized farmers buy at the maximum rate and sell at the minimum, although the consumer derives no benefit from the low price at which the farmer sells.

In a certain agricultural school the teacher of agriculture was made United States demonstration agent for the county in which the school was situated. Besides instructing the boys at the school and on the school-farm, it was his business to work with the boys and their fathers on their farms to increase production. The money crop in the county was potatoes, but while the teacher was able to help the individual farmers to increase their production, he was not able substantially to increase their incomes. The reason for this, he found upon investigation, was that each of the farmers was raising a different variety of potatoes, that they had no system of grading in preparing their product for market, and that they were therefore at the mercy of the local commission agents. By tact and patience he induced the farmers who had joined the demonstration clubs to fix upon one variety of potatoes, to agree in advance upon their acreage, and to follow his directions in the cultivation of the crop. At his suggestion the farmers appointed their own business agent to act with him in finding a market. Instead of producing odd lots, the farmers, through their coöperative agreement, produced carload lots of a single variety that could be shipped at a given time directly to the ultimate market. Their product has won a reputation for excellence, and they are getting good prices before their potatoes are loaded on the cars.

In this same way the demonstration agent induced the farmers to organize themselves into an association for the coöperative purchase of fertilizers, and he took pains to instruct them in the qualities of the fertilizers they were ordering. For the first time in their lives many of these farmers discovered that they had been buying a large amount of useless "filler" instead of real fertilizer, and that they had been paying the maximum price. The saving through the coöperative buying of fertilizer in the first year amounted to from 20 to 40 per cent. of their former outlay, while the increase in their receipts from their potatoes was equally great. The farmers found that through coöperation they were able to save both in buying and in selling. When a community of farmers has gone so far as this it does not take them long to look into the whole question of middlemen and individualistic production and buying. Coöperation means not only increased production, but better prices both to the producer and the consumer.

Realizing that scientific marketing is an essential supplement to scientific production, the same forces that inaugurated the coöperative demonstration work have succeeded in securing the creation under the United States Department of Agriculture of a bureau whose business it will be to gather information and to formulate plans for the coöperative organization of workers on the land. It will do for scientific distribution what the division of Farmers' Coöperative Demonstration Work has already done for scientific production.

VII

DEMONSTRATION WORK THROUGH THE RURAL SCHOOL

AN extended notice has been given of extension and demonstration work because they point to the inevitable next-step in the evolution, redirection, and transformation of the school program, the course of study, the daily program. The wide and rapid spread of boys' and girls' clubs throughout the nation is a sign of the times that the school authorities will ignore them at the risk of disaster to the public-school system, the country-school children, and the nation. Heretofore the "culturists" have excluded the "practical" things from the course of study; but the growth of the purely agricultural-domestic-science schools, which, going to the other extreme, are now excluding the so-called "cultural" studies, should show that they are now sufficiently powerful to "set up for themselves." There is no reason why the one should exclude the other. If the exclusion is to be kept up, the country is destined to have a system of schools as narrow and narrowing in one direction as they have heretofore been narrow and narrowing in the other. The child should get at the school and through the school everything that he needs for his normal growth as a citizen. While learning "culturally" the life of the race in general, he needs "practically" to learn the "life of the race" in Possum Hollow in particular. And because he comes from Possum Hollow it does not follow that he knows anything about its particular life or the conditions under which he must live and make a living there. Physical contact and superficial familiarity are not the same thing as knowledge. If he does not learn this life, and learn how to improve it, and have aroused in him the desire to improve it, he will either stagnate in or leave Possum Hollow. A course of study so arranged as to cause the school to become an active emigration bureau may be cultural, but it nevertheless depopulates the community or keeps it at a standstill. It is often said that a "practical" education is a bread-and-butter affair; that it destroys the finer spirit and vision of a people; and that "man cannot live by bread alone." It is undoubtedly true that without a vision the people will perish. It is also true that man cannot live by bread *alone*. But a man should not be trained to live on his own visions and on another man's bread. He should be so trained that he will be able to have both visions and provisions.

To isolate the "cultural" studies in one school and the "practical" studies in another is a distinct menace to our democracy. Each needs and must have the contact with, the sympathy and the help of, the other. Our "practical" activities need to be permeated with idealism; our ideals need to be crystallized into concrete results. The efforts to separate the two are based either on a desire to exploit labor or on effete class consciousness which desires to perpetuate class distinctions in industry. But in a democratic educational system, where the "cultural" and "practical" go hand in hand for the purpose, and the sole purpose, of producing efficient citizenship, there will be but two classes—the one including all efficient citizens, whatever their work; the other including all inefficient citizens, such as criminals, idlers, parasites, whatever their professions or occupations.

In what way can the demonstration work be made a part of the rural-school work? In what way can the rural schools do demonstration work? John Munroe, of the Cokato, Minnesota, schools, has said that "all good school work is extension work," and he here uses the word *extension* in the sense of *demonstration*. By including demonstration work in its educational scheme the school program will have an abundance of material upon which to concentrate the physical, mental, and spiritual energies of the children, and it will also enable the children, as citizens in the making, to realize through their own efforts, properly directed, the economic value of one necessary phase of their efficient citizenship—their efficiency as producers on a commercial basis. Moreover, directly and in coöperation with other forces, it will make the school program an integral part of the community program, and by helping the grown-ups as well as the children it will make the education of the children an integral part of the education of the community

"Demonstration" is the logical next-step by which to reach into every rural community and give every boy and girl who now has no such chance the opportunity to do the things they most need to do and most wish to do. It is one of the best ways yet devised to produce efficient citizens. And it is the method that "pays its own way" in poor communities as well as in rich, because it produces more than it costs.

If the United States Department of Agriculture can, in coöperation with a state, and with a county in a state, appoint a demonstration agent to teach agriculture to the adults and boys in one county in the state, why cannot this be made a part of the school program and the work be done through one or more central schools in the county? If the United States Department of Agriculture can likewise appoint a demonstration agent to teach gardening to the girls in that county, why cannot this be made a part of the school program, and the work be done through one or more central schools in the county? So far as the adult farmer and his wife are concerned, there is no reason why they cannot be reached on their farms and in their homes by the school agricultural instructor, or demonstration agent, and the school instructor in gardening and domestic science *as readily as by a similar agent working independently of the school.* Such agents or teachers can give to the great masses of our country people a new conception of the school as the center of constantly improving community conditions—the very heart that sends the enriched blood of economic and social improvement coursing into every avenue of the community life. In no other way can our school studies be so well linked with community activities, and a redirection be given the school program and courses of study.

It has already been pointed out that a plan which forces boys and girls to leave their homes and board at school, or go without a training in the activities of everyday life, cannot be the ultimate plan for reaching the vast majority of our oncoming citizens, because, in the first place, the very large majority of them should not leave home, and, in the second place, the very large majority of them cannot leave home. And if it be said that the cost of building and maintaining enough such central schools to give to all the children an opportunity would be too great, the answer is that the costliest scheme is the one that does not reach all the children, for the neglect to do so spells disaster to the citizenship of a nation. Besides, it is not necessary to spend as much on building and maintenance as may at first seem necessary. A county agricultural school that costs ten thousand dollars a year to maintain and to which the boys and girls of a large part of the county must go as boarders if they go at all is much more costly than, for instance, four such schools in the county costing twenty-five thousand dollars, and to which all the larger boys and girls may go daily *from their homes*. For in the first instance not one in four of the boys and girls of the county is reached, while in the second instance all of them are reached. And if in the first instance one child is reached and four are not reached, the county agricultural school with boarding facilities is 80 per cent. deficient. The cost is not in the money, but in the neglect. The purpose of education is not to save money, but to save citizenship. Saving money to the neglect of citizenship means losing both. Making citizenship, however much it costs, is making both. The fear of the cost of several schools in a county that will reach every boy and girl *in their homes* arises from the tradition that all school-work must be done *in* the school, and is a matter of childhood and youth. The democratic viewpoint is that school-work must be done both in and *through* the school, and is a matter beginning with the childhood and extending throughout life.

The experiments now being tried in several states to introduce the every-day work of the community into the school curriculum, to "link up" the school-work with the life-work of the community, sustain the views here expressed. If anything has been proved by all this experimentation, it is that in exact proportion to the efforts of the school to utilize the normal activities of the community as the materials upon which to set at work the normal activities of the children, has the course of study lost its deadening influence and unloosed the pent-up mental, physical, and social energies of the children; and in exact proportion to the efforts of the school to make education a matter of life for life, and to reach every human being in his home and on his place of living, has it succeeded in its one legitimate function of producing efficient citizenship.

The Cokato, Minnesota, experiment has shown that there are in that community, about nine miles square, many boys and girls, men and women, who have not attended the usual type of school, but who, when it was announced that a short course would be opened, beginning in the late fall and continuing into March, and that this course would be made to suit their needs, at once took advantage of this offer and attended the school. They are not required to be at the opening or to remain until the close of school. These pupils, ranging in age from thirteen to forty, do the necessary chores at home, then arrive at the school about ten-thirty, remain until about three, then go home and do the other necessary chores. While at school they are asked what they wish to learn —and they go right at it. They choose practical arithmetic, composition, spelling, reading, writing, civics, commercial law, farm accounting, agriculture, sewing, cooking, carpentry, blacksmithing. And each subject is full of purpose. The materials of study come from everyday life and conditions. The instruction points its finger to that home and that community as the place for its best application. The course of study is not made up for the applicants to fit themselves to it. It is made up on the demands and needs of the applicants. Too often schoolwork is merely mental—a mental gymnastic. But such work as this is both mental and fundamental.

That there are hundreds of thousands of boys and girls and men and women in this nation who are in similar circumstances will not be disputed. They must be reached, and reached now, if reached at all. It is in seven cases out of ten their misfortune, not their fault, that they have not had the proper chance. The boarding-school will not touch them. The academic school, with an outlook toward the Middle Ages and farther back, will not touch them. "The short course is the most valuable part of our school-work," says Principal Munroe; "the one hundred pupils last year ranged from thirteen to forty years of age, and they assimilated more material than an equal number of high-school pupils would have assimilated in nine months." George B. Aiton, State Inspector of High Schools of Minnesota, well says that "the organization of from one to half a dozen such schools in each county—no distant day-dream—is far ahead of a sparse system of schools, such as one for each congressional district." And he might have added, "or one for each county."

Thirteen smaller schools have associated themselves with the central school at Cokato to get the benefit of the industrial work done at the central school, by gaining access for the larger boys and girls, men and women, who can attend from the communities in which these schools are located.

The agricultural instructor at Cokato has also interested himself in the activities of the community. He has held to Principal Munroe's statement that "good school-work is demonstration work." Not only has the school program included an educational scheme that enables the pupils to concentrate their activities upon the community activities, not only are the materials of study gathered by both teachers and pupils in their surveys of the community occupations, but the school program has a definite plan of farm demonstration. A part of its work is "showing" the farmers on their own farms, on condition that they wish to be shown and will follow directions. These farms are managed by short-course pupils who live on them. Records of work are kept, and these records are used at the school as a basis of the farm accounting studied at the school. Improved and tested seed is furnished from the small school-farm. One short-course pupil found out from his studies and tests that there were fourteen cows on his farm that were not even self-supporting. The demonstrations include drainage, dairying, corn, alfalfa, infusion of good stock, etc.

The state of Minnesota, under the Putnam Act, gives state aid to the Cokato and associated schools on account of the teaching of agriculture, manual training, and domestic science in the central school. The demonstration work conducted on the farms is not yet required as a

DEMONSTRATION WORK

part of the duties of the school, but is recognized as an
essential part of the complete school program. The
testimony of bankers and business men at Cokato is that
this school has more than paid its way by the increased
production made possible and made actual by the school.

Another example of demonstration work done by and
through the school is found at Sparks, Maryland, where,
in coöperation with the principal of the school, a large
number of farmers are conducting experiments on their
own farms and a large number of boys are cultivating
corn. Over one thousand farms are using the seed recommended by the school, and the increase in yield has been
sufficient, to quote an enthusiast, "to pay for the entire
cost of the school." The school has been instrumental
in establishing a creamery and founding the first cow-
testing association in the state. Excellent work in seed-
testing has proven of much benefit to the farmers. Spraying demonstrations on the farms have been most helpful.
The school took a farmer's unproductive orchard and
made it bring a big yield.

An interesting feature of the school-work at Sparks is
the graduating exercises, which are held out-of-doors.
The program of 1912 will give an indication of the work
of the school:

Sparks, Maryland   1912
PROGRAM

The graduation exercises are intended to give expression to the
work of the school in all its phases. Because much of the work
is along practical lines a large part of the exercises are demon-
strational in character.

The graduation dresses were made in the regular sewing-classes
of the school. The amphitheater, in which exercises are held and
which seats fifteen hundred persons, was erected by the manual-
training classes of the school.

1. OVERTURE . . . . *Kennedy's Orchestra*
2. PROCESSIONAL

THE WORK OF THE RURAL SCHOOL

3. INVOCATION
4. SONG . . . . *Morning Hymn*
   By JOHN CRUGER
5. DEMONSTRATION OF AGRICULTURAL LESSONS
   Explanation by WILLIAM FREDERICK KAUFFMAN, Jr.
   Babcock Test . . . . C. F. BRUEHL
   Acidity Test . . . . . . A. L. PARRY
   Mixing Bordeaux . . . . . R. R. LORD
6. DEMONSTRATION OF COOKING METHODS WITH
   EGGS. Explanation by NETTIE PARKS
   Baked Custard ⎱
   Popovers   ⎰ . . . . ELIZABETH WILSON
   Sponge Cake . . . . . RUTH YOUNG
7. ORATION . . . . *Country Culture*
   By RUSSELL ROBBINS LORD
8. DEMONSTRATION OF HOME CHEMISTRY
   Explanation by IDA CHILCOAT
   Determination of Copper in Peas . ELIZABETH WILSON
   Determination of Glucose in Jelly. EVA AKEHURST
   Determination of Textiles . . . RUTH YOUNG
9. SONG . . . . *The Merry Heart*
   By LUIGI DENZA
10. DEMONSTRATION OF USES OF CARPENTRY TOOLS
    By ALBERT LEE PARRY
11. JUDGING THE DAIRY BREEDS
    (Illustrated with a Jersey Cow)
    By CHARLES FRANK BRUEHL
12. SONG . . . . *The Call of the Fields*
    Words by DEAN L. H. BAILEY
    Cornell College of Agriculture
13. ADDRESS   By Hon. W. M. HAYS
    Assistant Secretary of Agriculture
14. SONG FROM "PIPPA PASSES"
    Words by ROBERT BROWNING
15. PRESENTATION OF DIPLOMAS TO GRADUATES
16. CHARGE TO THE GRADUATES
17. SOPRANO SOLO . . . . *Farewell Song*
18. SCHOOL SONG . . . . *Mother of Farms*
    Words by the Senior Class, composed as a lesson
    in versification. Music by MISS ESTELLE THOMPSON
19. RECESSIONAL

DEMONSTRATION WORK

AT EIGHT O'CLOCK THERE WILL BE PRESENTED IN THE SCHOOL BUILDING

"THE TAMING OF THE SHREW"

Each year the English classes of the school produce one Shake-spearian play as a regular part of the required work. The manu-script was prepared in the school. The costumes of the period were designed and made in the sewing-classes. The three sets of scenery were prepared by the manual-training classes.

The principal of a county agricultural high school in Mississippi in one session has done a good deal of extension and demonstration work. Besides having farmers' institutes at the school, he lectures to the farmers throughout the county, doctors their sick stock, helps them to select pure seed, and holds himself ready to advise any who wish to improve farm conditions. As hog cholera has been rife in the county, he has taught all the boys in the school how to prevent the disease by inoculat-ing the hogs with serum. The state prepares the serum and sells it at cost. The principal advertised that he would inoculate all hogs free of charge if the owners would purchase the serum. In three months, with the aid of two boys, he inoculated nearly one thousand hogs in the county, saving to the farmers at least three thousand dollars. As his salary is eighteen hundred dollars a year, he seems to be making his demonstration work a paying proposition.

At some of the schools in Louisiana dipping-vats have been installed, and are largely used by the farmers. One principal says, "Our school-work is felt over the entire parish, but those within a radius of three or four miles are receiving the most benefit." There seems no valid reason, however, why the school-demonstration work for adults, boys, and girls should not extend over as much territory as is covered by the daily school patronage.

What is needed in every school of this kind is a definite plan to send the instructors in farm and garden work upon the farms and into the homes for demonstration work. In one school community the dairymen have followed the instructions of the agricultural teacher in making up a balanced ration for the herds, and the boys assist in this work. He is also showing the advantages of tested seed, pure stock, and diversified crops. Instances of this kind can be found in many states. In most of such cases, unfortunately, work of this nature is entirely voluntary, and is not yet a part of the definite school program.

Several schools have boys' pig clubs and as a result one community has, since the establishment of the new agricultural school, five times as many good hogs as it had two years ago. This is school demonstration of the right sort. It goes as far as the boys do. The garden clubs of the girls have the same effect. Another agricultural teacher, soon after his work began, induced the farmers and dairymen in the community to keep records of the individual cows—something never before heard of in that section. The results were an eye-opener to the farmers who had supposed that "cows is cows"; and a large number of cows fell from grace to disgrace. He also organized a corn club among the boys, with the result that several made over sixty bushels of corn apiece per acre, and one boy just missed one hundred bushels. He organized a boys' and girls' pig club, and in six months had seventy-five active members. Each member of the club was required to keep a record, to show gain or loss. Most of the children made money out of the enterprise. This work was all voluntary on the part of the instructor.

Another agricultural school undertook to raise thoroughbred pigs and poultry and to interest the school community in the raising of better stock. The success has been such that the school has been entirely unable to supply the demand. The organization of boys' and girls' pig clubs greatly stimulated this. One instructor got a grip on a boy by showing him how to do some gardening. The boy made a hotbed and raised all the young plants needed at home. He raised and sold twenty-two dollars' worth of onions on a small bit of ground. His father seemed surprised at the boy's interest, naïvely remarking that the boy "had never been interested in garden work before." How much would the father have been interested in his own farm work if he had gotten no pecuniary return?

Other examples of good extension and demonstration work cover the analysis of fertilizers for the farmers, and teaching them how to purchase and mix their own fertilizer ingredients; the value of tested seed and how to select seed; the use of improved implements; deep plowing; the value of peas, beans, and clovers; winter crops, the value of rotation; the value of breeding up stock. This work, heretofore done by the agricultural colleges, is being taken up not only by the regular agricultural high schools, but even by schools which make no pretense of teaching agriculture, but are blessed with teachers who believe that this is one of the important functions of school and teacher. One principal found that through the direct influence of his school more money had been spent in one year for improved farm implements than in the previous five years.

One teacher bewails the fact that his agricultural school, which has been in existence one year, "has had no effect on production of farm crops in the surrounding country," because the school-farm was not ready for use! How he might surprise himself and benefit the community if he would induce a number of farmers and farmers' sons to allow their home-farms to become school-farms, and thus have as many adult and boy students as he could look after!

A striking contrast to this attitude and an excellent illustration of the value of active extension and demonstration work may be found in this record of a two-year-old school:

The school has a farm which is used to train the boys and to be an object-lesson to the community. New methods of plowing, planting, and cultivating were introduced. Some of the farmers were persuaded to try them. One farmer remarked, "That acre of corn you raised on the school-farm last year made two thousand bushels of corn," meaning that this had been the effect on the community. The school has shown the farmers that "there are fertilizers—and fertilizers." The school is teaching them how to discriminate, and how to do their own mixing. This is saving thousands of dollars each year. One farmer declared that the instructions on this one thing had saved the farmers of that school community $5,000 a year. When the school opened there were few good hogs in the community. The boys in the pig clubs, starting in a small way, now have $2,000 worth of registered hogs and pigs in the school community. The hardware merchant states that he has sold more improved agricultural implements in the last two years than in the previous twenty years combined, and that this is due to the influence of the school. The boys' corn clubs and girls' garden clubs are directly under the management of the agricultural instructor of this school. The average for the boys in 1911—a dry year—was over 60 bushels of corn to the acre. One boy in 1910 made 120 bushels on his acre. The average in the state in 1911 was 18.5 bushels. The girls' canning clubs are in a flourishing condition, and are having a decided effect on the community.

At a school in Massachusetts the teacher encouraged project work at home. One of the boys kept 26 chickens, and in six months showed a net profit of $27. Another boy fed to his father's herd of 12 Jersey cows a balanced ration, keeping accurate accounts of feed, labor, interest on investment, etc., from November to June. He found that his best cow netted a profit of $54, while his poorest one showed a loss of $2.39. Another boy raised tomato, celery, and cabbage plants in a small hotbed, which netted him a profit of $35. The arithmetic, spelling, language, and bookkeeping work is largely based upon these activities.

At two agricultural schools in Virginia a rather unique plan of coöperation has been devised, and the results obtained have been in every way satisfactory during the short time the experiment has been tried. At the school at Driver, Nansemond County, Virginia, the instructor in agriculture is also the United States demonstration agent for the county. Under an agreement reached between the local school authorities, the state school authorities, and the United States Department of Agriculture, this instructor has scheduled his time so that he spends a portion of it at the school and a portion on the farms of the adults and the boys. Besides having a flourishing agricultural club at the school, he is kept busy visiting farms throughout the county. He is employed by the year, and of course his busiest seasons are the spring and summer, during three months of which the school is on vacation and he can give all of his time to demonstration work. During his first year forty demonstrations were made on as many farms, with from one to twenty acres cultivated under his direction.

A similar experiment has been tried at Burkeville, in Nottoway County, Virginia. The teacher of agriculture at the school is also the United States demonstration agent for the county. There are flourishing boys' corn clubs and girls' canning clubs. This coöperative plan has been under way only about a year. The school has its garden in excellent state of cultivation, and the instructor is already in great demand among the farmers. The boys in this school make a specialty of seed-testing, and the farmers are taking advantage of this by bringing their seed to be tested. The instructor has got excellent results from dynamiting land for purposes of orcharding and subsoiling.

At another school a one-acre apple orchard was purchased as part of the school-grounds. It is cultivated by the boys of the high school, working under an expert who occasionally visits the school. The boys are taught to cultivate, prune, spray, pick, and pack the apples. The proceeds of sales go to purchase library books and other equipment for the school. There are unlimited opportunities here for work in arithmetic, in spelling, in language, in the keeping of records, in bookkeeping, and in marketing. Would the following study of the apple have any educational value, or might there be the risk of "commercializing" the boys and girls with "common" things?

THE APPLE

Variety

1. *Shape*—Spherical, flattened, long, and egg-shaped. Does shape help in determining variety?
2. *Color*—Streaks, freckles, etc., blush cheek.
3. *Stem*—Long, slender; short, thick.
4. *Stem Cavity*—Deep, shallow.
5. *Blossom End or Basin*—Find remains of calyx, stamens, pistils.
6. *Skin*—Polish small section. Appearance? Cause? Proof that it is wax (apple wax). Heat, water.
7. *Experiment*—Peel one of these apples: place peeled apple and one unpeeled in contact, and third one near by, but not touching. Which one commences to decay first? Which next? Where? Lesson for care in harvesting and storing.
8. *Vertical Section*—Color of pulp; juicy, mealy; sweet or sour? Any odor? Spicy?
9. *Core*—Fibers connecting stem and blossom ends. Core-lines. Outer core-lines.

10. *Transverse Section* — Other core-line dots, how many?
     Where? Termination? What? Carpels, how many?
     How many seeds in each? Rudimentary seeds? Why
     developed?
11. *Seed*—Outer coat, inner coat, germ, meat.

A teacher of agriculture in a high school in which
agriculture and domestic science were introduced in 1908
states that the high school formerly had a purely classical
course, and that the new subjects were received with utter
indifference, or worse. There was ridicule of "book-
farming" and "cooking." This in a farming community,
too! But he has succeeded just in proportion to his
efforts to reach the farmers. A large farmers' institute
of men and women meets regularly at the school. Fourteen dairy herds have been cleared of tuberculosis by the
aid of the school, although the owners had resisted the
efforts of the board of health to compel a tuberculin test.
Eighteen boys in the school work their demonstration
acres at home under the supervision of the agricultural
instructor. Each year sees more farmers consulting him
about their work, about milk and cream testing; testing
cows for tuberculosis; spraying, pruning, and grafting
trees; seeding; alfalfa; mixing fertilizers; balanced
rations. The farmers' organization was imperative if for
no other reason than because the county is sparsely popu-
lated, the roads are bad, and the farmers belong to several
religious sects. The institute is served with lunch, prepared and served by the girls of the domestic-science class.
This has caused a revolution of sentiment in regard to
cooking in the school.

The many illustrations cited to show the possible effect
of the school on production might be multiplied indefi-
nitely. Such instances can be given from communities in
many of the states. The illustration from Minnesota has
been taken as a type from the Northwest that will prob-

ably be widely followed, with certain adjustments to suit local and state conditions. The illustration from Maryland has been used to show the success of school-demonstration work where a program has been arranged with this definitely in view. The illustrations from Mississippi and Louisiana have been used to show that where farm-schools and agricultural schools—the one purely a farm-school, the other embracing other studies also—have done actual extension and demonstration work among the people and on their farms, they have met with gratifying success in increasing production, in making the people look to the school for advice in regard to the every-day activities of the community, and in giving the school an outlook on present and future life instead of continuing the back-look on the past. The illustrations from Virginia are given to show the results of combining the agricultural instruction at the school with the agricultural demonstration work on the farms, and to show a plan of coöperation including federal, state, and county authorities.

The best school-farm is the home-farm where the worker is studying and working his own land under the direction of the school for his own benefit. This is as true of the child as of the adult. The little boy who had not shown an enthusiastic interest in working his father's garden, but who, when he saw that there was a chance for himself, made a hotbed, furnished plants to the household, and sold twenty-two dollars' worth of onions, is an illustration of a sane, natural, correct attitude in children that has been too long ignored. The little girl who joined the garden club because she wanted to make some money of her own is another illustration of the same wholesome attitude. To give children everything, without an effort on their part, is a sad mistake. To give them nothing after they have put forth efforts is an equally sad mistake. There should be a middle ground recognized by parents and by school authorities. There are some things that children should

do—and usually will gladly do—as a duty and privilege.
There are some things that children do for which they
should be paid. Exploitation, while by no means an
uncommon custom among adults, is least admirable when
the child is the victim of it at the hands of parent, guar-
dian, teacher, or employer.

To expect children to do all the hard things for nothing
but glory is to expect too much. It is utterly unfair, and
when forced on children is an exhibition none the less
mean and cowardly because sometimes unconsciously so.

It is a necessary part of training in citizenship to show
to children the economic value of citizenship in efficient
production. Children dearly love to "do" things like
"grown-ups"; they resent being always treated as
children, and that is one reason so many of them loathe
school. This treatment is one of the most fruitful causes
of the desertion of the school by the children after they
have endured it for three or four years. Trying as it is to
girls, it is intolerable to most boys. Growing up into
citizens, they are permitted to have little or no part in
the training process. With discipline, course of study,
and all else handed to them or thrust on them, their growing bodies and minds and souls cry out for an opportunity
to be not only in but of the every-day life.

If the children work in the school-garden and on the
school-farm, all production over a certain amount should
go to the individual doing the work. It is well to have a
part of the garden cultivated for the school. The proceeds from the rest of the work should be divided in fair
proportion among the workers. When boys and girls join
clubs to raise corn, cotton, vegetables, fruits, pigs, poultry,
or anything else, they should be treated not only as
human beings, but should be treated as citizens dealing
with citizens. Every transaction as to land, expenses,
records, etc., should be conducted with scrupulous fairness
and accuracy. It is the best of all times, and the best of

all ways, to train the citizen in the making. He is putting forth energy, muscle, thought, time—for what? To be exploited? For what does his father work—glory or a crop?

A school program cannot be complete which fails to include in its educational scheme a training in this necessary phase of citizen-making.

The objection raised that to permit the children to earn money by their school work will "commercialize education," will "commercialize the child," is based on an utter misconception and a shallow premise. The child is not under this plan taught to make money for the sake of making money. He is not trained to make money for the sake of hoarding it. He is not taught under this plan to make money by taking advantage of some one else. He is taught to transact business in a business way—to put forth effort and time, and to expect a fair return in terms of every-day commerce. Does it "commercialize" the painter, the sculptor, the architect, to allow him materials to work upon and tools to work with? The boy should have—and would have if he were treated sanely—the same attitude toward his corn crop or his pigs as the sculptor toward his work. That element of our citizenship which is fearful that teaching boys and girls how to work efficiently and how to express this work in terms of commerce will "commercialize" or degrade them is dangerous to the public welfare because it has a false and feudal, and not a social and democratic outlook.

A little fellow seven years old worked all summer on his corn crop—five short rows of popcorn. He worked hard. At the end of the summer one of the laborers on the farm carelessly turned a horse loose, and in a little while the crop was ruined. The child came to his father.

"Sam has turned one of the horses loose, and he has ruined my crop," he said.

"I am very sorry," said the father; "I'll speak to him about it."

"But, daddy, that won't help my crop!"

"You are right. We will estimate its value."

They did so, and the boy was paid the proper damages.

A little fellow raised an acre of corn, and exhibited some of it at the school fair. He was a very poor boy, and had probably never seen as much as five dollars in all his life. He won thirty dollars in cash prizes, besides owning the crop. Without the slightest suggestion from any one he went at once to his teacher and said to her:

"I would like to see some other boy have a chance, and I want to give two dollars toward raising prizes for next year."

Where was the commercialization of this boy's soul and vision? To teach a child to transact business on a money basis is one thing; to inculcate in him a spirit of greed or selfishness is another. It is superficial to confuse the two.

A training of boys and girls by the demonstration plan brings them into contact with community life; gives them material upon which to direct their physical, mental, and spiritual powers; and it brings them into a normal and not an artificial contact with life. It shows them what it should show: that education is not a matter of childhood for childhood, but of life for life. It can be applied to old and young, and it can reach wherever a human being on the land desires instruction.

VIII

THE SCHOOL-PLANT

THE school-plant — the site, the acreage, the size, number, and type of buildings and their equipment— will naturally be determined by the course of study, the purpose by which the school program is inspired, and by the community survey which must always be at the foundation of the school policy. To invest money in a school-plant without knowing the exact population, the rate of probable growth of the population, the economic and social needs and aspirations of the community, is as foolish from the point of view of good business management as it would be to locate an expensive manufacturing-plant in the center of the Sahara Desert.

The object of public education is to make efficient citizens out of the raw material of childhood, and the money invested in grounds and buildings is certain to be badly invested unless the school authorities know in advance how much raw material they have to deal with and unless they have decided in advance upon the best school program for the efficient use of the raw material in the particular community under their educational jurisdiction. No stereotyped plans will do; each community will have special conditions to meet, and these special conditions will require the most careful consideration and the best intelligence which the best educational authorities can give or can employ in the way of an expert school architect. For expert ability is as essential to the satisfactory layout of the school-grounds and the planning and construction of the school building or buildings as it is to the satisfactory formulation of an efficient school program and course of study. There are, however, certain fundamental considerations that apply to all school-plants whatsoever, whether of the isolated one-room type or the large centralized or consolidated school.

In selecting a site for the schoolhouse, in drawing the plans for the buildings, in equipping the grounds and buildings with sanitary conveniences and working apparatus, the controlling consideration must always be the welfare of the children as citizens in the making.

As long as the school trustees or the community look at the school from the penny-wise standpoint the children cannot come into their own. The old school of finance—in which the present as well as the past generations have been trained—thinks it unwise to spend a dollar without the immediate prospect of a money return on the investment. It gives the minimum required by law in providing for a school. Niggardliness is regarded as economy. School trustees—too often supported by community opinion—measure the efficiency of their administrations by the money they do *not* spend. They will prefer an inconvenient, inadequate, and possibly unhealthful location that costs fifty dollars an acre to a suitable one that costs one hundred dollars an acre. Or they will purchase a half-acre, when from two to ten acres are needed, to "save" from twenty-five to a few hundred dollars. As if money could ever be saved at the cost of the health and happiness and well-being of the children!

But, happily, the tendency to look ahead and to provide wisely is growing. In thousands of instances the school authorities have the opportunity to purchase not only enough land for all present needs, but enough for the years to come, and in increasing numbers they are taking advantage of the opportunity. Recently, on the edge of a small town of about six hundred people a well-treed, ten-acre tract was put on the market. The school trustees of the district bought it for five thousand dollars. The town needs a new school, and will have to wait two years to accumulate enough money to build, yet the trustees wisely decided to buy the tract and wait rather than to build on a plot too small for a school and a community playground. The property is beautiful and is being still further improved with trees, lawns, flowers, and shrubbery. These trustees realize that beauty in the school-plant has a positive value not only as a setting for the education of their children, but as an inspiration to the entire community. They have caught the spirit of true citizenship; they understand that efficient public administration is not to be measured by the amount of public money hoarded, but by the wisdom of its expenditure. They belong to the new school of finance, in whose view expenditure that gives the children a passion for beauty, that tempts them through self-activity to develop their muscles and grow into healthy animals, that conserves life and gives it tone and vigor, is money not only saved, but put out at a good rate of interest. For such expenditure means fewer sanitariums, fewer insane asylums, fewer jails and reformatories, fewer charities, fewer bums and hoboes—more good citizens.

There is, of course, no rule of thumb for determining the exact acreage of the school-grounds. The number of pupils and games in vogue in the neighborhood, the number of games that can profitably be played at one time, the size of the school-farm and school-garden, the amount of space that should be reserved for trees, lawns, flowers, shrubbery, outhouses, wagon sheds, and open-air classes —all these must be taken into account. And each one of these factors should be carefully weighed by the school trustees and the parents before a location is chosen. It should not require argument to show that no school is or can be satisfactory from the standpoint of the children unless all of these considerations are generously and wisely decided. For any one-room school with, or with the possibility of, from fifteen to twenty-five pupils, two acres at the very least should be provided, and this acreage should be increased with the increase in attendance. A good rule is to consider the school-grounds as a community playground, and, in addition to the ordinary requirements of the school-children, to provide space for those games that require a maximum of space and for as many games as the active members of the community, old and young, may need for their healthful recreation at any one time. For the school should be considered the social center of the community as well as the educational center for the children.

And because the school must be regarded as a community center it should be located as near to the center of population as practicable—by no means always the geographical center of the school district. It is of course both bad policy and undemocratic to choose a site with reference to the convenience of any one person or group of persons, however influential, as against the convenience or interest of the community as a whole. And here again it is the welfare of the children that must receive first consideration; if the center of population is not the center of the school population the latter should decide the location. Generally, however, in the long run, the two will pretty nearly coincide.

But centrality in itself is not enough. A site may be central, may have an ample acreage, and yet be so difficult of access as to make it difficult for the children to reach it. What possible excuse can there be for forcing children to go to school over paths and roadways that cause them to arrive with shoes and stockings and clothing bedraggled with mud, torn with brambles, or covered with beggar's-lice, sheep-burs, and stick-tights? Sometimes children who go from one to four miles to school are compelled to fight their way through one bit of path or road that is so bad as to do more damage to clothes or wagon than a year's ordinary wear and tear. If the regular legal authorities cannot be persuaded to mend such places, let a few of the citizens volunteer to repair them. In many instances the task will not be beyond the children if properly encouraged and guided, and, in addition to increasing their comfort, will furnish them good training in citizenship and coöperative effort.

And every now and again there will be upon the board of trustees or among the influential citizens of the community one of those ardent patriots who think that there is no profit in building a schoolhouse that cannot be seen like an electric sign by all who pass within a radius of miles. Especially if a railroad runs through the district he will insist on having the schoolhouse on the peak of a hill so steep as not only to preclude the possibility of playgrounds, but also to make its attainment by the children a labor of Hercules. If accused of sordid motives he will ordinarily plead the symbolic value of such a sky-towering site, forgetful of the difficulty the human spirit has in grasping the meaning of such subtle appeals when the muscles of the legs are aching and the lungs are panting for breath. A slope of more than one inch in three feet means not only erosion and the preclusion of playgrounds, but the foolish waste of the children's energy.

The most important consideration of all is the moral and physical health of the children, their protection against vice, disease, and physical injury. Is the site healthful, or can it be made so? If not, it should under no circumstances be considered. Marshy places or places that breed disease-bearing insects; railroads and factories, with their noise and dust and danger, are undesirable neighbors and should by all means be avoided. Nor should the presence of unsightly and immoral settlements, saloons, or groggeries be permitted in the vicinity of the school. They are a curse to any community, and the children should not be exposed to their degrading influence. But if a site is otherwise satisfactory, the interests of the children should not be sacrificed to their existence; such places should be closed or removed by law.

The school site should be ample for the convenient location of the building and outhouses; it should offer abundant opportunity for the development of school-gardens and open-air classes; its soil should be susceptible to the highest cultivation; it should be well drained; it should be readily accessible; its approaches should be safe and easy; it should provide space for school and community playgrounds; it should be made beautiful with trees, lawns, flowers, and shrubbery; it should be quiet and sheltered from all immoral influences.

The site having been chosen, the size of the building—the number of rooms it shall contain—should be carefully considered by those in authority before the plans are drawn or the position of the building on the site determined. This may sound like a trite statement, but, as every one who has had wide experience with country schools knows, it is the exceptional community that considers and settles these elementary matters in the best interests of the children. The ordinary lack of foresight is really astonishing. The problem requires not only foresight, but intelligence, a highly sensitized intelligence. Is not the fact that schools are constantly being erected that herd children to the number of from forty to one hundred and ten in a single room conclusive proof of this statement? Such practices are survivals of the time when the schools were regarded as a species of prison and the teacher as principally a custodian of the police power of the community for the "discipline" of the children during school-hours. Herding is not only ruinous to health; it taints the moral sense of the children, destroys their finer sensibilities, and makes it impossible for even the best of teachers to develop their normal individual and social impulses into free and purposeful action.

If, then, the school authorities are confronted with the problem of providing a building for the community, they should first ask themselves: How many teachers will be necessary to give the children of this community the best possible opportunities for development into efficient citizens? Can the children of this community make better progress under one teacher or under more than one? The stock replies rattle like dried peas in one's ears: "We've got along for a good many years with one teacher for fifty children"; or, "We've made out pretty well for twenty years with two teachers and seventy-five children, and we guess that will do well enough"; or, "Anyhow, this community won't stand for so much expense"; or, "I guess those of us who went to a one-room school average up pretty well." These are not arguments, they are unmistakable signs that all real forethought has degenerated into sleepy stupidity and indifference. As often as not citizens who make such statements will make better provision for their stock than they make for their children.

It may be taken as a sound rule, and one that works for the best interests of the children, that an attendance of twenty children and up to forty requires two teachers and two rooms; that an attendance of more than forty-five and up to seventy-five requires three teachers and at least three rooms; of seventy-five to one hundred, four teachers and at least four rooms. This estimate does not include workrooms and auditoriums. The exceptions to this rule will be brought about by the variations in the advancement and the ages of the children and the number of activities included in the school program, but the exceptions will always be in the direction of more rooms and more teachers — never less. If the school survey shows that there are fifty children in the community and the growth of the community is not at a standstill, then provision should be made for all fifty and a certain allowance in addition should be made for probable growth in the near future. It does not meet the situation to say that "All of them won't attend"; or in states where attendance is not compulsory to declare, "Oh, well, there are fifty children in the community, but there are never more than thirty or forty present at any one time." Compulsory attendance will soon be the universal law; if the states do not see to it, the federal government will. But even where compulsory attendance is not the law of a state, there is something wrong with a community that will listen to such specious arguments. If there is no legal compulsion, there should be the persuasive compulsion of a building and a school program that will draw children to the school, backed by a public sentiment sufficiently strong to overcome any supposed reasons or excuses for keeping the children away from school. Progress cannot be made by resting quietly under wrong conditions or by tolerating conditions that do not constantly make for the ideal of community life. A community that does not provide ample grounds and adequate housing for its children is blind to its own best interests as well as to the best interests of the children and the nation.

The size of the schoolrooms must be determined by the maximum number of children allowed in them at any one time. The minimum floor space for each person, including the teacher, is fifteen square feet. The minimum air space for each person is two hundred cubic feet. This means absolutely clear space; in calculating the air space, allowance should be made for cloakrooms, vestibules, desks, chairs, tables, stoves, bookcases, and the like, and for all of these additional space should be provided.

If, for example, 20 children constitute the maximum allowed to use a room at one time, the proper floor area will be found by multiplying 15—the number of square feet required for each person—by 21—for the teacher, ordinary practice to the contrary notwithstanding, does occupy space. This will give 315 square feet. Each of these 21 persons would require 200 cubic feet of air in the clear, or 4,200 cubic feet of absolutely empty space. Dividing the number of cubic feet of free space—4,200— by 315, the floor area, and we have the height of the room —13.33 feet. The width of a schoolroom should ordinarily be from two-thirds to three-fourths of its length; a room 18 x 20 x 12 will give a floor area of 360 square feet, and an air space of 4,320 cubic feet. But this does not make sufficient allowance either in floor space or in cubic content for the usual "fillers," and it would therefore be safe to enlarge the dimensions to 18 x 24 x 12 for 20 pupils and the teacher. It should always be borne in mind that up to a reasonable limit no harm can come from making a schoolroom too large. The height should never be less than 12 feet, and for the sake of good light especially a greater height is preferable.

An abundance and proper diffusion of light is as important as an abundance of floor and air space. Recent investigations have revealed an appalling number of school-children with defective vision. The repeated testimony of eye specialists has been that but for the schools many of them would have to go out of business. Even to-day, when so much has been written upon the subject and when the science of proper lighting has made such great progress, buildings are erected with not enough windows, with windows whose streams of light fall at the wrong angles and make conflicting shadows, with windows that come neither close enough to the floor nor near enough to the ceiling.

In planning a schoolroom the amount of clear glass

surface—and it must be remembered that window frames make no part of a *clear* glass surface—should be from 20 to 25 per cent. of the gross floor space. A room made for twenty pupils and a teacher—to revert to the illustration already used—should have seventy-two to ninety square feet of clear, unobstructed lighting surface, and, of course, if buildings or trees or other unavoidable objects obstruct the light, the surface should be correspondingly increased. It is always better to have too much than too little light. If inadequate provision is made when the building is constructed, it is almost impossible to increase it, while its regulation if the light is excessive is a simple matter. The roller-shade curtain which can be raised or lowered either from the top or bottom of the window is a satisfactory controlling device.

There is no difference of opinion among those who have studied the matter scientifically that the pupils should never be seated facing the light, or with their right shoulders toward it. When the light strikes directly into their faces it not only injures the eyes, but stops the thought processes. When it falls over their right shoulders it casts shadows that make ease and accuracy of workmanship difficult. When the light comes from the left through windows that are properly "bunched" so that there are no walls or supports between the sashes it makes no shadows. So that expert opinion is unanimous in favor of left-side lighting. There is some difference of opinion as to whether light should be admitted from the rear of the room, but the preponderance of authority is to the effect that rear light is valuable so long as it is admitted in a way to supplement the light from the left, not conflict with it. To secure this result the rear-window surface should not exceed one-half of the left-side surface, and the windows should not come so close to the floor as the left-side windows.

Teachers sometimes object to rear windows on the

ground that they make *them* face the light. This can happen only when the teacher's desk and chair are at the front, a position warranted by nothing but the obsolete police-power tradition of the teacher's function. A teacher who is interested primarily in teaching will find the side or the rear of the room quite as convenient as the front. In fact, even in a schoolroom arranged on the desk-in-a-row plan it would seem that "order" might be most easily maintained by a teacher stationed at the rear. This is the testimony of many teachers who have tried both positions. If Johnny is disposed to be mischievous he is at a disadvantage when he is unable to see whether the teacher is watching him or not. Teachers who are convinced that children will not grow without having a symbol of discipline constantly before them are close spiritual kin to the university graduate who recently changed the position of the desks in his room so as to make the children face the light on the ground that this would strengthen their eyes!

To secure the most satisfactory diffusion of light the windows should always be placed within six inches of the ceiling. The upper fourth of the window furnishes one-third of the light, and when the ceiling is too far from the upper sash the light is absorbed instead of being given back into the room. For similar reasons the color of the walls should be selected with reference to a maximum diffusion of light and a minimum tax on the eyes. Yellows and buffs absorb little light, but they produce visual fatigue. Probably the best color for the walls is a light green-gray, and white is best for the ceilings.

It need hardly be said that arched windows defeat the purpose for which school-windows are built. The esthetic ends which arched windows are intended to serve are much more satisfactorily attained by a carefully considered scheme of decoration. Some of the most attractive schoolrooms are made so by a simple frieze in soft-colored chalks along the upper edge of the blackboard. A picture-molding running around the entire room is indispensable, and of course its appropriate use is equally so. But pictures are likely to do more harm than good when they are covered with glass. There are few more subtle instruments of torture than the plates of glass that flash darts of light into the eyes of the children from pictures that are meant for their delight and comfort.

Why should not the schoolroom be the most gracious and homelike of places? Nothing will so certainly bring to the surface the generous impulses, the enthusiasms, and the sweetness that are innate in all children as an air of "homey" coziness; just as nothing will so certainly stifle these impulses and arouse temper and irritation as the bleakness, the chill, and ugliness that are so wide-spread in the schoolrooms of the country.

But ampleness, brightness, and beauty will fail in a room that is ill-ventilated. The query of the five-year-old girl who went to school with her mother soon after she had been to the circus would be justified in probably 85 per cent. of the rural schools of the country.

"Mother," she asked, "where is the elephant?"

"What elephant, child?"

"I can't see him, but I smell him, mother."

The three greatest tonics in the world are fresh air, sunshine, and wholesome food. Two of these have not been affected by the high cost of living—they are free. This is probably the reason why we value them so little. Most people—school-teachers are no exceptions—seem to think that windows are made for ventilation and are all-sufficient for that purpose. Windows are really made for lighting, though many of them, judged by their size and position, do not appear to be made for any useful purpose. Of course, window ventilation is better than nothing, but it is altogether inadequate. No school can be made fit for use without a good system that will force fresh air into the schoolroom and force foul air out at the rate of thirty cubic feet of air each minute for each child. Such a system is not easy to devise, but it is more vital than difficult. Air that has been breathed and given off again by the lungs is poison, and it is an unpardonable sin against health and decency to compel children to breathe it. What would be said if children were required to quench their thirst with sweat from each other's bodies? Why, then, should they be forced to drink foul air that has been rejected by their bodies? It is an unhealthy, indecent, and filthy wrong that is prevented by law in some states and cities, and should be made a penal offense everywhere.

Tuberculosis, pneumonia, grippe, and colds are bad-air diseases, and cannot thrive in fresh air. The initial cost of installing forced-draft systems in every schoolroom in America would not equal by half the annual cost of doctors and hospitals made necessary by foul air—the lack of good ventilation—in the schools. And this takes no account of the suffering, the heartache, and funeral expenses that follow the sacrifice of teachers and children to indifference, ignorance, stupidity, and greed.

The forced-draught system is the best means of getting fresh air into and foul air out of the schoolroom. It consists of a dynamo or a gasolene engine, a fan or fans, and a proper system of flues. More and more small towns, villages, and country districts are having the wisdom to install it. Its cost is not prohibitive; indeed, a community that values the health of its teachers and children will consider its cost very reasonable. If we only had some universal system of social bookkeeping that would make the community see its share in the expense of individual doctors' bills and in the waste of human energy that doctors' bills so often stand for to-day there would be a revolution in school ventilation. For no one can be sick or below the standard of efficiency without being a charge upon the entire community.

The jacketed stove has come into wide use in recent years, and when properly installed and managed is a considerable factor in ventilation. There are several good systems on the market, but, like most good devices, none has been made that is fool-proof.

The lack of knowledge about the simplest rules of heating and ventilation among school trustees, superintendents, and teachers is wide-spread for a number of reasons: The great majority of them received their schooling in an environment and at a time when no attention was paid to hygienic matters because no one knew anything about them. The intimate relation between bad air and such diseases as tuberculosis, colds, pneumonia, and grippe was unknown. In fact, fresh air was considered bad for such maladies, and night air was regarded as especially dangerous. The discovery that they are germ-diseases and that fresh air and sunshine fortify our resistance against them and, with nourishing food, are the only remedies for them is comparatively recent, and has yet to impress itself upon the consciousness of the great mass of the people who are slow to break with the habits and traditions not only of their own lifetimes, but of centuries. The young person who is slow to accept a sound new idea is the exception; the old person who is quick to take one is equally the exception. The schools are mostly in the hands of men whose ideas and habits were long since fixed. It is thus the misfortune of the children that the schools lag two generations behind, not only in courses of study, but in the healthfulness of their equipment and environment. In nothing is it more vital to keep open the eyes and ears of the mind and spirit for the reception of sound new ideas, and in nothing is it more important to keep open the pores of the mind and spirit for the discharge of effête ideas, than in this matter of the intimate relation between the amount and constancy of fresh air and sunshine and the bodily and spiritual health of the children.

Another reason—which is a corollary of the first—for the appalling lack of knowledge of the simplest rules of heating and ventilation is that not only the primary schools, but the high schools, colleges, and universities have been slow to include instruction in these matters in their courses of study. The consequences of this attitude are tragically manifest on all hands.

A graduate of a leading college was recently appointed principal of a new consolidated rural school that had been built according to state specifications regarding floor space, light, heat, and ventilation. The jacketed stoves had been ordered and delivered, but as the trustees had never seen one of these "new-fangled" things, they asked the principal to install them. He did! Seeing the hole provided for the inlet of fresh air and the hole for the outlet of foul air, he cut two squares of tin and nailed up both holes. He then set up the jacketed stoves, had fires built, and after opening the school with the Lord's Prayer, in the recital of which he blandly petitioned "Forgive us our trespasses and deliver us from evil," he called up the Cæsar class, followed the campaign in Gaul with a lesson from the text-book on physiology and hygiene, and gave Mabel and James, the two leading pupils, perfect marks for their explanation of the effects of carbonic-acid gas.

This is not an unusual instance. Scores could be cited as ludicrous and equally tragic. There was the school board that put in a six-inch flue to carry out the foul air that had been breathed by forty children in one room—as sensible as installing a six-inch waste-pipe for a three-foot discharge of water; and the janitor who nailed up the fresh-air inlet of an elaborate fan system for fear the fresh air would cool the furnace!

The heating and ventilating problems must be settled together. Most schoolrooms are overheated, yet even when the thermometer registers high the room often feels cold. This is because the room lacks fresh air. Not one teacher in ten takes account of the fact that it is much easier to heat pure, fresh air than it is to heat air that is stale and foul. The reason is obvious: fresh air is elastic and a good conductor, foul air is full of carbonic-acid gas and is difficult to penetrate. The heat diffuses itself readily through the one and with great difficulty through the other. It has been proved that children invariably make better progress in a cool or moderately heated room than in a room that is overheated; they are less liable to colds and kindred ailments, freer from irritation, rest-lessness, and a spirit of mischievous discontent.

The final objection which stands in the way of modern heating and ventilating systems in many country districts is that their proper operation and repair require the services of a janitor, and that this means additional and unusual expense. There is only one answer when this question is raised—they do require not only a janitor, but an intelligent one. An intelligent janitor is as important an adjunct of the school-plant as the teacher, and it is as foolish to try to get along without one or with one that is "cheap" as it would be to get along without a teacher or with a "cheap" teacher. Here, as in all things, the determining consideration should be the welfare of the children. Money "saved" at their expense is worse than wasted.

The same spirit should govern in the matter of seating.

"How many children will be in the school?"

"About twenty-five."

"Well, order twelve double desks, assorted sizes."

This usual method may save the trustees time and trouble, but is it to be commended? Careful investigations have shown that seats that are not adapted to the sizes of the individual children cause physical injuries and diseases that sometimes result in serious physical handicaps, sometimes in death. Spinal curvature, rounded shoulders, flat chest are all the products of improper seating, to say nothing of the torture that children are compelled to endure when their legs are too long for the seats to which they are assigned, or so short that they dangle for hours at a time.

The old-fashioned home-made benches were unspeakably bad, and they have by no means gone out of use. The "patent" desk and individual seat are undoubtedly an improvement, because, especially when they are "adjustable," they are designed with a serious aim to fit the individual shapes and sizes of the children. But even better than these, particularly for the primary grades, are the simple unattached chairs and tables which are as old as the nursery. These are inexpensive, they can be had in every community in as great variety of sizes as the individual needs of the children require, they can be moved about in obedience to the will of the teacher or the exigencies of class work or study, and where the activities of the room are properly organized they are as silent as the fixed seats and desks, and much less of a hindrance. Tables and chairs of all sorts and sizes for schoolroom use are being manufactured to meet the growing demand.

The motor activities of the children not only require more room than is usually provided, but more freedom for the body and limbs than is usually allowed. The "patent" desks and chairs always tend to cramp the body, and in most cases actually do cramp it. That this evil is so prevalent is astonishing in view of the amount of authoritative criticism that has been directed against it. This entire subject of proper seating is one that should receive the early and thoroughgoing attention of state and local school authorities, and especially of state boards of health, which in some quarters are doing such vital work in regard to lighting, heating, and sanitation.

In what way should a child be seated to encourage the best development of his mind and body? That is the sole point at issue. The usual desk-in-a-row plan is a relic of medievalism, of an age when the democratic spirit had not penetrated the schoolroom. It was adopted for two purposes—first, to maintain discipline, and, second, to save space. Saving space is not one of the essentials of child growth. And so far from the desk-in-a-row arrangement helping to "maintain discipline," it is the enemy of that essential discipline which is the spirit of self-management, self-control, and self-development. If the schoolroom is to be a miniature democracy—what else should it be?—where the children are to develop their own powers of self-discipline through their own activities under the guidance of the teacher, they should not be rigidly confined to seats that are screwed to the floor in rigid, ugly rows. For a church this arrangement may answer, or in a college lecture-room where the students are concerned in nothing but hearing a lecture and taking notes, but for the use of children it cannot be successfully defended.

If a teacher had but one pupil, does any one suppose that she would seat the child in an uncomfortable chair screwed to the floor and make it sit there for hours at a time in the usual wooden way? Would she not permit it to move about, to ask questions, to be more at ease, more natural? But if one child, why not two? And if two, then why not twenty? The inevitable answer will, of course, be that such freedom would destroy discipline. And an autocratic, undemocratic discipline it might destroy. Such discipline depends upon the leather strap, the hickory stick, indiscriminate "keeping in after school" for all manner of transgressions against a specious code of rules, quite as much as it does upon desks in a row. Happily, the abolition of the "patent" seat and desk in favor of the unattached chair and table is not an untried experiment, and where it has been tried the results have fully justified the best predictions and hopes of those who desired the change, and have shattered the gloomy prophecies of those who knew that chaos would certainly follow. There is probably no more beautiful, interesting, or inspiring sight than a schoolroom of children seated in chairs that comfortably fit each child, at tables of just the right height, happy in an air of busy order that is the only good order—an atmosphere of work whose sunlight kills every lurking germ of autocratic discipline.

But if "patent" seats and desks are to be used, the greatest care should be taken to provide sizes that will, as nearly as possible, meet the individual requirements of the children. There is no longer any excuse for purchasing double desks, except the disgraceful excuse that they will save money. Single desks and seats that are in some measure adjustable can be bought of all the leading school-supply houses. And where they are adopted the following rules should be followed:

1. Desks range in size from 1 to 6, No. 1 being the smallest, No. 6 the largest. The rural school should contain a single row of No. 2, a row of No. 5, and two rows each of Nos. 3 and 4.

2. Only single adjustable desks should be used.

3. Only desks of the same size should be placed in the same row.

4. The smallest desks should be placed nearest the windows.

5. The desks should be placed so that the distance from the edge of the desk to the back of the seat will be: For Nos. 5 and 6, nine inches; No. 4, ten inches; No. 3, eleven inches; and No. 2, twelve or thirteen inches.

The children's feet should touch squarely on the floor.

6. The aisles at the sides and rear should be about three feet wide, and the others about twenty inches.

Even after the desks and seats have been arranged to fit the sizes of the children it does not follow that John should be placed on the front seat to keep him out of mischief and Mary on the back seat because she is "good." There are thousands of semi-deaf and near-sighted Johns and Marys sitting in the rear of school-rooms who are having their time wasted and are considered dull because the teacher does not know that their vision or hearing is defective.

A superintendent visiting a second-grade schoolroom in a small village noticed a boy sitting near the back of the room.

"How did Larrie Jones get into this room?" the superintendent asked.

"His father moved into the district, and he was transferred," the teacher answered.

"How long has he been here?"

"About ten days."

"How does he get along in his classes?"

"Only fairly; he doesn't pay good attention much of the time, and he makes irrelevant answers."

"How about this boy in front here?"

"Oh, he's quick as a flash!"

"Suppose you ask them to change seats," the superintendent suggested, "and then see how Larrie gets along."

A week later the superintendent visited this same room.

"How is Larrie doing now?" he inquired.

"Oh, very much better," the teacher immediately replied; "he has come to be one of my best and most attentive pupils."

"How do you account for the change?" the superintendent asked.

"I don't know, unless he feels himself more under my discipline now that he is nearer me."

The fact was that the boy's hearing was defective, and he hadn't been able to hear while he sat on the back seat.

"I hadn't the remotest idea of such a thing!" said the teacher, when the matter was explained to her.

In this case, as in many more of the same kind, the

fixed platform for the teacher was equally responsible with the desk-in-a-row arrangement of the seats for the mischief done the child. Like the rigid seats, the fixed platform is a relic of medievalism and should be discarded with the leather strap, the hickory stick, and the autocratic ideal of discipline. The teacher should dwell with the children and guide them through their self-activities, not sit over them and endeavor to fill them with knowledge after the most approved methods of fattening chickens and geese.

To build a schoolhouse and then save money by refusing to buy plenty of blackboard is on all-fours with building a buggy and then saving money by refusing to buy taps for the wheels. Nothing is more essential to progress in studies than abundant blackboard space and its use by the children. Aside from the fact that the blackboard is of great assistance to the teacher in keeping children busy, it is often a relief to the pupils to leave their seats and do blackboard work.

Slate is the best material for blackboards, and in the long run is the cheapest. But there is bad slate, and a great deal of it is used in the schools. The best place to get good blackboards is from a thoroughly reliable dealer. Under no circumstances should a slick, shiny, glaring surface be tolerated. Its effect on children's eyes is distinctly bad, and its use should be forbidden by law.

In setting blackboards, care should be taken to set them to the sizes of the children. To place all the blackboard so high that the small children cannot reach it without stretching their arms and necks is utterly bad. It is not generally known that bending the head back and looking up for any length of time interferes with the circulation of the blood and stops the thought processes. Dustless crayon should always be used. No other kind is healthy.

Every schoolroom should of course have ample cloak-

"WE, CAN'T SEE"

BETTER BIG LETTERS AND A GLASSY BLACKBOARD

room space separate from the sitting-room, but easily reached by the children. The cloakroom should be well ventilated so as to prevent dampness and odors. Under no circumstances should it be dark. It should be well lighted, well ventilated, and should have little troughs, with catches for holding umbrellas and rubber shoes, so that the water will run off and out-of-doors. For a few dollars such devices can be made and installed and they greatly add to the healthfulness and convenience of the children.

Most cloakrooms are too small by from one-half to one-third. The space should be so ample as to preclude the possibility of the hats touching each other when hung on pegs. The coats and cloaks should be suspended on hangers so as to be entirely free from contact. The custom of hanging cloaks, coats, hats, and umbrellas in the schoolrooms or hallways should never be permitted. To force children to hang these things in the schoolroom or pile them up on chairs or put them in their desks is to exhibit gross indifference to ordinary decency.

In many schools it is entirely practicable to have provision made for the children to eat their lunches at table in a regular and orderly way, out-of-doors in good weather, indoors in bad. The necessary plates, dishes, knives, forks, spoons, paper napkins, etc., can be secured and kept at little cost, and folding-tables and folding-chairs will take up little room during study-hours. Where the patent desks are used the schoolroom will have to be large enough to offer the extra space for the table or tables. Where the work-tables—for writing, study, etc.—are used with movable chairs, which, as already stated, is much the best arrangement, especially for the first four or five (primary) grades, these tables can easily be utilized for luncheons.

The plan of having the luncheons served in orderly fashion is especially valuable in schools where cooking is

—as it should be everywhere—included in the school program. If in schools already erected it is not practicable to provide lunchrooms the teachers should improvise plans for having the luncheons eaten from the desks, and in a way that will make the noon-day meal a source of pleasure and good breeding. This will be for days that are too inclement for the children to have luncheons out-of-doors. Whenever the weather permits, the best place to have luncheons served is out-of-doors. Folding-tables and folding-chairs are cheap and can be quickly set up and quickly put away.

The moving picture is destined to be a great factor in the schools of the future. Some rural schools are already using them for educational purposes.

IX

SOME NEGLECTED FACTORS IN RURAL-SCHOOL EQUIPMENT

THE rapidly increasing use of electricity and gasolene for generating power makes it practicable to-day as it never was before to have a water system for the toilet, shower-baths, and drinking-fountains. In fact, it is the exceptional school which cannot now have such a system, and every school that can should have a system of running water. Where no public water-supply can be tapped either a running stream can be used with a water-ram or engine, or a well or cistern can be used with a dynamo or gasolene engine. For a small sum of money a good well can be drilled, and all machinery and apparatus, including a pressure-tank, closet system, shower-baths, and a sewer or sanitary well for waste, can be installed. A number of one-room schools have installed pressure-tanks operated by a hand pump with entirely satisfactory results and at remarkably low cost.

The sanitary condition at most of our country schools in the United States is not merely bad—it is too vile for description. The varying conditions may be described on a pyramidal plan: At the bottom are tens of thousands of schools that have no outhouses for either sex, and tens of thousands that have one insanitary outhouse for the girls and none for the boys. Above these there are tens of thousands of schools that have one insanitary outhouse for each sex. Here the building of the pyramid ceases, for the number of sanitary, properly located outhouses is relatively so small that they must be counted by the thousands, and not by the tens of thousands. Indeed, there are still many states in which the properly located, thoroughly modern and sanitary outhouses can be counted only by the hundreds or the scores.

This horrible condition has existed and has been tolerated since the foundation of the public-school systems for the same reasons that the bad-air conditions have existed—lack of knowledge of their menace to health and morals. So hardened to these unspeakable conditions has the male portion of the population become that it is almost impossible to eradicate the prevalent idea that sanitary and clean outhouses are not possible with boys. The truth is, boys are innately clean, refined, and modest —just as girls are—but they soon have their finer instincts killed by the example of older people. What frightful wrong we do the children by such conduct!

It is a comparatively recent discovery that typhoid fever is a germ-disease, and that it is contracted only by the swallowing of water or food that has typhoid germs in it. It is now known that typhoid germs come from the discharges of people who have typhoid fever, and from nowhere else. It is known that drinking-water is infected by these discharges through improper drainage. It is known that the common house-fly is the greatest carrier of this disease from night soil to the foods of people. It is now known that the greatest distributing center of typhoid fever is the usual type of home and school privy, where the flies feed by the billions between meals, and then carry the germ-laden filth on their feet, legs, and bodies to the house when they join the families at breakfast, dinner, and supper, besides sampling all the food in the kitchen and bathing in the milk. Some one has said that many flies have suicidal tendencies and choose milk as their medium of destruction.

Flies breed mostly in stable manure, but also in almost

any kind of filth, or decaying matter, such as meats and vegetables.

It is fortunate that it has been proved that stable manure which has been hauled to the fields fresh, or that has been protected from the weather, is much superior to manure which has been thrown out from the stables or barns in a pile waiting to be hauled out in the fall, winter, or spring. When this once gets into the consciousness of the American farmer the greatest breeding-place for flies will be eliminated; and while he protects the manure his boy or girl will, incidentally, be safer from the disease, which is still largely regarded as a mysterious visitation of Providence instead of a perfectly natural result of filthy conditions. It takes ten days for flies to breed. If all the manure is removed even once a week this breeding-ground is eliminated.

It is very easy to interest children in the fact that decaying meats and vegetables, and dirty paper, and unclean outhouses form breeding-places, and that all filth in which flies breed should be carefully put in a covered receptacle and destroyed at regular intervals. This training not only causes them to protect the schoolrooms and grounds and keep them in clean condition, but the good effect of the training is soon seen in their homes, and especially when they set up homes of their own.

It does not cost much in money to build sanitary outhouses at the school. The price varies from nine to thirty dollars each for two dry closets for one and two-room buildings. For larger buildings the price will vary from fifteen dollars up, depending on size and material. The closet can easily be made fly-proof, and if the boys and girls are formed into committees to look after the good order and cleanliness of these places they will be kept in perfect condition. A boy accustomed at home to see immodest, careless conditions will very naturally debauch the conditions at school. Why shouldn't he? Train up a boy in the way he should *not* go, and when he is old he will rarely depart from it.

Two sanitation committees were once formed at a large school. One committee was composed of the larger boys, the other of the larger girls, the members being chosen so as to include some boys who were very careless but who were leaders. Proper and improper conditions were frankly explained. These houses were their property, built for their convenience. They were expected to protect their property from any who showed a tendency to deface or soil the walls or floors. It is never difficult to form an efficient committee of girls. They have usually been protected at home, and their inbred refinement goes to school with them. But with a little tactful oversight and inspection, and with kindly criticism and wholesome commendation and suggestions, the boys catch the idea promptly, and, considering the rearing they have had, it is astonishing how quickly they bring decency and cleanliness to the front and keep them there. And so this committee of boys did. One day at recess a boy came crying to the superintendent with the plaint that some of the boys had bumped him. The boys were promptly summoned.

"Why did you bump this boy?" was asked.

"Because he befouled the closet," was the answer.

"The next time he does it don't bump him too hard, but just hard enough," said the superintendent. And there was no more trouble.

It has been found that hookworm is the direct result of insanitary conditions resulting from a lack of good home and school privies. This disease is thus a filth-disease and is enormously prevalent in a belt all around the world extending about thirty degrees on each side of the equator. That it does not take a wider sweep is due to climate alone. The hookworm victims become an easy mark for tuberculosis, pneumonia, and other germ-diseases, since the disease weakens the resisting power of the persons infected.

The lack of decent, sanitary closets is the cause not only of typhoid fever, but of constipation, with its long train of bodily miseries, and of numerous other troubles that go with the victims through life. Many a boy and girl, not knowing the terrible evils that grow from retention, prefers to remain in the school rather than go out in the woods or go to a filthy closet.

A fearful responsibility rests upon the teacher who fails to teach in the proper way the physiology and hygiene of this subject. There is no need for squeamishness on the one side or lack of tact on the other. A natural function can be treated in a natural way. A "refinement" that cannot tolerate a mention of how to improve conditions, but tolerates the bad condition, is hardly skin-deep. Prudishness and stupidity are not refinement at all. The rule prevailing in tens of thousands of schools of refusing to let a child leave the room upon request should be forbidden by law, and any teacher who violates this law should be prosecuted and dismissed.

The menace to the morals of children is of course as threatening as the menace to their health when they are forced to submit to these intolerable conditions. A mere roof and the four walls of a school privy, so far from protecting health and morals, are often breeding-places for disease and an invitation to vice.

Why should the closets be placed so near each other that the boys and girls must pass each other to reach them? Why should they be so close that conversation can be heard from one to the other? Or why should they be stuck in the yard, looking like two huge warts on the face of the school-grounds? Why should they be windowless and dark? Where on earth are sunshine and light and fresh air more needed? Why is it apparently a crime to have a trellis with flowers or vines banked between the school and the closets?   Flowers and evergreens make ugliness beautiful, turn coarseness into refinement; and when children are allowed and directed how to prepare and plan, and how to grow these, they come quickly, remain permanently, and add to the sum total of happiness.

Many state boards of health and the United States Bureau of Education are glad to send plans and specifications for sanitary privies and their surroundings.   To fail to use them is immoral, because it tends to degrade our future citizenship.   It is curious that even these boards recommend the same kind of closet for boys and girls.   Different kinds are obviously needed.

Taking a financial view of the matter, the building of decent and sanitary closets of ample size and equipment in or at every schoolhouse in this country would not cost as much money as the neglect to do so causes each year in illness and vice.   Again it may be said that if the community could only realize that, after all, not the individuals affected, but the community, pays for every bit of this illness and vice, there would be a revolution in this matter.   And it should be preached and declared by every teacher and every wide-awake citizen that the community does that very thing!

Throughout the United States there are many days during the session when lessons can be heard out-of-doors or can be learned out-of-doors.   Every rural school should be located on the school-grounds so that just next to the school, on one or more sides, the children, or a part of them, can sit for study or recitation purposes.   There are several ways of arranging this.   On warm, dry days the children can sit in chairs on the grass; on colder days, or when the ground is wet or damp, they can sit on fixed or movable platforms.   A concrete platform slightly elevated, and with gentle slopes for drainage, can be made by the larger boys, who would consider it "great fun" to do the work.   Arrangements on three sides of the school

152

would meet almost every problem of wind and sunshine and of two or three grades of children. If there are no trees—as there should be in every yard—a covered roof with posts might be used in some places where rains are frequent or the sunlight too glaring. They should, of course, be made attractive with growing vines or flowers covering the posts and running along the roofs.

If all the children are not seated out-of-doors it should often be possible—and best—to let the children who are studying sit out, while those who are reciting could be inside. There should be no iron-clad rule about it in any school. Children don't grow according to iron-clad rules, nor should they be tortured into fitting them.

Every school should have one or more workrooms on the school-grounds, either as a part of the school-building or as a separate building. Not infrequently when a new building is to be erected the old one can be utilized for workroom purposes.

What is the object of the workroom? In a small school it can be used as a place in which to teach cooking and sewing; as a place in which to teach certain handicrafts; as a place in which to teach the use of the indispensable tools of the home, with simple woodwork and work in iron. In larger schools the workroom should be large enough to be divided, if necessary, so that besides the sewing and cooking room there may be a carpenter shop for the boys and a place for the collection and examination of soils, seeds, and plants. The number of workrooms, their sizes, their uses will be based upon the life activities of the community in which the school is situated. No elaborate finish or equipment is needed. The building or room should be simple, clean, and comfortable. For the carpentry and iron work a shed is often sufficient—where the lumber and other materials can be kept and where a roof will protect from weather. The building can be built by the boys, and can be relieved of bareness by getting the boys and girls to paint or whitewash it, and to plant and cultivate flowers and shrubbery and climbing vines about it.

Some localities are including distinct workrooms in their school plans, and these are meeting with great success. It has been found that the children, when allowed to have and use a workroom, take more interest in the usual book program, come more regularly, and remain in school longer. It is not impossible to do sewing, cooking, and simple handicraft in a one-room school, but it is so easy to add the workroom that there seems little excuse for its not being done. The quick response made in most communities, when the citizens are asked to help erect and equip a workroom, shows the interest the public takes in this vital feature of real education.

The importance of a school-garden and a school-farm has already been considered under "The Widening Outlook of the Rural School." It may be added, however, that one of the essential uses of a school-farm is the training of the boys in the right use and care of farm tools and machinery, and this requires that the school should own a variety of tools and machinery so that the boys may learn how to take them apart and set them up properly. There should, of course, be included the care and use of farm animals. A valuable adjunct is a good smithy, which should be conducted as a business for the use of the neighborhood. If there is a smithy in the neighborhood the school should secure the coöperation of the smith in the teaching of the boys.

The lack of an adequate conception of the function of the school-plant—its uses, its relation to the every-day life, and its large part in that life—is in no way more clearly shown than in the almost universal absence of school-cottages, a vital unit in the physical equipment of the school center.

Just as the school-building should be planned with great

care as a model for the convenient use of the children, so the school-cottage should be planned as a model of what a home should be. In architecture it should be—as all buildings should be—on simple and classical lines. It should be built with a view to saving steps for the house-keeper. It should be built to accentuate the idea that housekeeping should be, not a tradition, but a science. It should be a model of ingenuity in securing a maximum of labor-saving, time-saving devices at a minimum of cost. From front door to kitchen, from cellar to garret, from front yard to back, it should show purpose in every detail.

In connection with the school the cottage should have a water system. Its kitchen should be utilized as a center of the cooking and home-keeping activities of the school. Its dining-room, one of its bedrooms, its living-room, its bathroom and closet, could be used in the same way. As a training-center in housekeeping and home-making, in the making and keeping of the daily budget, it should be a model to the community.

But "Who would keep it in vacation?" It would be the home of the principal and his family—or of the teacher or teachers, according to its size—and would tend to minimize the evils of that *wander-lust* which seems to have infected the great mass of country teachers, not because they like to wander, but because the low pay and often unsatisfactory living arrangements force them to "move on."

The development of the school-library as an essential part of the complete school-plant has been very encouraging in recent years, yet only a beginning has been made in most of the states, if the full extent to which a library can be used is considered. Having a collection of books in the schoolroom is one thing; making the most of the collection may be quite another.

The state teaches children to read. With the many excellent school-readers, full of good literature, now used it is hardly possible for a child to read a series of books and not have his desire for reading awakened. What then? Does the state provide the means to gratify this desire? Does it help the child to get something good to read? In some cases, yes. Most states or communities have made only the smallest beginnings in this direction. Yet to teach children to read, to give them the desire to read, and then to fail to provide anything with which they may gratify the desire is not right. The consequence is that the boys and girls read what is most easily obtainable—the dime and half-dime novels filled with utterly false views and with low standards of life. It would seem that the more vicious and nasty a book is, the cheaper it is and the more accessible it is. Why are not interesting, wholesome books accessible to children either free or at very low cost? A child who gets into the habit of reading wholesome books will not care for vicious ones.

The idea in the past has been that a boy should learn to read so that he may be able to read his ballot. But what candidate on the ballot will he be most apt to support when he is saturated with the ideals of the *Police Gazette* or idealizes the gambler hero or the prize-fighter? More important than the power to read the ballot is the power to discriminate between persons and principles; more important still is the developed passion for personal and civic righteousness.

Who can see the barely perceptible line between the man who cannot read at all and the man who does not read at all? What is the difference between the literate who does not but can read and the illiterate who neither does nor can?

Good books in good bindings are now offered at so reasonable a price that poverty is no longer a valid excuse in any rural community for the absence of a well-selected library. The literature of the world has been searched for material suitable for children; and so much has been found that there is almost an embarrassment of riches.

Unfortunately, along with the gold there is much dross. The desire of the publishers to be represented in every school-library has led to an output that is bewildering in quantity, and it has become increasingly difficult to winnow the wheat from the chaff. Chaff is not poisonous, but it is anything but nourishing.

Some of the books issued in series, giving false ideals of life and stimulating the appetite for highly seasoned stuff, should not be allowed in libraries. A visit to libraries containing such books discloses the fact that they are read to pieces, while other books that should be of interest to healthy-minded children are but little used. The fact that a child finds a book "interesting" or that he "likes it" is not always a safe criterion of merit. Goody-goody books filled with moral lollypops and candied priggishness are utterly out of the question, and, fortunately, are not so much in vogue as in former days.

Many of the state educational departments issue lists of books suitable for young people's libraries, and these, as a rule, are good guides, though the tendency seems to be toward a generous inclusion rather than toward a selection that means reasonable exclusion.

The traveling library, in use in some of the states, has proved a great boon. It has been especially helpful in small and remote communities where the indifference of the local school authorities or of the people makes it difficult to interest them in a permanent library. In some communities it is of advantage for the traveling library to precede the permanent one: first, because a taste for good reading is created by it and because in many communities it is difficult to raise money for libraries until the young people and old have acquired this taste; and, second, because there is a rigid requirement that the books must be handled with care and must be returned in good order.

If a well-selected library is placed in a community, a taste for reading good literature is created or developed. This result rarely, if ever, fails if the library is for the children. It is then comparatively easy to get the young people and the older members of the community to work for the establishment of a permanent library. The children are then eager for more reading - matter, and intelligently eager. They know just what they are raising money for, and just why they are interested in succeeding.

Quite as important as developing this taste for reading good books is the careful training of the children and adults in handling the books. A book must not be abused. It must be handled with clean hands. Its leaves must not be dog-eared or turned down. Its back must not be strained or broken. It is a clean, pure guest in the home, and must be treated with the respect, the courtesy, the thoughtfulness due such a guest. This requirement has a tremendously elevating effect on a child. Few children treat a book maliciously, but most children, unless trained, treat books carelessly. The rules of the traveling library train the children away from malicious and careless treatment of books.

There seems no sufficient reason why the library at the school should not be the community library, unless the community already has a well-equipped library elsewhere. There could rarely be a more convenient place for a library than the schoolhouse. The teachers and older boys and girls can act as librarians, while the facilities for getting and returning books are excellent. The children can easily take the books home for the older members of the household and return them to the library. This constant medium of communication encourages the use of the library. In places where this plan has been tried it has met with success.

SOME NEGLECTED FACTORS

The teacher who uses the school-library as an adjunct to the school studies has a decided advantage over one who does not. It is impossible for the most talented of teachers to obtain a maximum of efficiency in teaching without a constant and intelligent use of well-selected library books. Teaching is made much more interesting and effective both to teacher and to pupils. If the teachers are not well trained in the use of these tools they should consult with those who are. To select books of reference, books for side reading, and books for general reading without a thorough knowledge of the subject is to make blunders and waste funds. Many of the state normal schools include in their course of study a training in the use of library books in the daily school program. All normals should do so, and it would be well if the states would require a knowledge of this subject before granting certificates to teach. It is amazing that in this day, with books for reference and books for sup- plementary and general reading so excellent, a teacher should be permitted or compelled to teach without their use. It is pathetic to see so many children utterly un- trained in the use of reference books and supplementary reading. Unless the habit of consulting reference books is cultivated in childhood it is not likely to be acquired at all. This habit helps to make study a delight; gives a wide and varied information; makes the child stronger and better able to help himself; gets him into the habit of looking up every word and expression that he does not understand, and thus leads him away from the slovenly habit of passing these over when he knows he does not understand their meaning. The text-book publishers pub- lish excellent books supplementary to the texts on geogra- phy, history, hygiene. Where these cannot be used in class work—as they should be—they should be in every school and community library, and should, under the direction and encouragement of the teacher, be read by the children.

One of the worst of sinners is the teacher who solemnly glass-cases the library, locks the door, and keeps the key. Books are intended to be used, not to be gazed at through a pane of glass. There should be strict rules as to the treatment of books and as to their prompt return. Carelessness in these things means the disintegration and ruin of the library. But these rules should be few and simple though rigidly observed. The distinction between the use and the abuse of a book should be clearly understood by the teacher and the pupils. But restrictions should be few. No one, young or old, in the community should be denied the privilege of reading the books; indeed, every one should be encouraged to read them.

An all too common mistake in the selection of a library is to forget the smaller children and have books only for the larger ones—as, for example, the high-school pupils. Nine children out of ten never get into a high school; most of them never get beyond the fourth grade. The majority of the books should be for the majority of the children. There is no reason why there should not be an abundance for all. Children should be given books as soon as they enter school, and should be encouraged to use them. They should be encouraged to take books home even before they read fluently, so that their fathers, mothers, sisters, and brothers may read to them. A library should be started, not with an encyclopedia, but with a well-illustrated copy of *Mother Goose*.

Another mistake that is too common is to regard a "library," when it has arrived, as complete. A true library is never complete. It should be allowed to grow like boys and girls—all the time; and with that end in view it should be constantly nourished.

The time will come—it should be here now—when no state, no community, will permit a single school to exist without a well-selected library. It is as necessary a part of the equipment as blackboards, text-books, and seats are. The time will come—it should have been here ere now —when a teacher who is not intimately acquainted with the functions and familiar with the uses of a library will not be granted a certificate to teach.

Relaxation is as much a part of life as work. Children should not be kept at close attention to one subject for a long period. When the line or point of fatigue is reached, that work should stop at once. A continuance after that does harm; the children lose more than they gain. Fatigue produces a poison in the system, and a continuance of the work that is producing the fatigue means more poison to the system.

The evil of overcrowding children with work is a wide-spread evil. It comes largely from the attempt to "do" so many pages and subjects and pass the examination and go to the next grade.

The school authorities pay too little attention to the proper proportion of work and relaxation among children. The belief that time is gained by "keeping right at" a piece of work for a long period, and that time is lost by taking a rest or relaxing, is not only an error, but an error that leads to serious results. Nervous headaches and nervous irritation are only two of the evils. Physical growth is not regular—nor is mental growth, nor spiritual growth.

It is not difficult to tell when a child is fatigued, as has been pointed out. And when he is he should be allowed to relax, and to relax in plenty of pure, fresh air. A change of work from a quiet study at the desk, or a period of recitation, to play on the school-grounds, or to a period of work in the school-gardens, or to a period in the workroom, making something, is definitely beneficial.

Then, too, children should be allowed periods of their own. Periods should be given them to use exactly as they wish. They may prefer to remain at some bit of work— in the workroom; in the garden; in the library; on the playground; to visit another room or class, a thing many of them take great delight in; to make a trip home for some special purpose; or simply to roam abroad, across the fields, through the woods, down to some interesting spot where they have found a squirrel's nest or been watching a couple of birds with their young.

Usually, if there is a nest to see, or the home of some wild thing, they will wish their teacher to go with them, which, of course, the teacher will when opportunity offers. A boy shows his innate generosity of spirit, his fine sense of comradeship, his craving for acted but unspoken sympathy and love when he asks "teacher" to go to see his rabbit gums, or his little field of corn, or the squirrel's nest he has found, or the trout-pool down in the woods. What an opportunity for a teacher who knows, and who, knowing that a boy's spirit is as shy as a woodsprite, draws that spirit to him with a tact that seems to draw nothing.

And when the *wander-lust* comes on the boy, and he wishes just to tramp, to see nothing and nobody in particular, but to be by himself for a while, he should have that privilege—nay, that right. A tramp through the woods and over the hills crystallizes many a fluid impulse or thought, brings to consciousness many a new one, unravels many a tangled mental skein, enables many a child to "catch up" with himself, and brings him back to civilization with a glow on his cheeks and with his blood charged with oxygen; with a clearer brain, a purer heart a finer spirit and vision.

Often in his tramps and in his quiet dreamings he walks with God, even when not conscious of it. Often, when communing with himself, God communes with him. Often, when battling with himself, God helps him. The deep silences are the vestibules where the Maker meets man in the making.

Let the child go, then, and have his dreaming—his moods of silence and solitude. "When are these?" you

ask. Watch him with love, and know when. He will
go with joy. He will go upon the mountains and into
the valleys of related things; and he will return with
gratitude in his heart and with a new light in his eyes.
It was in his day-dreams that Samuel heard; it was out
on the hills that David could open his heart to wisdom;
it was in the fields that the voices spoke to Jeanne.

In the making of our cities and towns the children have
been forgotten. The children's acre—the playground—
has been filched from them; and the value of land in
terms of money has so obsessed the hearts and minds
of our man citizenship that the value of land in terms of
healthy-bodied and healthy-minded youth has been
overlooked.

The results of this violation of the laws of child-nature
are seen in that fearful product of the cities, the Apache—
the embodiment of energies suppressed where they should
have been directed, and run riot in wrong ways; in the
"gang"; in weak bodies, in contracted chests, in physical
and mental dullness and moral stupidity or degeneracy.
The playless child—the child who does not know how
to play—is one of the most pathetic of sights, and is in
line to be the father of the weak-minded and the mother
of the dependent. The energies of the play-deprived and
play-denied child, if there be in him the virility of the
race, will be suppressed in only one way—in his play; for
they will certainly break forth in other ways that mean
reformatories, penitentiaries, policemen, and courts.

These results are at last forcing themselves on the
attention of the nation. The awakening in some of the
cities and towns is in every way encouraging, for it means
a vigorous start and is the prophecy of a steady, healthy
growth of sentiment.

Play is instinctive; it is as much a law of nature as
growth, for it is an essential part of growth. Without play
no animal can be or become normal in its functions.

Play is not just "play" in the sense of being an unnecessary sort of pastime or amusement. It is a necessity of life. The dumb child is no more abnormal than the playless child. It is as senseless, as cruel, and as wrong to forbid play (and it is forbidden when the opportunity is filched) as it is to forbid speech.

In the rural districts the opportunities for play are of course far greater than in the towns and cities; but the wide-spread belief that the only value of play lies in the working of the muscles makes it difficult for people to realize the importance of ample playgrounds at the school as an essential part of the educative process.

"I don't send John to school to play. I send him to be educated. I can give him plenty of exercise at home" (meaning the wood-pile and the plow) is a typical attitude.

The agitation for playgrounds in the rural districts and the insistence that it is essential to John as a part of his education are awakening the people to the importance of playgrounds. The fact that work-exercise of the muscles is good, but does not take the place of play-exercise of the muscles, is becoming better known. The wood-pile and the plow are a good training for John's muscles and character, provided he doesn't get an overdose; but to substitute these for play-exercise is to deprive him of physical, mental, and moral health, and to run the risk of making him surly and unsocial.

Play is usually expressed by games; and those games which best strengthen body, mind, and character are the best. A game which injures body, mind, or morals is, of course, vicious.

Physically, an outdoor game should give free play to the muscles, make supple the back and limbs, and develop deep breathing. Morally, a game should develop initiative, a sense of justice, honor, and fair dealing. It necessitates restraint, consideration, good manners, truthfulness, a mastery of self, the capacity to follow and

A KANSAS SCENE

A MAY-POLE DANCE, LAKE COUNTY, OHIO

A CHILDREN'S FREE-FOR-ALL RACE, IN NEBRASKA. (By the courtesy of the International Committee, Y. M. C. A.)

ORGANIZING PLAY

obey, and, therefore, to lead and control. Mentally, a game should develop concentration, close attention, alertness, the ability to decide quickly and accurately, good judgment, imagination, memory. Many a successful life is based on play experiences.

In play there should be instruction and direction. Great tact is needed—nowhere is it more essential. The instruction and direction should be entirely informal. The teacher must not be *over* the children, but *with* them; and if officiousness cannot be laid aside, the teacher should be. Spirit and spontaneity are the soul and body of play, and these wilt and die in the presence of Jupiter Pedagogus or Stern Juno. Leading-strings are not in order on the playground.

"Go and play!" is sufficient in command but deficient in instruction. There are so many good games, and often the children know so few. They need a more varied play-diet than they usually get. As a rule, those games which have stood the test of time are best. A few good ones are: The Bird Catcher, Klondike, Skip Away, Jumping Rope, Cat and Mouse, Leap Frog, Anthony Over, Roly Poly, Hide and Seek, Finding the Switch, Prisoners' Base, Fox and Geese, Old Cat.

The playgrounds should be so arranged as to give all grades of children recreation during the day. The recesses need not come at the same time for all. But, as they usually do, there should be play spaces for the smaller children and other spaces for the larger children, and play spaces for several different play groups at one time. Unless this provision is made the smaller children and the timid—the ones who most need development by play—will be crowded out.

If a sufficient acreage can be secured—as in most rural communities—and there is no community playground it is very desirable to have this provided for at the school. The school thus becomes more of a community center.

THE WORK OF THE RURAL SCHOOL

Land is steadily increasing in value everywhere. School boards and the communities they represent should therefore be constantly on the lookout for the opportunities to purchase land for playgrounds. In some cases, especially in villages and small towns, a good school is already established, but is lacking in play space, and none can be obtained next to the school. In such instances playgrounds should be purchased elsewhere *as a part of the school equipment* for educating the children. There is just as much reason for purchasing and building playgrounds for educating the children as there is for purchasing material and building a schoolhouse. A school program that does not definitely include organized and directed play is lopsided.

School athletics are happily coming into vogue in a large number of country schools—notably in the consolidated and union schools. But there is no reason why they should not become a regular part of the school program of any school. And plays and games now abound that give opportunity to all the children. The competition of athletic teams is becoming a feature of the rural school. In many of the states the schools of a district or of a county send teams to a central meet to compete for prizes. In some counties these meets are the events of the year, and attract thousands of visitors. Several of the state departments issue bulletins containing rules and descriptions of plays, games, and athletic contests. One of the best of these is issued by the Bureau of Education of the Philippine Islands,[1] and is in itself an illustration of the extent and value of play and games in the public schools.

Every location for school-buildings should have trees, and if they are not already there the layout should be

[1] Bulletin No. 40. Athletic Handbook for the Philippine Public Schools.

planned with them as a part of it. The children should always have a hand in planting every tree and in caring for those already on the grounds. It is not unnatural for children to neglect or injure trees in which they have no sense of ownership. A boy does not hack a tree or otherwise injure it because he is "bad." He does it because he is thoughtless. But why should he be thoughtful about something that his thought or attention has not been called to? He wishes to let out his pent-up energies; what material shall he use? Every way he turns is the sign-post, "Don't!" He hunts for something he can *do*. Pent-up energies cannot be used through channels of *don'ts*.

The same principle applies to flowers and grass. At every school a reasonable—not a large—amount of space just in front, and usually a narrow strip around the sides, of the building should be sacred to grass and flowers and shrubs. They should be planted and kept in order by the children, working under the guidance of one who knows how to beautify the grounds. In the same way walks can be built and kept in order. The custom in many places of devoting a large part of the school-grounds to flowers and grass is an unfortunate one, as the children become discouraged in trying to care for them, and they are deprived of that much play space.

The front of a school-building is not the place for play; the grounds are made to look bare, and the appearance of the most beautiful building is seriously marred by an ill-kept or bare front yard.

One principal writes of his school that last year "two beautiful plots were planned and executed in the school-yard, and to-day two gardens show the work of the children in helping to make and keep the school-grounds beautiful."

A teacher, writing of her first experience at a school, says:

I had been employed to do the primary work. When I reached the school-yard and saw that there were about four acres of school property, yet directly in front of the school was a basketball-ground on which it seemed a sprig of green had never grown—a real clay spot—I felt homesick.

Everything in nature seemed to preach to me that it was really a beautiful spot; it just lacked a little human nature, and in the mean time the human world would get as much benefit as the plant world.

I suggested to the principal that the basketball-ground be changed to the back of the campus and that the front yard be beautified and be used especially for developing the esthetic taste of pupils. He said: "yes, we'll change the ball-grounds, but you could never get grass or flowers to grow on that spot, and then you'd never keep the children off. They'll pull all the flowers even if you succeed in getting them to grow." I said, "Well, if you say I may do it I'll risk it." "Certainly, certainly; I have no objections," he said. As soon as we got things straight on the inside of school I began to plan for the outside. I talked to the boys on what could be done to the yard. They said, "We'll help you if you want us, but the flowers will bloom here just in time to go on our graves." I said, "Well, it would be nice to have a hand in putting flowers on one's own grave, so we'll try." One boy brought a spade, one a shovel, one a pitch-fork, then we borrowed some tools and started. Our first task was to remove rocks and old bricks. The walks were very narrow, so every brick was taken up and the walk made so wide that there would be no excuse for walking on grass and flowers. We worked a little every day, and in a few days the chairman of the school board noted what we were doing, and he said: "Get any tools you need, and charge them to the trustees. You have an awful job before you, but I guess you can make something of it." A very few tools were gotten. Some of the boys brought horses and plowed. It required plowing a number of times, and very hard work to break the soil, but we got it in condition for weathering during the winter. A near-by citizen saw what we were doing and said: "I'll send you a flower catalogue, and I want you to select the flowers you want. Inclose the list and catalogue to me, and I'll give you the flowers." He gave twenty-seven rose bushes, four dozen hyacinth bulbs, and a great many other seeds. Another man gave five hundred jonquil bulbs. Two women sent cuttings, plants, and seeds for the yard. The plots were laid off and seeds planted at the right times through the late fall and winter.

The man who gave the rose bushes said, "I am going to give the fertilizer when you are ready to plant your grass in April." Another man gave the lime, and a seedsman gave the seed. The boys plowed, cultivated, dragged, and rolled the seed-beds for grass. It was just exactly the right time to sow the seed. A rain was coming, and they must be gotten in before the rain. It was a holiday; a man could not be secured to sow them. The boys, two girls, and I sowed the fertilizer, lime, and seed, and it rained just as we finished. That summer the yard was as green as velvet, and we had flowers in profusion—too soon to go on our graves.

It was just this first work, this strictly voluntary work, on the part of pupils and teacher that paved the way to our first year of school-garden and agricultural work.

Every care should be used to have the entire school-plant—the buildings, the grounds, the interiors, and immediate approaches, the background—as beautiful and as attractive as possible. This will require much thought, constant attention, and sometimes a little money. The children will furnish the time and attention, if permitted and guided. There is no better way to train them than through their directed activities.

Beauty has great cultural value. In fact, an appreciation of beauty is one of the essentials of culture. All children have an appreciation of beauty; and a little direction and encouragement will soon develop in them a passionate appreciation of beautiful things—trees, flowers, birds, streams, pictures, statuary, buildings, furniture; of beautiful music; of beautiful literature; of beautiful deeds. It is strange, then, that in our rural schools so little attention is paid to this phase of life. And it is especially disheartening to see some of those who insist on what they term a "cultural" education satisfied with schools that are ugly, unkempt, and neglected inside and outside; satisfied with the utter neglect of the training of the children to appreciate and preserve beautiful objects. Certainly there is little that is cultural in an education that insists on the three R's and neglects beautiful buildings, beautiful pictures, beautiful books in the library, beautiful school-grounds, beautiful trees and flowers and grass, beautiful birds, and beautiful music.

From a purely financial standpoint beauty is of immense value. The most hidebound embodiment of selfishness in a community knows that a beautifully kept place will attract more money than an ill-kept one. He knows that a home with beautiful trees is worth more than a home placed in a barren spot; that a home with flowers and shrubbery and a beautiful view is worth more than a similar home without these. And yet he generally resents the training of the children in the appreciation of beautiful things as an unwarranted extravagance.

Paris has thousands upon thousands of visitors because it is beautiful Paris. And who travels across oceans and continents to see ugliness in California?

The auditorium is increasingly becoming a feature of the school-building as the rural school increasingly becomes the center for the social activities of the rural community. Wherever the school is conveniently located for community gatherings an auditorium or assembly-room should be included in the plans and specifications. In such cases, where the school-fund is insufficient, the cost of the auditorium will usually be shared gladly by the citizens. Even where the school is not the social center it should have a common meeting-place for the children of the neighborhood; the one-room schools should be constructed and equipped with this in view, and in a two-room building the partition between the two rooms should be a rolling-door, so that they may be thrown into one when desired. The needs and advantages of such meeting-places will be discussed at length in the chapter on "Consolidation and Transportation."

Many communities are wisely including in their school-plant a shed or sheds in the rear of the school-grounds for horses and vehicles. This provision not only serves the adults when they drive in to community meetings, but it has been found that it almost invariably increases the attendance and the regularity of attendance. There is good reason for this. Children living at a distance can get to the school if they can ride; on bad days they will come if they have a horse, but not if they have to walk. The owner of a horse and vehicle very naturally objects to having them stand in cold and rain. These sheds cost very little; often the patrons who desire to send their children from a distance will furnish the necessary ma-terials. The sheds should be built by the school board or trustees in order that they may be uniform and of adequate construction.

The study of school planning—of the lighting, sanita-tion, ventilating, and proper location of school-buildings— has made great progress in recent years. In view of the fact that the science of school construction has been worked out to great perfection by specialists in school architecture it is inexcusable that so many buildings are erected throughout the country in disregard of established high standards. It pays to consult a competent and honest lawyer in regard to legal matters; it pays to con-sult a competent and honest physician in matters of health; it pays to consult an honest and expert apple-grower in regard to the planting and care of an orchard; it pays to consult an honest and expert agriculturist in regard to the raising of crops; and it pays to consult an honest and competent *school* architect—not merely an architect—in regard to a school-building. To save money by cutting off the architect's fees is as sensible as buying patent medicine to save a doctor's bill. It is the acme of ignorance, and is about as certain to turn out right as purchasing a "gold brick." Moreover, to suppose that a man can draw correct plans for a schoolhouse because he is a contractor is on a par with getting a carpenter to pull a tooth because he can draw a nail.

Most of the state departments of education now issue plans and specifications of school-buildings of one, two, three, and four rooms. These have lifted the standards of school-buildings throughout the country from the bare box type to a less unattractive style. But some of these plans and specifications are not correct, according to the best standards, either as to lighting, ventilation, or attractive appearance, and should not be sent out as models to be followed. In fact, some of them have no attractive features whatever, though they are printed as "models." A school-building should have but one standard, and that the ideal. It seems strange that, when so much accurate knowledge has been discovered and printed in regard to the proper location, size, style, lighting, ventilation, and sanitation of school-buildings, anything but the ideal should be tolerated. The United States Bureau of Education is hoping that in coöperation with the various state departments of public instruction it may be able to contribute toward making the best models universally available.

X

CONSOLIDATION AND TRANSPORTATION

THERE are few rural-school workers to-day who have not accepted the theoretical advantages of consolidation and transportation. The multiplication of consolidated schools and transportation-wagons in all parts of the country has been one of the most striking of all the later developments in rural education. And yet there are thousands of trustees and superintendents and teachers who, while accepting the advantages of consolidation in principle, still believe that consolidation and transportation would not work in their particular communities. It is true that there are still communities in the United States so sparsely settled that they need the one and two-room schools, and will need them for generations to come, but these are rapidly becoming the exceptional communities. More often than not the failure to put the principles of consolidation into practice is due to timidity and fear of obstacles that are more imaginary than real. The literature on the subject of consolidation is so abundant and so easily accessible that it would be superfluous to repeat the general arguments in its favor. What school-workers want to-day, I find, is not general arguments; their almost invariable question is, *How has consolidation worked in your state*[1] *and under what condi-*

[1] Because of this demand, this chapter is Mr. Eggleston's account of the development of Consolidation and Transportation in Virginia, where he was for seven years state superintendent of public instruction.

tions have consolidation and transportation succeeded or failed?

The term "consolidated school" is used in this chapter to mean the merging of two or more schools into a central school.

When consolidation and transportation were adopted as definite policies in Virginia they were greeted with the usual prophecies of certain failure. I suppose the same objections are raised everywhere. It is said that the people will not agree to give up their little near-by schools; that the distances are too great for the children to reach the central schools without great hardship; that the roads are too bad to haul the children; that the children will freeze to death, or at least be frost-bitten, while waiting for the wagons or while being transported; and that the cost is too great.

Each of these objections has been successfully met. I shall not attempt to take them up seriatim, but I hope to answer each objection while discussing this subject.

During the fifth year of this policy we have over two hundred wagons running in all sections of the state, and under almost every possible condition. We have routes as long as eight miles and as short as two and a half miles. We have wagons on good roads and bad roads, on level roads and mountain roads, on rocky roads and sand roads, on macadam roads and red-clay roads. We have transportation-wagons of the latest and most modern type, and we have ordinary farm-wagons fitted up for the new and precious freight. We have one-horse and two-horse wagons, and in one instance we have a four-horse transportation-wagon—or "kid-car," as it is called—which hauls between forty-five and fifty children to school every day. In addition to this we have in one place in the state the use of a dummy line which hauls a large number of children back and forth each day. The railroad and electric lines are largely used, special rates being allowed the children. In some of the communities where there is consolidation without public transportation the children ride horseback or use private vehicles, wagons, buggies, and "jumpers." One little group of children drives a large calf to school. To encourage the children to use horses we build sheltered stalls at the rear of many of the school-grounds.

Last fall I visited a new consolidated school in H—— County, and at some distance to the rear of the school-house I counted twenty-one horses in covered stalls eating their dinners. Five schools were merged into this central school, which is situated on seven acres of land. This is a country school, and the farmers themselves inaugurated the movement for consolidation. To this school, as to most of the other consolidated ones, children will go a long distance, and in so doing will pass by the doors of smaller schools which they formerly attended and which in some instances have not been closed. Such schools soon starve for lack of attendance. The children desert them for the larger school. This is one method of closing them; and this is a sufficient answer to the objection that the people will not consent to give up their little schools.

Is consolidation essential to a proper solution of the rural-school problem? I believe that it is, and I believe that this is now universally admitted among thinking people. This does not mean, of course, that we shall not always have the small school. In fact, so far as we can now see, we shall always have one and two-room schools, and a great many of them. But that the consolidated or central school has great advantages over the one-room school, in turning out its product in terms of efficient citizenship, is evident.

Consolidation means much more than the mere grouping of a number of small schools under one roof; it means much more than the usual grading of the children according to their capacities and advancement in the study of books.

Its deeper and more significant meaning may be found in the fact that it makes possible a more dignified and beautiful structure, which in itself enhances the respect of the community for the school; that it makes possible the school-garden and the agricultural plot and manual training and domestic science; that it makes easier the teaching of arithmetic, physics, chemistry, geography, history, language, and composition that look toward, and not away from, the farm and country life; that it makes possible the formation of children's debating societies, of coöperative industries for the women and for the men, and of citizens' leagues for the continued oversight and improvement of the school; that, by bringing together larger groups of children and larger groups of citizens, it tends to socialize the isolated districts by taking the children and their parents out of their small and narrow environment and giving them an enlarged social vision and contact; it therefore not only makes the boy and girl dissatisfied with a deficient and uninviting environment, but it can take the next logical and necessary step of giving the boy and girl both the capacity and the desire to return to that environment and improve it.

The consolidated or central school tends to minimize the influence of the anti-social patron who, unless he can control the small school, may threaten to break it up by withdrawing his patronage—and it therefore tends to maximize the community life as against the individual. It is a great advantage of the large school over the small one that it is not dependent upon the whims and prejudices of one parent or even of several to keep it alive. To be able to break up the school by withdrawing or transferring four or five children is more power than some human nature can stand. A one-room school sometimes makes one man larger than the community. A larger school enlarges the influence of the community and tends to diminish a spirit of truculence on the part of the individual.

CONSOLIDATION

The consolidated school also tends to group homes around or near the school, thus tending to break up the isolation of the large plantation. It makes easily possible the inclusion of auditoriums, thus providing meeting-places for the children and for the people of the community, and encouraging the introduction of series of lectures, which are now confined almost entirely to the cities and large towns. The rural people need meeting-places for educational, economic, and social purposes. The consolidated school provides a proper center for such meetings.

In other words, the deepest meaning of the consolidated school is that it tends to socialize community life; it tends to break up unsocial and anti-social tendencies. Its very erection is a form of coöperation, which makes easier other coöperative efforts. If this consolidation of smaller schools, and therefore smaller communities, is accomplished solely by means of taxation, it is still a distinctly coöperative step, because it is the merging of these smaller school communities into a larger community. But in at least one-half, and probably in two-thirds, of the instances of consolidation in Virginia the people are asked to contribute from one-third to two-thirds of the amount by private subscription for the erection of the new consolidated building and the purchase of the land. They are asked for two reasons; one is that the taxes, as a rule, are not sufficient to make the consolidation. The other is that all those who are induced to subscribe become much more interested in the welfare of the school.

Let me give two or three illustrations of the use of the consolidated school as a meeting-place for community purposes, of the use of them as community centers. I know of a two-room school of about forty pupils in the little, sparsely settled county of C——, which was erected last summer. It is provided with cloakrooms, with good lighting, and with good ventilation. It is painted. It is pleasing to look upon. It is something to which every

13

man and child in the community can and does point to and speak of with pride. It is situated on two acres of land, so that there is not only room for a nice front yard, but good playground for the boys and girls. This building took the place of a little rectangular box with a roof on it, unpainted, badly lighted, poorly ventilated, provided with no cloakrooms, situated on a small plot of ground—a thing regarded with indifference and even contempt. The land for the new school was given by a gentleman who stated to me one month after it was open that he thought his farm had been increased in value at least two thousand dollars by the erection of the new building. The two schoolrooms have a folding partition between them. This partition can be rolled up, and an assembly-hall thus provided for neighborhood meetings. During the week-days the two rooms are occupied by the school-children. On Sundays, as there is no church in the immediate neighborhood, the ministers of the various denominations take turn-about to preach to the people in this double room, while during the rest of the day the school is used as a community Sunday-school for old and young. At other times the farmers or the ladies of the neighborhood can use the building for any purpose that has in view the improvement of the community. This school is eight miles from a railroad.

One of the things that has surprised us is the effect of the consolidated school on enrolment and attendance. It had been predicted by prophets of evil that the consolidated schools would cut down the enrolment and that the attendance would be even worse than in the smaller schools. We put our faith in the reports of other states that had tried consolidation and transportation; and, so far from being disappointed, we have been surprised at the showing made by the consolidated school. It has been much better than we expected. The following illustration is only one out of scores that might be mentioned.

CONSOLIDATION

On the outskirts of a small village of about three hundred people in a sparsely settled county was a two-room building of the old type. Sometimes there were enough children for two teachers, and sometimes there were not. The year before the consolidated school was opened there were forty-two children enrolled in the old building. It was determined to erect a building of six rooms and an auditorium. It was thought that it would take about eight or ten years of growth to fill this building. There was so much opposition to closing the small schools two or three miles away from the village that the school authorities, aided by the state, decided to open the new school with four teachers and to do some high-school work, leaving the small schools open to those who wished to attend them. Although no public transportation was provided, there were during the first session one hundred and twenty-five pupils, and a fifth teacher was added. The new school had in its second year one hundred and thirty-two children and six teachers; in its third year it added a seventh teacher, and had an enrolment of one hundred and seventy-four pupils. A school-wagon was put on in the third year and hauls about thirty pupils. The small schools have died of starvation—that is, the pupils passed by them to attend the central school, and they were closed for lack of children.

The new spirit that is put into the schools and into the community by the consolidated school is really the difference between life and death. In this school, for example, there is a spirit of progress that was entirely absent in the old schools; and the community which had never taken the slightest interest in school affairs under the old conditions now looks upon the new school with the greatest pride and interest and shows a willingness at all times to improve school conditions. Then, too, the new school can do so much for the community. The help is mutual. Let me illustrate:

The drinking-wells in that community have for generations been the surface-wells running down some forty to sixty feet. In the rear of the school-yard a well was bored through earth for sixty feet and through solid rock forty feet to an abundant supply of pure water, a pump was put in, pipes were laid in the building, lavatories for the boys and girls were placed in the basement, and a drainage system inaugurated. The total cost, including the digging of the well, the machinery, the piping, the pressure-tank, and the lavatories, was less than five hundred dollars. Up to that time there was not a bored well in that county. The man who did this work states that he has never been able since he sank the well at the school to take his apparatus out of the county, and that he has been boring wells steadily, except on Sundays and on days that were too bad to work. It might be said that this could have been done under the old conditions. The fact is, however, it was not done.

The spirit of improvement that came with the new building caused the organization of the patrons into a school-improvement league. This league has improved the three acres of school-grounds, has helped to install a school and community library, and to purchase a piano and pictures. It helped to put a nice fence around the school-grounds.

The principal and boys put down concrete sidewalks around the school, and this started concrete walks in the village. The school and the school-yard looked so pretty that the County Board of Supervisors planted a privet hedge around the court-house grounds, which were near by. The principal and the boys secured tools for a workshop in the basement, and at a small outlay the equipment was purchased for framing pictures. This is good manual-training work, besides which the boys get from it good lessons in language, arithmetic, and geometry. The pictures are framed at a small margin of profit, and the result is that a large number of good pictures have been resurrected and nicely framed, and large numbers of new pictures have been purchased, framed, and hung in homes for many miles around. A corn club in the school captured every prize last year offered by the county fair.

It would be easy to mention fifty instances similar to this one.

Where transportation-wagons are used to haul the children to the new consolidated school the increase in attendance has in many cases been phenomenal; in fact, it is the custom now in the state when building a consolidated school to include from one to three rooms more than seem to be needed. They are almost invariably filled, either at once or in two or three years. In one community, for example, two small schools were merged into a central school of four rooms, and two transportation-wagons were started. In a few weeks the demand for seats in the wagons was so great that a third wagon was started, and a few weeks later it was necessary to put on a fourth wagon. Before the session was out the school authorities had begun to figure on adding two new rooms to the new four-room building. The two old schools of one room each had a combined enrolment of fifty children.

Another thing that has surprised and gratified us has been the return to school of a large number of the older boys and girls who, after a few years' attendance at the little schools, had quit and gone to work. There have been many very striking instances of this, and I do not hesitate to say that large numbers of boys and girls who had quit school and who returned to school when the new consolidated schools were opened are now attending state normal schools and colleges, while many others have taken three or four years of good high-school work before going out into life.

The consolidated school with auditorium gives an unrivaled opportunity to the school to serve the community

THE WORK OF THE RURAL SCHOOL

in a very practical way. I believe that it is the duty of the school to help make the economic life of the community profitable while it is raising the intellectual and moral life.

The consolidated school can be of great help to the farmers and their wives in many ways. Here is one way: the State Department of Agriculture holds farmers' institutes throughout the state. These usually last one day at each place. We have induced this department to hold a large number of these institutes in the auditoriums of the new consolidated schools, thus bringing the farmers and their wives to these schools and giving them an illustration of how the schools may be used for the benefit of the community outside of the regular school-book work. The agricultural college holds in various parts of the state what it calls "movable schools." These schools last about three days in each of these communities. Teachers from the agricultural college have charge of these schools; they are widely advertised; and every one of them is being held in some consolidated school. The farmers and the high-school boys, to the number of from fifty to three hundred, attend these three-day sessions, and are instructed by these teachers as to improved methods of agriculture, such as seed-selection, subsoiling, fertilizing, corn-growing, potato-growing, grass-growing, apple-raising, the spraying of orchards, the feeding of cows, poultry-raising, etc., etc. It is indeed "a new thing in Israel," so far as this state is concerned, for the school to become the center of such meetings and to do such work in behalf of the community.

We have found, too, that it is a comparatively easy matter to organize the boys and girls of a consolidated school into corn clubs, poultry clubs, pig clubs, garden clubs, etc. And in many of our consolidated schools the children have clubs of one sort or another and are doing excellent work in them. It is so much easier to organize them and it is so much easier to look after them after the organization is effected. Of course the same thing applies to literary and debating clubs, and scores of these are in active operation throughout the state since the consolidated schools have been started. Every consolidated school with as many as three rooms does some high-school work. This brings in the larger boys and girls who cannot be found in the one-room schools.

There is no use talking about making the small school the community center unless the population is so sparse that it is not practicable to merge this small school into a larger school. The consolidated school has an unrivaled opportunity to make country life socially attractive. Not only have debating clubs been organized in our consolidated school, but a system of lectures has been organized for many of these schools to the lasting benefit of the community. Then, too, the children in these consolidated schools eagerly avail themselves of the opportunities to join athletic and play clubs. These have become an essential and attractive feature of our school work in the small towns, villages, and country districts.

We realize that the small schools should stand for all these essential things that have been mentioned, but we have found out that it is so much easier to turn these ideals into realities through the consolidated school. To accomplish these things in the one-room school usually means a maximum of effort to get a minimum of results.

In the average one-room school the teacher has from thirty to forty classes in the six-hour school-day. This gives ten minutes to a recitation. Thousands of teachers in the South have not even eight minutes for a recitation; sometimes not over five. The time of the children is thus largely wasted. Tens of thousands of children sit in the schoolroom day after day, waiting two or three hours for the next recitation: thousands of these get disgusted and quit, and who can blame them? No one knows these things better than the teachers, who are powerless to remedy the conditions. These facts alone are sufficient to demand a change from the crowded one and two-room schools to something better, and to demand a merging of the small schools that are near enough together to be consolidated.

The increased number of children begets an enthusiasm and interest that are often lacking in the small schools. It is universally conceded that the behavior of the children is much better; there is more earnestness of purpose; the children are mentally alert; they are more ambitious, because the higher grades give them something to look up to; they pay more attention to their personal appearance and dress better. In fact, complaint has been made by some parents that the children demand better clothes for attendance at the better schools. One parent could not see why his boy desired a fairly good suit of clothes and good shoes to attend school, when he had been attending the one-room school in his overalls and brogans. The boy stated to his father that he did not object to wearing his working-clothes before school and in the afternoons when he returned home for work, but that he did not feel comfortable in these working-clothes in the new school. The boy was, of course, right.

It is the universal testimony that the progress of the pupils in the consolidated school is rarely less than twice as rapid as in the one-room school. This is because the children can be better graded and because the teachers can give more attention to them than in the one-room school, unless this one-room school has very few children in it.

It is much easier to secure a good teacher to fill a vacancy in a large school than in a small one. She has more association with other teachers; her work is far less trying and wearing; she has the satisfaction of seeing the children make better progress; and she stands a better chance of specializing—something that every teacher wishes to do. This attitude of the teacher toward the small, isolated school is no inconsiderable factor in the rural-school problem. The time has passed—let us hope forever—when the economic conditions in our rural communities are such that the community can dictate the wage and be satisfied with a poor school-building and always find worthy applicants to teach. A new condition has arisen, and to-day the competent teacher can—and in an increasing number of counties and cities does—dictate that the wage and the schoolhouse shall be good.

There are ten objections to consolidation and transportation—eight of these are imaginary; the other two are real. These two are bad roads and sparsity of school population, and they are applicable in only a comparatively few communities in this state, although 76 per cent. of our people live outside of incorporated places (and everything in this state is incorporated that has as many as five hundred people).

There are one hundred counties in Virginia; in at least ninety of these there are communities where one-room and two-room schools can be merged into larger schools, and the children be transported to the great advantage of the children.

Most of our roads are bad in winter, but it takes even worse roads than the average to prevent transportation of children. Good roads and good schools should go together; but, since neither exists in many of our communities, the advocates of good schools have gone right ahead consolidating, knowing from the experience we have already had that good roads will follow. We have refused to be deceived or misled by the frequently uttered statement that consolidation of schools and transportation of children should wait until good roads are established. It is true that some of the roads are bottomless, and consolidation and transportation in such cases are out of the question. It is also true that good roads make it easier to have consolidation and transportation, provided the people are intelligently interested in their schools, but experience and observation show that good schools do not necessarily follow good roads. In fact, in this state, with the exception of one county, the counties which have the best roads have schools which are below the average in quality and above the average in quantity.

On the other hand, experience and observation have shown that good roads do follow good schools. This is especially the case when the schools have been consolidated. The consolidation of schools invariably brings to bear on the county road authorities great pressure for the improvement of the roads leading to such schools. I could mention numbers of counties where this has been demonstrated beyond a doubt. In one school district where all the schools except one were merged into a central school and four wagons started, the agitation for good roads grew so pressing that the people of the district met in the auditorium of the central school and by unanimous vote asked that their road taxes be raised, and that all the roads in the district should be improved, and that this improvement should begin at the schoolhouse.

How did we begin in order to get the people into a frame of mind favorable to consolidation? In two ways: by having laws enacted that have encouraged consolidation, and by a campaign of education to convert the people from an attitude of hostility or indifference to an attitude of sympathy and coöperation. I may add that we did not wait to get the whole state, or a whole county, or a whole district into a favorable attitude before beginning. We picked out communities where we believed consolidation would be of benefit, and then proceeded to reason with the people of these communities. The movement is now well under way, and we find it less and less difficult each year to bring the people to see its advantages. There are still hundreds of communities that would strenuously oppose such a movement, but there are dozens and scores of communities with an open mind on the subject, which two or three years back were earnestly opposed to it. In fact, it is not infrequent that communities initiate movements for consolidation and call upon the school authorities to show them how to proceed.

Even after the wagons have run a year or two, however, the voice of the chronic kicker may still be heard in the land, and care must be taken to prevent the school trustees from mistaking a large quantity of noise for a high quality of noise, and taking the wagons off before the new plan becomes a permanent habit. If left to the children, 95 per cent. of them would favor the continuance of the transportation-wagons. Eternal vigilance is the price of permanent progress. It is a significant fact that for every ten wagons started hardly one is taken off, and when it is taken off it is invariably because there is a lack of funds or because it should not have been started, owing to the wretched condition of the roads.

In some instances the people have preferred to furnish the transportation for their own children, as they were afraid that public transportation would increase their school taxes. It is easy to see that in a short while the very people who are opposing higher taxes for school, and who now prefer to furnish their own transportation, will see that this is costing them more than the extra tax for public transportation. If we find that a community can be persuaded to consolidate schools and prefers private transportation we encourage the first step. The next step will inevitably follow. It will not take twenty parents long to see that it is much cheaper to hire two or three wagons at public expense to haul fifty to seventy-five children than it is to use twenty horses and twenty buggies for the same purpose.

In some instances where we find a mere handful of children subjected to hardship by the consolidation of schools the local school authorities arrange to pay a patron to haul his own children or to haul his own and his neighbors' children, allowing him a certain per diem on attendance, not on enrolment. On some routes the large boys who are attending the schools drive the wagons. As I stated above, we have no iron-clad rules. The sole object is to get the children to the most efficient school at as low a cost as is consistent with reason and comfort. In a few cases only the larger children attend a consolidated school while the smaller children attend the small schools near their homes.

While I am writing this there comes to mind the experience of the school trustees and superintendent in one county. They persuaded the patrons to allow them to try two wagons for a month on the understanding that if they were not successful they would be taken off. They were to be given a fair trial. There was not sufficient money to buy regular transportation-wagons, so two farm-wagons were purchased and covered and fixed with seats. In two years there were fifteen wagons running in that county, and people in several sections were complaining because wagons were not provided for their children. In one community in this county, when the school trustees announced that they would put a wagon on a certain route, a lady on that route who had been sending her little girl to the near-by one-room school employed an attorney to prevent the trustees from carrying out their nefarious purpose of breaking up the one-room school and hauling the children to the consolidated school. The trustees won the case, and the wagon was put on. At the beginning of the next session, when it was rumored that the trustees might take the wagon off the route, owing to lack of funds, this same lady employed the same attorney to prevent the trustees from taking the wagon off.

TRANSPORTATION

One of the most striking things we have observed is that almost invariably when a new consolidated school is erected the patrons demand a better quality of teaching than they have had in the small schools. I think the psychological explanation of this lies in the fact that the average man forms his estimate of the school by the outside appearance of the school, which is the only part of it he usually sees; and if he has a contemptible-looking schoolhouse in his neighborhood he becomes indifferent to the quality of the teaching on the inside; whereas, if the outside of the schoolhouse is attractive to him, if he has put money into this school by private subscription and by increased taxation, he wishes the quality of the teaching to be at least equal to the quality of the building, and he wishes to get his money's worth.

It remains to consider the cost where consolidation and transportation are now in vogue, and the cost in the same communities when the old conditions prevailed. The stock objection that the public roads will not permit consolidation and transportation, and that the people will not favor the change, has been ruthlessly overthrown by the actual use of over two hundred wagons in over one-third of our counties, with every variety of roads—good, bad, and indifferent. The people in these communities have placed an unqualified indorsement upon the change from the old conditions to the new; but the last remaining objection—the cost of the wagons and drivers—which has looked so formidable, and which is still a cause of battle in many of our communities where consolidation and transportation are on trial, has been shown in at least half the cases to be a man of straw—a scarecrow.

In the gross amount of money expended it does, as a rule, cost more. That fact might as well be faced; but it has been proved beyond contradiction that the cost per month per pupil in daily attendance in the small schools

189

before consolidation is greater than the cost per month per pupil in daily attendance after the consolidation of these schools. As one of my coworkers has said, "A four-teacher school with two wagons will cost more money in the aggregate than five one-teacher schools without the wagons, but the five one-room schools cost more per child upon the basis of daily attendance." And he adds this very pregnant statement, which should be preached every day, and all day, until it burns itself into the hearts and brains of people everywhere: "It is the daily attendance that counts!"

The only correct basis on which to figure the cost of a school is the attendance of the children. It is the child present in, not the child absent from, the school that counts in reducing the cost. It is the child absent from, not the child present in, the school that counts in increasing the cost. Any other basis of estimating the cost is absurd and utterly foreign to the real purpose of school levies. If it costs forty dollars a month to employ a teacher to hold a school enrolling twenty children, how much does it cost per month to educate each one of these children? "Two dollars," says some one. But this answer is probably incorrect. The cost to educate depends upon the attendance of the children. If the enrolment is twenty, and the daily attendance is ten, the cost to educate each child is four dollars per month. The other ten are not being educated.

"But," says some one, "the community has to pay the forty dollars to the teacher, anyway; so it's the same thing so far as the community is concerned."

There are two answers to this statement, either of which seems to me to be sufficient:

First, in the large majority of the communities, in this state at least, the community doesn't pay the forty dollars. The state (which in this matter means the cities, the few rich counties, and the corporations) pays a goodly part of it, and pays it on a basis of the children in the community, whether they attend school or not.

Second, it is a sufficient answer to the above statement to point out that if "forty dollars have to be paid, anyhow," common sense should dictate that the community see that every dollar shall serve its purpose, shall attain its object, shall not be wasted. The object is not to expend the forty dollars, but to get the children into the schoolroom. That method which is the most practicable for getting the largest number of children into a good school for the greatest number of days is the cheapest.

If this argument is a sound one, if the school is the place where the child, and not the money, is the central consideration, then the schools will be consolidated and children transported, not because money will be saved thereby, but because the children will be benefited thereby. If the children are benefited it is economy to make the change, even though the cost is greater. Economical expenditure is expenditure; it isn't hoarding. Economical expenditure is not parsimonious expenditure; it is wise expenditure, or expenditure without waste. That school economy is ideal which gives to the children the largest opportunity and spends every dollar that is necessary for that purpose.

Two years ago one of my assistants worked out a table of certain communities in which, before consolidation, the number of teachers was 56; after consolidation, 45. The gain in enrolment was over 50 per cent. Another table showed that in a given number of communities the enrolment before consolidation was 3,185 children; after consolidation 4,814 children, a gain of 1,629 in enrolment. For the same communities the average attendance before consolidation was 2,107; after consolidation it was 3,617. This included consolidations both with and without public transportation. Where public transportation exists the average daily attendance is, of course, very much better.

THE WORK OF THE RURAL SCHOOL

While I was dictating these statements I received a letter from a school trustee in which he says:

Our school district has seven schools consolidated into one school, and seven schools unconsolidated. The seven unconsolidated schools have enrolled (this session) 162 pupils, with an average daily attendance of 125. The seven consolidated schools [and by this he means the one large school into which the seven small schools have been consolidated] have enrolled 264 pupils, with an average daily attendance of 240. The character of work done in the consolidated school is far superior, and, besides, 41 of these pupils are doing high-school work. The central school is doing twice as much work as the seven separate schools.

It may be of interest to state here that this school after one year of consolidation had to double its capacity.

The public transportation of children means better behavior on the way to and from school. The drivers of the wagons are made responsible for the conduct of the children. These drivers are chosen with great care. In a transportation-wagon a boy is not permitted to smoke or chew tobacco; he is not permitted to use profane or unbecoming language; he must not indulge in bullying. If he fails to conduct himself in a gentlemanly manner he is put out of the wagon and must walk until he can give assurances of proper conduct. And when their daughters are safely ensconced in the transportation-wagons under the protection of good men there need be no uneasiness on the part of fathers and mothers lest some dreadful calamity befall them.

Do not for one moment suppose that this "Jordan is an easy road to travel." It is not. But the more we travel it the easier it gets. There is always a lion in the path until we begin to travel it. This thing of getting the people into a favorable attitude toward the consolidation of schools and the transportation of children is hard work, but it is none the less glorious.

XI

THE TEACHER WHO IS THE CITIZEN-MAKER

IT is an old proverb, and as true as old, that "*the teacher makes the school*"; which, being interpreted, means that the future of our democratic citizenship depends upon the ability, training, and patriotic devotion of the men and women to whom the homes of the nation have intrusted the education of their children. To say that the success of the public school as the instrument for the transformation of the raw material of childhood into an efficient citizenship depends upon the efficiency of the teacher is so obviously true that no one is likely to question it.

Why, then, have we not placed a discussion of the teacher as the citizen-maker at the beginning of this book? The answer is that in spite of the splendid achievements of rural-school teachers scattered throughout the country, in spite of individual instances of heroic devotion to which the progress of rural education during the past decade is so largely due, rural-school teachers as a body have not been measuring up to the responsibilities that the nation has laid upon them; and there is small hope that they will so measure up until their outlook upon the problems and opportunities of rural education has changed. This conclusion is justified, not only by personal observation in many states, but also by the statistics of the United States Bureau of Education, which show that the rural-school teachers, as a body, are a migratory flock, that a very small proportion of them "stay put," as the phrase goes, for more than a session or two at a time—in other words, that very few of them hold their positions long enough to become acquainted with their communities or to exert any lastingly beneficial influence upon them.

Every one who has had any experience in rural education knows that there are scores, even hundreds, of exceptions to this rule. Time and again one finds communities in which the majority of the teachers have worked faithfully and well under trying conditions for five and ten and twenty years. But that such teachers are the exceptions the facts recently published by Mr. A. C. Monahan, of the United States Bureau of Education, prove beyond question. The instability of the teaching force in our rural schools is most strikingly reflected in the intensive studies made by the State Superintendent of Public Schools in Missouri and by the State Board of Public Affairs in Wisconsin. The State Superintendent of Missouri found that of 9,883 teachers who were in charge of the one and two-room schools of his state during the year 1910–11, 6,804, or 69 per cent., were teaching their first year in the positions they then held; 2,071, or 21 per cent., their second year; 860, or 7 per cent., their third year; 180, or 2 per cent., their fourth year; 67, or less than 1 per cent., their fifth year; and 72, or less than 1 per cent., their sixth or more than their sixth year. Of these 72, however, only 55 had taught six or more years in the same school in consecutive years. The average length of service of the Missouri school-teacher in one and two-room schools—the great majority of all rural-school teachers—is, according to the State Superintendent, *one and four-ninths years*, or *233 school-days*. In 443 of these schools teachers were changed during the session.

The Preliminary Report on Conditions and Needs of Rural Schools in Wisconsin—an educational document that it would be well if every rural-school official and every legislator in the United States should read—states that of 128 teachers, canvassed in this intensive investigation, 56 had taught in their present schools less than one year; 39, one year; 20, two years; 9, three years; and 4, more than four years. Moreover, it was found that the great majority of these teachers had contracted to teach for one year or less.

The investigation of the United States Bureau of Education leaves no doubt that with slight variations the facts in Missouri and Wisconsin are reproduced in practically all of the states.

Is it not obvious that so long as the rural-school teachers are here to-day and there to-morrow they can never become, in any true sense, the citizen-makers of the nation?

When one seeks an explanation of these distressing facts one is told that the fault lies with the one-room school—that conditions will never change for the better until the one-room school is abolished. Certain enthusiasts invite us to adopt their slogan: *The one-room school must go!*

Now, no one believes more earnestly than we do that consolidation should be effected whenever and wherever it will work to the best advantage of the children and the community. But there are thousands of communities in the United States where if the one-room school did "go" the children could not follow it. While great stretches of America are so sparsely settled as they are to-day, and as they are likely to remain for some decades to come, it is deliberate self-deception to believe that every one-room school can be abolished. We must look the facts squarely in the face and be guided by them.

In 1913 Mr. A. C. Monahan, of the United States Bureau of Education, published the results of a searching inquiry into the status of the rural schools in thirty-two states. He found that the "total number of one-teacher schools is 80 per cent. of the total number of 183,824 public schools in those states." On the basis of careful estimates Mr. Monahan concludes that the enrolment in the one-teacher schools is "37.6 per cent. of the total enrolment in all the public schools of the country, and 60.2 per cent. of the total enrolment in all rural schools."

While the multiplication of consolidated and union schools will undoubtedly decrease this percentage, it is still obvious that for the next generation or two at least, from 30 to 40 per cent. of all children who live in the open country will remain in the hands of teachers in one-teacher schools. To say that "the one-room school must go" sounds impressive and shows a valiant spirit; but if the stability of the rural teaching force is dependent upon the elimination of the one-room school it is to be feared that true efficiency in rural education will be a sadly long time coming.

Again, it is said that the rural teaching force will never become stable or efficient so long as the rural-school buildings are badly constructed and poorly equipped, so long as the teachers are underpaid, so long as rural communities fail to provide decent and comfortable homes for their citizen-makers. Certainly, there is much truth in all of these declarations. The investigations of the United States Bureau of Education show that the rural-school teachers, and especially the teachers in the one-room schools, are wretchedly and disgracefully underpaid. The table printed at the top of the next page is eloquent on this point. A yearly salary of only three hundred dollars is a most ungenerous reward for the ability and devotion essential to the success of our rural schools. This same investigation of the United States Bureau shows further that the rural-school buildings are, as a rule, dingy, insanitary, badly lighted, miserably equipped. Moreover, the living accommodations provided for most rural-school teachers, especially in the open country, are a great bar to the development of teaching efficiency.

SCHOOL SESSIONS AND SALARIES

	ONE-TEACHER RURAL SCHOOLS			ALL SCHOOLS, URBAN AND RURAL		
States	Number of days in annual session	Average monthly salary	Average yearly salary	Number of days in annual session	Average monthly salary	Average yearly salary
Connecticut ..	184	$47.21	$434.33	185	$58.95	$545.20
Colorado.....	141	53.33	375.98	156	63.22	493.12
Illinois.......	151	42.00	317.74	171	69.51	594.31
Indiana......	140	52.20	365.40	147	65.93	484.58
Iowa.........	160	38.63	309.04	172	47.92	412.11
Kansas.......	131	49.11	321.67	164	63.36	519.15
Maryland ...	180	44.44	400.00	184	52.84	502.38
Michigan.....	170	43.53	370.00	171	56.01	478.88
Minnesota....	140	43.51	304.57	149	52.56	391.57
Mississippi ...	117	34.44	201.46	123	42.50	261.37
Missouri	140	31.72	219.26	155	57.18	443.14
New Mexico..	90	48.21	216.94	100	67.82	339.10
North Carolina	90	31.94	143.73	102	34.40	175.44
North Dakota	130	48.73	316.75	147	52.95	389.18
Ohio.........	160	46.00	368.00	165	58.66	483.95
Oregon.......	119	53.44	317.86	138	80.13	552.90
South Dakota.	135	47.63	321.50	166	55.21	458.24
Tennessee [1] ...	111	39.25	217.83	130	40.90	265.85
Texas........	116	55.03	320.57	131	59.69	390.97
Mean......	137	$44.76	$307.51	150	$56.83	$430.60
Median ...	135	44.44	317.74	149	56.01	443.14

[1] White schools only.

We have a letter from Mr. J. C. Muerman, of the Field Service in Rural Education of the United States Bureau of Education, in which he states his belief that the absence of teachers' cottages or other proper homes for country teachers is a far more serious matter than is generally realized.

I have been told by excellent teachers [says Mr. Muerman] that they much prefer the work in the rural schools were it not for the fact that it is practically impossible to get a good board-ing-place. The wealthy farmers do not, as a rule, care to take the teachers except as an act of charity, and no self-respecting teacher wants to feel that she is imposing upon any one. The poorer families in the district are usually in a position where they cannot accommodate the teacher even if they so desire. I believe that this point is fundamental and is one of the main reasons why some of our best teachers are going out of rural work. . . . A teachers' home is a recognized part of every school-plant in Switzerland—why not in the United States?

It will be noted that the mean salaries paid to all teachers in these 19 states is lower by $1.28 than the mean for the entire United States. The mean of the monthly salaries for the rural one-room teachers in the 19 states is $44.76. This is $12.07 less than the mean monthly salary for all teachers of the same states, and $13.35 less than the mean and $16.94 less than the average monthly salaries for all teachers in the United States. The mean annual salaries for these schools was $307.51. This is $123.09 less than for all teachers of the 19 states, and $137.03 less than the mean, and $176.72 less than the average for all teachers of the United States. In the 19 states the monthly salary of the rural teacher is 78.7 per cent. of the mean salary for the 19 states, but the annual salary of the rural teacher is only 73.7 per cent. of the mean annual salary for the 19 states. The greater difference in the annual salaries is due, of course, to the difference in the length of the annual session. The mean number of days in the annual session of the rural schools was 137, while for all schools of the 19 states it was 150, and for all schools of the United States 153 days. The average length of the session in 1909–10 for the United States was 157 days.

It will be noted that the figures given at the bottom of the table are not averages, as averages could not be found without the number of teachers being known. The mean, obtained by dividing the totals for each column by the number of states, is given; also the median found by arranging the states in order according to the length of session, or the amount of salary, etc., and taking for the median the middle figures.

All these things are unfortunately only too true: we do need better rural-school buildings, better equipment, more adequate salaries, more attractive and adequate living accommodations. But how are these improvements to be brought about? No great service was ever rendered by men or women who faltered before such obstacles as these. And the problem of citizen-making in our rural schools will never be solved until the teachers themselves develop a new outlook toward their work, a new sense of patriotic consecration toward the great responsibilities the nation has laid upon them.

"Investigation seems to show," says Mr. A. C. Monahan, in the report of the investigation already referred to, "that where the greatest advance has been made in rural schools *improved buildings and equipment have followed better teaching*."

Who that has followed the progress of rural education during the past decade can doubt that this is so? And it is because we are convinced that the future of rural education depends primarily upon the development of a new outlook, a new vision of the scope and possibilities of rural education on the part of the teachers in our rural schools, that we have placed the discussion of this new outlook before the discussion of the qualifications of the citizen-maker and the problems of normal training and field supervision.

The modification of the course of study, its adjustment to the daily activities of the children as normal members of the community, is generally the first manifestation of a vital outlook on the part of the teacher. A wide-awake teacher, speaking of the excellent results she obtained by going to the community for the materials of study, says:

In our overcrowded course of study it would be ridiculous to add more; so I work on the elimination-by-substitution plan. Girls and boys in the country need certain things; those in the city others. We must connect the school with the home. Hence we substitute for the "stock work" (in the book) some real live country problems. We find that the industrial work (boys' corn clubs and girls' garden clubs) is a stimulus instead of a drawback to book work, especially when the children can see the relation between book work and *their* work.

How many children see this relation? Whose fault is it that they do not see it? They do not make the course of study; and, sad to relate, in most instances they do not see any purpose in the course of study. Is this the fault of the children, or is it not rather due to the fact that there is really so little relation between the book work and *their* work? With the present course of study only a teacher with extraordinary courage and initiative can be expected to succeed.

But it is not courage and initiative alone that are needed; great consecration is also needed—a consecration that can face the warped outlook of a decrepit tradition and refuse to accept defeat.

In 1906 the president of a state normal school said to the graduating class:

The world is full of people who can do the things that can be done; but rare are the people who do the things that cannot be done. The country school of permanent influence has never been set up in our state, and rarely enough in any other state. Can you do it?

One of the graduates thought she could. Returning to her county, she began her work in a country neighborhood eight miles from any railroad. The majority of the people of this community are renters. There was a two-room schoolhouse which an old gentleman and his wife and a very few other courageous people had persuaded the patrons to build instead of the wretched one-room affair to which the children had gone in previous years.

The new teacher began by calling the patrons together, outlining her plan, and telling them that if she taught the school she would look to them for coöperation. A good deal of objection was raised. Her plan was something new. A few of the patrons were, however, ready to follow her. She asked for an extra teacher, for a school-cottage where she and her associate might live and where domestic science and household management might be taught, and for sufficient money to insure the necessary supplies.

The extra teacher was secured, and three weeks after the opening of the school the principal called another meeting of the patrons to discuss the building of the cottage. They informed her frankly that they thought they had made a mistake, that the school was proving too expensive, and that the original plan would have to be modified. She answered with equal frankness that she was not surprised at their changed attitude, but that she had come to that neighborhood at their invitation and that she would not work for them unless they would abide by their agreement. She and her assistant would pledge fifty dollars apiece out of their salaries for industrial equipment and would undertake to raise the balance of the money if the patrons would build the cottage, support the industrial department, and agree to help the work. Her firm stand and her liberal offer so impressed the patrons that they agreed, although with many shakings of the head.

The two-room building had cost one thousand dollars; the industrial cottage was built at a cost of three hundred dollars. Those who had agreed to support the school remained true to their contract, but others in the community became hostile, and the consequent struggle was very hard. This, of course, made the management of the pupils hard. The principal and her assistant organized a school-improvement club. The boys and the men and women of this club met at the school and spent a day removing stumps and rubbish, scrubbing floors, and cleaning up generally.

During the first year several entertainments were given to raise money for pictures and a library and also to get the patrons on speaking acquaintance with the school. The teachers took an active part in the Sunday-school work, and spent some weeks during vacation in visiting from home to home. A class was organized to interest the men who, as in most other communities, did not at first attend. For two years it was all the teachers could do to keep this class of men alive. After that it flourished, because the men were put to work at many things that were of practical benefit to the community.

These teachers tried to get a grip upon every phase of life in the neighborhood, and, in fact, they went outside the neighborhood and got in touch with the people of the county-seat. The preachers, doctors, lawyers, and business men of the town helped in many ways to get over obstacles that seemed small, but that were very large in that little community.

While the work was exceedingly hard, there were enough patrons recognizing the importance of it to invite the two teachers to return the second year. "Very well," said the principal; "but you must build a third room to the school before the next term commences. I will be responsible for the third teacher's salary." The room was built.

The school has never enrolled more than seventy-two pupils in any one year, because the district is small.

THE TEACHER THE CITIZEN-MAKER

The principal suggested to the county board that a transportation-wagon should be provided for some children who were remote from any school; that started transportation in the county, and it has since been adopted by other schools. *She saw what is now being seen everywhere, that a home for the teachers (either of one school or of the scattered schools in a district) and a few pupils should be built on the school-grounds.* It was hard to secure board, and, besides, the teachers could not have at a boarding-house the freedom and quiet that is essential to efficient work. It took four years to get the people to see the need of that home for teachers. They looked upon it as a fad and a luxury, but the principal was determined. From the State Federation of Women's Clubs she secured a ram for pumping water, from another source she got the piping. She then showed an amount of courage that makes the proverbial "bearding a lion in his den" look like an innocent pastime. She persuaded a plumber to help the teachers and pupils install the ram and piping. She secured good plans for the building. Even then she had to furnish three hundred dollars without security to get the cottage completed and furnished.

But this was not all. An effort was made by the surviving opposition to break up the school by building a one-room school near at hand. Unfortunately, the county board of education decided in favor of the new school. This was so discouraging that the principal decided to resign, but now the trustees said, "You have the same strong friends you had in the beginning; why resign now?" The teachers stayed.

The work in this school had now won such a reputation that the board of trade of the county-seat presented the school with a check for five hundred dollars, which enabled the teachers to cancel the debt on the cottage and to equip it for domestic science. A water-tank with a capacity of five hundred gallons was installed. A laundry-room was built and water piped to it. This laundry-room has not yet been equipped. The purpose of it is not only to have economical apparatus to lighten the work of those who live on the grounds, but chiefly to show the people of the community how the wives and mothers who are drawing water out of wells or bringing it from springs and doing their laundry work under adverse conditions may do the same work with very much less labor and time. It is proposed to have a laundry that can be duplicated in any of the homes of the county, or which can serve as a community laundry.

The industrial work flourished from the first year. The children became so interested in it that all opposition on the part of parents ceased. At the end of the second year the patrons were asked to provide a piano. They did so. The patrons were now so much interested that they agreed to assume the financial responsibility for all three teachers. The county board pays each teacher forty-five dollars per month for five months. The patrons are doing the rest with some help from the outside, and the school has never run less than eight months in a year.

Such is the record of six years' work in a small country community which is below the average country community in financial resources. The school is now "a going concern." This country teacher and her associates did not wait for adequate salaries and an ideal equipment.

Some of the best bench work we have ever seen is being done in a one-room school in Indiana. In answer to a question as to how he introduced the work and what the results have been, the teacher of this one-room school writes as follows:

At the time I introduced industrial work in my school I was taking summer courses in manual training at Valparaiso, Indiana. The first winter after beginning my summer courses

THE TEACHER THE CITIZEN-MAKER

I told the trustee if he would get a bench I would furnish the tools (as I had a set of carpenter tools), and we would try the experiment of introducing manual training in a one-room school. He secured a bench, and we went to work. I made the course elective for grades five, six, seven, and eight, and all the boys of those grades elected to take the work.

We had no official course of study to follow. I made my own course. We made small useful articles, nearly all of which were on straight-line construction, making only one piece of curved-line work. I had two boys work each day, and in that way each boy had about two hours per week of bench work. They worked in the morning before school, then at recesses and noon. They could hardly wait for their turn, so interested were they in the work.

The boys sent some of their work to the county-fair exhibit, and during the two years that I was there secured ten prizes.

Since I started the work of manual training in the district school in 1909–10 there have been several one and two-room schools in this county that have taken up bench work, and this year I think more than half of the schools have had some bench work.

This teacher did not wait for a new building and modern equipment, nor for an adequate salary. These things follow consecrated teaching; they rarely precede it.

That school progress does not always follow adequate equipment, but does follow a teacher with consecrated purpose, is further shown by the following instance:

The people of a small country village were persuaded by the state superintendent to erect a new building and to equip it for future growth. A principal was secured. He was a graduate of an academic college, and he conducted his classes in an academic manner. To him a school meant opening at nine o'clock, holding a certain number of recitations, and closing at four o'clock. The school was a failure. It did not grow. Another principal was secured. He also was a graduate of an academic college, but somehow he had a vision of what a school ought to mean to a community. He began by getting acquainted with all the patrons of the school, and, not satisfied with this, he kept extending his visits until he had pupils coming from all the homes for miles around. If a pupil was absent he made inquiry at once, and if the absence continued he went to see what was the matter. The people soon got the idea that if a child was absent there would be a visit from the principal. Not only did the enrolment grow, but the attendance began to get very close to the enrolment. Not satisfied with this, he advocated transportation-wagons, and in the face of all sorts of objections he persisted. To-day the back yard of the ample school-grounds is filled with vehicles of all descriptions, including public transportation-wagons. By means of entertainments and a school league he has purchased all kinds of necessary equipment for the school. One hard-headed business man in the community says of this principal, "You know, our community never did get together on anything before. We were nearly always having a row about something, and were always split up, but I want to tell you that man has everybody working for the school, and we're learning how to pull together."

Here is what a live teacher in a one-room rural school in Massachusetts was able to do. We give the story in the teacher's own words:

In a one-room rural school in western Massachusetts sewing, cooking, carpentry, gardening, and typewriting were correlated with the other subjects. In sewing, the girls first learned all the stitches with which they ornamented lamp-mats and work-bags. The latter were made of Ada canvas and worked with peseidon silk. Then followed the practical application of the stitches. Dish-towels and table-napkins were hemmed; cooking-aprons, cooking-caps, and carpenters' aprons were made. Some of the upper-grade girls took measurements, drafted patterns, and made blouses for lower-grade boys. According to the daily time-table, half an hour a week was devoted to the sewing. During this thirty-minute period the teacher could only give brief instruction regarding the advance work. Consequently, most of the sewing was done by the children in leisure moments. Each day an older girl was appointed monitor of a group. Usually this girl was very glad to go to the teacher a few minutes before the opening of school in the morning for criticisms and instructions in sewing. During the day, when any girl had satisfactorily finished her work—arithmetic or writing, as it might be—she took her sewing from her desk for seat work. If she needed help she went to the group monitor. During the noon-hour the teacher herself inspected the work done in sewing.

The cooking in this rural school occupied an hour a week. At the beginning instructions in detail needed to be given the girls. But later they were able to work much alone. The recipe was written on the board, read by a member of the class, and discussed about five minutes with the teacher. A certain part of the lesson was assigned to each girl. Immediately after the discussion of the recipe the girls of the upper grades proceeded with their cooking, while the teacher heard lower-grade arithmetic or reading. A housekeeper was appointed, whose duty it was to see that everything was clean and in order after the lesson. This cooking class made jellies and preserves, cooked cereals, vegetables, soups, made bread, cakes, ices, beverages, and candies. A dinner was given to the parents, the following menu being served:

Tomato Bisque		*Croutons*
Roast Beef	*Mashed Potatoes*	*Green Peas*
Peach Pie	*Coffee*	*Cheese*

Other dinners were served to the State Board of Education and visiting superintendents. The remuneration for the latter dinners, together with the proceeds from the school-garden, was used in purchasing pictures for the school. The ordinary lessons were made more interesting to the child because of correlation with the cooking. Spelling-words were taken from the recipes, which were also often used for writing-lessons when copied to put in booklet form. In geography the children were delighted to learn of the preparations of tapioca. It was interesting arithmetic to estimate the cost of a cake or a dinner and to find the per cent. gain on the different dinners.

While the girls enjoyed their work in cooking, the boys worked at the bench. After a study of the tools they made match-boxes, whisk-broom holders, coat-hangers, and bread-boards. Preceding the actual working of each problem, working drawings were made. In an old woodshed adjoining the schoolroom was the possibility of a model workroom. Accordingly, the eighth-grade boys estimated the amount of material needed, then sheathed the room. Because of projecting beams the walls had to be built out by "two-by-fours," making a difficult proposition. Later these boys made a table for the typewriter. Whenever a window-pane was broken by a ball the unfortunate boy in good spirit got his tools and at once went to work to put in a new pane. The boys took up, put down, and adjusted the chairs and desks, making more room, yet seating more pupils. In these ways the boys became handy in the use of the tools of a carpenter and were prepared to help in the home as well as at school.

All the gardening was done as busy work. A boy was appointed as superintendent, and was held responsible for the work done during the day. Now and then at recess or a few minutes after school criticisms and suggestions were offered by the teacher. The older boys mixed the fertilizer used. Some very good arithmetic problems were evolved, as:

How many pounds of fertilizer·are used per acre?

How many pounds are needed for your garden-plot, which is 17 x 67 feet?

If you use 8⅓ pounds nitrate of soda, 18 pounds acid phosphate, and 6⅔ pounds high-grade sulphate of potash, how many pounds of nitrogen, phosphoric acid, and potash are used if 15½ per cent. nitrate of soda is nitrogen, 14 per cent. acid phosphate is phosphoric acid, and 50 per cent. high-grade sulphate of potash is potash?

If you used in 33 pounds of fertilizer 1.29 pounds nitrogen, 2.52 pounds phosphoric acid, and 3⅓ pounds potash, what per cent. of each was used?

What kind of fertilizer did you use?

In the school-garden were raised peas, radishes, lettuce,

onions, swiss chard, beets, corn, and potatoes, half of which were scabby and half good. Some of the scabby ones were planted the next year after being treated with formaline solution, mixed at school. The treatment proved successful, for from the scabby seed sound potatoes were raised. For blight the boys treated the potato vines with Bordeaux mixture, also made at school. More problems, in weighing lime and sulphate of copper and in measuring the right proportion of water, were derived for the eighth-grade arithmetic. And so again in gardening, as in other industrial subjects in school, correlation made the other work more interesting.

The question is: How can these subjects be taught in a rural school? There must necessarily be so many classes in the three R's. The keynote of the whole situation is in the words "seat and group work." Inculcate in the child a feeling of responsibility. Give him more freedom. Encourage team work. Make the schoolroom a home, not a workshop.[1]

If any one thinks that a one-teacher school with a wide-awake teacher cannot improve community conditions he should change his mind after reading the following account of what a teacher is doing out in the open country in Minnesota. Again we set down the story in the teacher's own language:

This is a one-teacher school located in the open country. The principal's home is close by the school, and his home and wife have been of much assistance in developing its social and community service.

Following the lead of several progressive educational institutions, the school set about to remedy its shortcomings. The principal interested privately the school board in the study of agriculture as applicable to the little school, and soon every one had become interested, the idea seeming to be contagious. We secured from the creamery at M—— a large Babcock milk-and-cream tester, and soon the boys and girls of most families weighed the milk every day twice and had each cow tested at least once a month. This alone has led to the building of two silos, the only ones for several miles around here, the weeding out of poor cows from several herds, and a better standard of and interest in dairying as an essential branch of agriculture. We won the first, the second, and the third prizes awarded by the Minnesota State Dairyman's Association, and this in competition with any boy or girl in the whole state.

At different times I visit the pupils to see how their cows and records are getting along. Sometimes a member of the faculty of the County Agricultural School comes to see them in their homes. Their gardens are inspected in the same way in the spring and at other times. Several of these are in the state one-acre corn contest.

These activities led our patrons to look upon the school more as a social center. Whenever there was something to be done there was little trouble to secure some patron to do it. The children carried home with them the spirit of improvement and change of things generally for the better. The parents caught the spirit. Good seed was sown, even in the hearts of the fathers and mothers.

About once a month an entertainment was given by the school. There were basket socials, necktie socials, pound socials, etc. The schoolhouse was nearly always filled to its capacity. We raised considerable sums of money in this manner. Often we would have some noted speaker or some instructor from the agricultural school address us, giving valuable helps and hints on agriculture and home affairs. While the people were enjoying themselves they were also profiting greatly by this pleasant experience.

Soon we started debating on live and suitable topics. This can easily become a most powerful agency in community school-work. Pleasure and profit are properly and happily united in it. Some things were learned in these debates which would not have been learned by other means.

On Saturdays we used the building for sewing lessons. At other times the girls would come to my house, where my wife gave them instruction in sewing. They seemed to enjoy the social part of these meetings very much, as well as the instruction.

THE TEACHER THE CITIZEN-MAKER

Once every month the older boys and girls met as the "School Progress Club." They learned parliamentary rules and practices. At these meetings some members read papers of their own production on subjects selected by the president. Some of our work was illustrated by pictures in one of the agricultural papers, and the effect was "great" on the boys and girls.

Music, singing, comedies, debates, discussions, other musical entertainments, etc., formed a large part of social gatherings for the people.

Even those somewhat indifferent at first soon became thoroughly a part of our merry-making and social activities. Every one felt helped, and they expressed this sentiment oftentimes to me personally. This alone is a large part of a teacher's compensation.[1]

A teacher looking about for a place that would try her mettle landed in a mountain country. She found a wretched little hovel for a schoolhouse, and on the day of opening she was confronted by about one hundred children. Nothing daunted, she went to work. She went after the trustees and superintendent, and, finding that their intentions were good but their performance a little slow, she got in touch with the state superintendent. He made a week's campaign in the county, carrying the county superintendent and some of the trustees with him, and at the end of the week he had them pledged to erect a modern schoolhouse of three rooms and a workroom to take the place of the hovel. In the meanwhile the teacher on visiting the homes of the community saw that these were run on a basis of drudgery. She determined to introduce sewing and cooking in the school if possible. She began by organizing the larger girls into a sewing class, and found that not one in five of them knew the use of a thimble. In a few weeks the girls had become so enthusiastic that the boys complained that they wanted to do something, and, as the teacher did not at the time

[1] *Atlantic Educational Journal.*

have any carpenter's tools for them, they insisted on being allowed to join the sewing class. The mothers soon became interested, and are being taught to sew by the teacher and girls who are learning. The new building has been completed, and the workroom is equipped for sewing and cooking for the girls and manual work for the boys. Garden work for the boys and girls will be introduced during the vacation, and this teacher is determined to work the year round. She is interested in the transformation of that community through the school. It is through such teachers that the transformation must come.

Another teacher in the same county relates this incident:

It is hard to get a teacher to come to this county because the living conditions are not good everywhere. It is still harder to get them to stay, for the same reason. One day last fall I went with a new teacher to a neighborhood where they had not had a school for some time. I wished to put heart into her, because I felt that the schoolhouse and the surroundings would depress her. When we arrived in the community she saw the place where she would have to stay, and then she looked at the schoolhouse. Both almost indescribable! As soon as we arrived a manly little fellow about twelve years old came out and took our horse and fed him. Knowing me, he asked, "Is that the new teacher, and will she stay?" The question was pathetic, because several teachers had come and looked and gone away. After dinner the new teacher told me she could not stand it and that she would not remain. I asked the little boy to hitch up the horse, and with an eager look in his face he again asked me, "Will the new teacher stay?" When I told him that she would not, a look came into his eyes that haunts me yet.

"Ah, yes," said a rural-school superintendent to whom we were relating this story one day, "but the conditions you describe are very exceptional. There are not many communities in America that have such difficulty in securing and holding teachers."

Possibly there are not a great number where the conditions make such heavy demands upon the courage and consecration of the teacher; but do not the facts published by the United States Bureau of Education sufficiently show that what our rural districts everywhere most need is the teacher who will "stay"? Such instances of courage and consecration as these we have cited have occurred and are occurring in every state of the Union; but they are unfortunately occurring only in spots. Why should they not occur everywhere? Why should they not be made the rule instead of the exception? Is it not obvious that because they are the exceptions they have made an extraordinary and even cruel demand upon those qualities which should be encouraged and not discouraged in every teacher? If such results can be obtained with little or no encouragement from the state or local communities, what results might not be obtained with adequate encouragement and support? Why should the task be made so difficult that only the exceptional teacher is able to surmount the obstacles and work out a successful program in harmony with the normal activities of the children and the normal needs of the communities?

It may be true that many teachers who have not done so might have shown more initiative and courage and consecration than they have shown, but a criticism of this nature begs the question. These instances have been mentioned to show that, after all is said, it is not *the one-room school*, but *the one-room teacher*, that fails to improve the community; and that the teacher with many rooms in her mind and many windows to her soul will transform the one-room school and the one-room community. They have been mentioned in order to show the really heroic qualities of a very large number of our country teachers. They have been mentioned as an encouragement to teachers because they show that adequate buildings and adequate salaries almost invariably follow the exhibition of these qualities; but, inasmuch as such instances have occurred in every state in the Union, it is incumbent upon the states and local communities to take the necessary steps to erect adequate school-plants and to pay adequate salaries to real citizen-makers, and then to demand that the product be forthcoming. To make every rural teacher in every rural community prove what has already been amply proved in other communities is not only unreasonable, but puts the states and the communities in the attitude of neglecting their own children; and, indeed, where discouragements and opposition are placed in the way of the teachers, the states and the communities assume the attitude of "stoning the prophets" who come with the desire to turn the raw material of childhood into citizenship for the benefit of the state and the community.

It is probable that no one factor has done so much to break down the barriers between a bookish program and every-day life as our normal schools. They have been of incalculable service in freeing our citizen-makers from a musty medievalism. Their graduates are in great demand, and this demand is increasing more rapidly than the supply.

The normal schools have done much in child study; they need now to do much in community study—to lead their students to make community surveys, and to show them how to base the course of study upon the activities of the community. They have taught how to correlate one study with another, they need now to teach their students how to derive the materials of education out of the every-day activities of the children as normal members of the community.

Many of our normal schools are, as a matter of fact, reshaping their training courses to meet the modern conception of the teacher as the citizen-maker. The state normal schools of Michigan, for example, are required by legislative enactment to give special courses for students preparing to teach in the rural schools. At the Western Normal School at Kalamazoo the course for rural-school teachers covers four years. Besides twelve weeks of required work in psychology, methods, and management, there are thirty-six weeks of required work in nature and agriculture, twenty-four weeks of elective work in domestic arts and science, and a course in rural sociology. A one-room rural school near by provides opportunities for practical experimentation.

At the Kirksville (Missouri) State Normal School special courses offered for rural-school teachers include sanitation, nature study and agriculture, rural-life problems, rural-school organization and management, industrial arts, and observation in rural-school work.

At the State Normal School at North Adams, Massachusetts, students preparing for rural work may elect two years in agriculture and extra work in domestic science. Besides professional courses in education and methods, courses are required in music, drawing, child study, nature study, cooking, sewing, sanitation, and social economics.

The State Normal School at Athens, Georgia, besides giving the professional courses in psychology, methods, etc., gives instruction in school-gardening, agriculture, outdoor plays and games, manual training, domestic science, rural sociology, and rural economics. Training in community surveys is given through the Georgia Club, a volunteer organization in which the members are studying the problems of agriculture, population, taxation, farm ownership, farm tenancy, schools, churches, coöperative enterprises, etc., with reference to the development of Georgia. Not only students at the State Normal School, but teachers in the field, are working on these surveys, which are being made by counties. These studies are changing the attitude of the teachers and of the normal students toward their work; they are giving them a knowledge of actual conditions and both the power and the purpose to reorganize and transform actual conditions through the schools. There could be no better way to begin to link up the school with the life of its community, to break down and eliminate the barrier of isolation now almost universal between the school and the teacher on the one side and the community on the other, and to prevent the building of a barrier between the children at school and their experiences and interests at home. There could be no better way to encourage the teacher to stay in the community and to be a citizen-maker and a community-builder. There could be no better way to make the teacher sympathetic toward country life and toward the school-work as a factor in that life. The Wisconsin report already alluded to, in speaking of the attitude of teachers toward country life, says that of one hundred and thirty-one rural teachers visited, eighty-five took no part whatever in the community life—that is, did not live with the community, although they did live in it. This is a picture of conditions everywhere. Here, then, is an opportunity that might well be grasped not only by normal schools, but by agricultural colleges and, indeed, by every educational institution that is interested in vital citizenship.

The Harrisonburg (Virginia) State Normal School includes in its four-year regular normal course subjects for special preparation in rural work. In addition a two-year course is offered, which includes training in rural sociology, home economics, sewing, cooking, gardening, agriculture. Observation and practice work is done in a number of country schools. President Julian A. Burruss, of this school at Harrisonburg, has admirably expressed the point of view that is inspiring the leaders in normal training everywhere:

The most potent influence in modern educational thought [he says] is the awakening of educators and the public generally to the necessity of bringing the school into closer touch with the life of the people, their work, and their interests. It is properly expected of our schools supported by public funds that they train for good citizenship, and it is generally recognized that this implies productive efficiency on the part of the individual so that he may be a self-supporting and contributing unit in the social whole. In fulfilment of this expectation the public-school education of the future must be brought close to the lives of the people, it must result in industry and thrift, it must make homes more sanitary and attractive, it must pave the way to productive work with skilled hands, clear minds, and pure hearts. In our cities our boys and girls must be put into possession of the elements of handicraft, and in our rural districts they must be given the elements of agriculture and kindred subjects.

To meet the demands of the new education it is obvious that the work of the Normal School can no longer be confined to theory and books, but must seek its material in *real* things, in nature, in the practical activities of industry and commerce, in the business, civic, and social interests of life. Without neglecting the limitless stores of useful knowledge bound up in printed volumes, it must also draw from the outside world—the home, the farm, the workshop, the office, and the marts of trade.

The complete normal school must be equipped to train teachers in agriculture and other rural arts, in cooking and sewing and other household arts, and in drawing and other manual arts.

As the factory has taken out of the home many of the materials of education, it becomes the more necessary to train the children through the schools in the knowledge of those things which bring them into every-day contact with the factory. The citizen-maker, then, must know, and must know how to teach, food values in order that the future citizens may know these values and may be able to detect and prevent the subtle sabotage of adulterated foods and of poisonous ingredients and extracts. The citizen-maker must know fabric values—the difference between the shoddy and the genuine—in order that the future citizens may know these values and be able to detect and to black-list the products of greed and fraud. These values were once known in the home; the factory has taken just so much of this knowledge from the home as was of educational value, and is offering products the real values of which those in the home who should know do not and cannot know unless in and through the schools they learn them. The citizen-maker must be able to use and teach the use of all labor-saving devices in the home, that the future citizens may be educated in the use of them before they become "fixed types," unable to escape the habit of using the tools and methods of drudgery.

To those who cry out that these things have not true cultural value—that we must teach our children to look up at the sun and the stars, and not down to the earth—the answer is that, fortunately or unfortunately, the feet and the stomach must remain on the earth, and the attempt of centuries to subject them to the star-gazing process has invariably led to disaster. The girl who acquires at school the desire to look up at the sun and the stars only and who spends the rest of her life awkwardly drudging is certainly not better off than the girl who, while learning at school the inspiration of looking up, also learns those things which enable her to do her daily work quickly, easily, efficiently, so that she may have an abundance of time to look up. The home-making and the home-keeping of the future must include a knowledge of food values, of fabric values, of labor-saving devices, of sanitation, of sex hygiene, of the laws of health. The home is in a stage of transition. The modern home must be organized on a basis of social efficiency, and not restored to a basis of sentimental drudgery.

Besides reshaping their training-courses so as to prepare their regular students for rural-school work, many of the normal schools are providing special summer courses for rural-school teachers, and in this a very considerable

TRAINING RURAL-SCHOOL TEACHERS THROUGH WEAVING, UNIVERSITY OF WISCONSIN

number of colleges and universities are following their lead. The United States Commissioner of Education has published a list of eighty-three state normal schools and more than four hundred colleges and universities that now offer courses of from three to twelve weeks for the special benefit of rural-school workers. And the movement has gone even further than this. A number of states have established special county training-schools and have organized training classes in connection with rural high schools. In 1912 Wisconsin had twenty-seven county schools and classes in connection with six high schools for special training in rural work. New York, Michigan, Minnesota conduct training classes for rural teachers in connection with high schools; and Arkansas, Iowa, Kansas, Maine, Nebraska, North Carolina, Oregon, Vermont, and Virginia conduct such classes either in connection with public high schools or private academies. In 1912 New York graduated 1,156 students from ninety of these special classes. Nebraska in the same year had extended this work to one hundred and ten high schools, and Kansas to one hundred and sixty. In April, 1913, Iowa passed a law requiring that after July, 1915, all teachers must have had at least six months' experience or twelve or more weeks of normal training. This list makes no pretense to completeness; it is introduced simply to show how the wind is blowing.

But in spite of all this encouraging progress it must still be evident to the close student of rural-school conditions that the facilities for the special training of rural-school teachers remain far from adequate both in number and in the quality of their instruction.

There are still, unfortunately, normal schools and college - training classes that send their graduates out to teach before giving them a thorough understanding of the basic rural-life problems, before giving them a mastery of the methods by which to familiarize themselves with the peculiar conditions of the particular communities to which they are called, and before imbuing them with the spirit of consecrated service that will make them "stay" on the job until the job is at least in the way of being done. Such institutions not only waste the money of the state, but inflict an unpardonable wrong upon the community to which the "graduate" flits for a short interval, heedless of the great responsibility and equally great privilege that has been awarded her. No institution can meet the demands of our generation if its aim is merely scholasticism. It is only when the normal or training school is fired by ideals that are not only high, but sanely directed, that it is in a position to lead to effective results. For it is too often forgotten that ideals may be both high and misleading.

For example, the ideals of a certain state normal school were very high, but when several teachers who had attended the school stood an examination on geography under a county superintendent their ideals seemed unable to function properly when an attempt was made to give them a practical application. All of these teachers lived amid the eroded and gullied lands from which, on account of bad farming, the soil was carried by tons into the branches and creeks and small rivers, and thence into a larger stream that was noted for its muddiness. The question was asked: "Why is the ——— River muddy all the time, and what relation has its muddiness to the farming in this section? How could the farmers lessen the muddiness, and how would this affect the land and the crops?"

Beyond the bare statement that the muddiness was caused by the rains, not one answered the question. Had the conventional geography question been asked, "What is erosion?" there would probably have been perfect answers from each teacher.

One could easily imagine that one of these normal-trained teachers, with the very highest of ideals, had wandered from her home in search of a better salary and had finally traveled across several states and began to teach in a rural district in Wisconsin, and that it was she concerning whom *The Report on Conditions and Needs of Rural Schools in Wisconsin* gives the following account:

Coming into one school, the investigator found a class of two boys and one girl reciting in geography. The children ranged in age from twelve to fifteen years. The oldest, a boy, was asked to name the exports and imports of England. He was unable to give any answer, and, although the teacher struggled with him and with the other children, she failed to get the replies she sought. She explained that they were embarrassed because a visitor was present.

The investigator asked if he might ask them a few questions, and the teacher consented. Turning to the boy first called on by the teacher, he asked him what the exports of his father's farm were. The boy still hesitated, but replied with the question, "Do you mean what we raise?" Encouraged by a partial assent, he went on and became quite enthusiastic in telling about the various crops grown. Another question brought out what was retained on the farm and what was sold. Asked as to imports, he again hesitated, not knowing the meaning of the word "imports." When asked what was needed on the farm that they could not raise, he again started off and gave a very clear statement, suggesting farm machinery, groceries, harnesses, and also spoke of buying seed-potatoes and seed-corn. This opened up a new field. Before leaving the subject the visitor asked the children to compare "export" and "import," asking them to give the meaning of the words. Without hesitation one of the boys said, "Exports mean what you take off the farms; imports, what you bring in."

During the lesson the rest of the school were interested, and when at last the original question was brought up, the pupils were eager to recite, and did so intelligently.

The content of normal-training courses should be two-fold: Instruction in right methods of securing vital materials for study, and instruction in vital methods of presentation. Just as the children should be directed to concentrate their activities upon the materials of community life, so the prospective teacher should be directed. The methods of making accurate community surveys and of winnowing the materials of study from these surveys; the methods of guiding the children in similar surveys; the methods of evolving the materials of instruction in reading, writing, spelling, arithmetic, drawing, geography, botany, biology, language, geometry, out of the children's normal activities; the methods of making hygiene and sanitation and civil government every-day affairs of every-day life instead of unrelated subjects of academic gymnastics—these, with the high and definite purpose of making efficient citizens, are the things that will put life into the normal schools and into every institution that would train the citizen-maker for effective service through the school. The training-school will thus become the place not only for the preparation of the teacher in accepted practices, but for constant experimentation. It will anticipate needs by searching out sound tendencies. It will base its theories upon actual conditions, and will apply them to the problems of every-day life for the improvement of that life. It will follow its students into their communities and teach them and inspire them in the handling of their particular problems, as the demonstration agent follows the boys and girls to the actual home and farm.

In fact, it is in the direction of such demonstration work that much of the most hopeful progress in the effective training of rural-school teachers is being made. If all the normal schools and other institutions for the training of our citizen-makers should adopt the best of methods and should succeed in securing the best of normal teachers they would yet be unable to reach more than a fraction of the men and women who are actually at work in the rural schools, just as our agricultural schools and colleges, with all their farmers' institutes and movable schools and demonstration trains and circulars and bulletins, are unable to reach more than a fraction of the men and women who are actually at work on the farms. It is a recognition of this fact that is leading normal schools and similar institutions to coöperate with state departments of public instruction in the development of a system of supervision, through state supervisors and supervising teachers, that promises to do as much for the improvement of rural-school teaching as the Farmers' Coöperative Demonstration Work has done for the improvement of methods of agricultural production.

XII

FIRST AID TO THE CITIZEN-MAKER

IF all the teachers in our rural schools were competent citizen-makers; if they were men and women not only with energy and foresight, but also with the proper training and the vision of the country community as it might be; if they were all backed by school boards anxious and able to make their work effective, then it might be excusable to drop them down into their respective schools to do their work with only such help as the county and state superintendents can give them, supplemented by teachers' institutes, summer normal courses, and the various forms of extension work which the states offer. But, however well the modern normal schools may fit the teachers of the future for rural work, few of the teachers actually in service have had any normal-school training or, indeed, any professional training at all.

A study made by the State Superintendent of Public Instruction of Kansas in 1910 shows that:

Of the total number of rural elementary teachers in both one and two-room schools less than 5 per cent. were college or normal graduates; 31 per cent. were high-school graduates; 4 per cent. had a partial college or normal course; 24 per cent. had a partial high-school course; and 36 per cent. had no high-school education. The number of inexperienced teachers was 24 per cent. of the whole.

According to reports made to the United States Bureau of Education, of the 15,042 rural elementary teachers in

New York State in the "school commissioners' districts," 139 were, in 1911, college graduates; 3,272 had normal diplomas; and 6,018 were graduates of teacher-training classes in public high schools. Five thousand five hundred and sixty, or considerably more than a third of the total, had no professional training.

In Texas, 10,564 of the 13,116 country-school teachers in 1910 had never attended college, normal school, or high school, according to the report of the State Department of Education. The state superintendent reports, further-more, "that 2,965 of them held the first-grade certificate, which is 'not at all equal to the requirements for gradua-tion from a reputable public high school of this state'; that 8,740 held second-grade certificates, to obtain which they must have the equivalent of the education of the seventh grade in the public schools of the state; and that 530 held third-grade certificates, to obtain which they must have completed the work of the fifth grade of the public schools or its equivalent. Four-fifths of these teachers are white."

The State Supervisor of Rural Elementary Schools in South Carolina has recently published the results of a study made by him covering twenty-six of the forty-three counties of the state. Complete data could not be obtained from the other counties.

In the twenty-six counties [he says] there were employed in rural schools for white children 301 graduates of 17 South Carolina colleges, 71 graduates of the state normal college, and 29 graduates of colleges in other states. The total number of rural teachers in these counties was 2,023. Most of the college and normal graduates were in union and consolidated schools, and practically none were in one-teacher buildings.

The report of the Better Iowa Schools Commission of 1912 says:

There are in round numbers 12,500 rural schools in Iowa. Almost 40 per cent. of the teaching force have had less than one year's experience. The average tenure of service is about three years. There are comparatively few normal-trained teachers. Last year 60 per cent. of the Iowa teachers who were certificated were inexperienced.

And this year thousands more of inexperienced young men and women in every state in the Union are leaving grade schools, high schools, and colleges, and are being installed in the rural schools because they are able to pass the examinations. In the very nature of things they cannot possibly know the business of conducting a country school—if they are to become efficient citizen-makers they must be taught while they teach.

Now, fortunately, most of these teachers are willing, and even eager, to learn. But to expect them to adopt a social outlook and to evolve a course of study outside of the text-books without help is to expect the impossible. What, actually, do they face when they enter the school-room for the first time? A variety of "subjects," required by law, and usually required to be taught from a prescribed text-book! These "subjects" are so numerous that in extent they are sufficient to produce anything from leadership to lunacy. For example, the courses of study include reading, writing, arithmetic, spelling, language, geography, history, civics, grammar, physiology and hygiene, music, drawing, cooking, sewing, woodwork, gardening, agriculture, geometry, algebra, physics, chemistry, botany, English and American literature, Latin, French, German, and Spanish. There are probably no rural schools that attempt this entire menu; but some of them approximate it.

This duck-and-goose method of stuffing the children with materials scooped out of a text-book will never justify the faithful labor of the teachers, trained or untrained; will never justify the faith of the children;

will never justify the financial outlay of the taxpayers. And yet the great majority of untrained and inexperienced teachers are as little capable of freeing themselves from it unaided as the average farmer is capable of freeing himself from outworn and inefficient agricultural methods without the aid of a demonstration agent. So long as teachers are unable to attend the normal schools it is essential to the development of efficiency in the rural schools that the normal schools or their equivalent should go to them. Demonstration methods must be used with them as with those who have received the traditional training in agriculture. They need *not merely to be told, but to be shown*, how to base the course of study upon the activities of the community; how to derive the materials of education out of the every-day activities of the children as normal members of the community.

Who is going to be the actual demonstration agent for the country teachers? Hitherto we have relied principally upon the county superintendent, not only to administer the business affairs of the school system under his jurisdiction, but also to supervise the work of the teachers—to give them the outlook and the training which only the few have been able to secure from the normal schools. It has become increasingly evident that the county unit is so large that not even the most competent superintendent can attend to both the administrative and the supervisory work.

To carry inspiration and technical training to the teachers who cannot go to the training-schools several states have made statutory provision for closer supervision than the unaided county or township superintendent can possibly give. In different states these new officials go by different titles—supervisors, inspectors, supervising teachers—but under whichever name, their work is to carry first aid to the rural teacher while she is on the job of citizen-making. One of these supervising teachers says in her first report:

There can be no cut-and-dried plans for this work, since the conditions in each school are so largely controlled by the environment of the particular school. We have selected five schools which we are trying to raise to the highest degree of efficiency in order that they may serve as demonstration schools for our normal school. This seems to us to be one of the quickest and most effective means of bringing a normal school into touch with the existing conditions in the rural schools.

The schools have been made more attractive for the children by using cleanliness and comfort as the foundation on which to build "beauty in the schoolroom."

Such decorations as appropriate pictures, flowers, blackboard decorations, and an exhibition of the children's work have been used most effectively. Care has been taken that the pictures should be well chosen and that they should mean something. These cost no more than the meaningless and occasionally vulgar pictures that are found on the walls of some schoolrooms. A few large pictures are better than many small ones. If the latter are used they should be arranged in effective groups. The following is a suggestive list: "The Horse Fair," by Bonheur; "The Gleaners," by Millet; "The Angelus," by Millet; "Pilgrims Going to Church," by Boughton; "Christmas Chimes," by Blashfield; "Madonna of the Chair," by Raphael; "Spring," by Carot; "Aurora," by Guido Reni; "Can't You Talk," by Holmes; "Feeding Her Birds," by Millet. These can be obtained at a nominal cost.

Children's work should be used for decorative purposes on special occasions and then put away.

Once a month the teachers of these demonstration schools assemble to discuss their different problems with the supervisor. In addition to these problems some definite work is assigned.

To awaken the interest of the children clubs have been organized in some of the schools. The children have been very responsive to this work, and many improvements have been made which otherwise would not have been made. Besides

FIRST AID

keeping the schoolroom and yard clean the boys hav
and crushed rock enough to make walks in the school-yard.

The school-garden is one of the very best means of connecting the rural school with the rural life. Realizing this, we are
making preparations now for a garden at a one-room school.
The teacher, with the assistance of her senior class, will operate
this garden and thus prove to the average rural-school teacher
that it can be done successfully.

Sewing and manual training are working successfully in four
schools, and cooking in one.

While the girls are sewing and cooking, the boys have manual
training. In the manual training as much of the native material
is used as possible. After making their own looms the boys
have woven rag rugs. Now they are making shuck mats.

In a three-room school the little people are furnishing a doll-
house, thus bringing in paper-cutting, designing, weaving, and
cardboard work.

Other phases of the school-work are not being neglected for
this practical work.

The supervisor tries to arrange to do some teaching in the
other subjects every time she visits the schools. Then she
plans and makes suggestions to the teachers. Her work takes
into consideration all the things which pertain to the physical
and social environment of the rural community.

The following is a list of articles suggestive of what
might be considered an average equipment for a cooking
laboratory for a one-room rural school:

COOKING EQUIPMENT

1 one-burner blue-flame oil-stove with oven	$6.50
1 kettle	.50
1 coffee-pot	.20
1 bread-board	.20
2 dish-pans	.40
1 wire sieve	.10
1 frying-pan	.20
2 egg-beaters	.10
1 dust-pan	.10

1 baking-dish . . . . $.20
2 measuring-cups 10
2 white bowls 20
2 kitchen spoons 10
1 scrubbing-brush. 10
1 towel-roller 20
2 dry-goods boxes for cupboards 10
1 quart cup 05
1 stew-pan 10
2 cake-pans 20
1 teapot 10
1 soap-shaker 05
2 strainers 10
2 muffin-tins 10
2 frying-pans 10
1 cake-tin 10

SERVING OUTFIT

6 cups and saucers 50
6 plates 50
1 flat dish 15
6 teaspoons 25
6 tablespoons 25
6 knives and forks 50
3 dessert-plates. 30
1 cream-pitcher. 10
1 sugar-bowl . . . .
Table-cloth and 6 napkins (made by the
    children) 50
4 glasses. 20
2 salt-shakers 10
1 waiter 05

Total $13.70

COURSE OF STUDY

COOKING

The first lesson is given to a study of the cooking equipment,

COOKING EQUIPMENT FOR ONE-ROOM SCHOOL IN VIRGINIA; COST, TEN DOLLARS

FIRST AID

including the use and care of the stove, also the washing of dishes, etc.

Fruit
1. Kinds.
2. Composition.
3. Food value.
4. Methods of cooking.
5. Stewed, baked, and scalloped apples.

Vegetables
1. Kinds.
2. Composition.
3. Food value.
4. Methods of cooking—salads and onions.

Potatoes
1. Kinds.
2. Composition.
3. Food value.
4. Preparation—boiled and baked potatoes.

Cereals
1. Kinds.
2. Composition.
3. Food value.
4. Methods of cooking oatmeal, cornmeal mush, and rice.

Sugar
1. Composition
2. Food value.
3. Cooking candies—fudge and peanut-brittle.

Milk
1. Analysis by experiments.
2. Composition.
3. Food value.
4. Products of milk.
5. Making junket pudding.

Cream Soups
Tomato, potato, and celery.

Eggs
1. Composition.
2. Food value.
3. Testing eggs.
4. Methods of cooking illustrated—soft and hard boiled, poached, scrambled, and stuffed.

Combination of Milk and Eggs
Baked and boiled custard.

Flour
1. Kinds.
2. Composition.
3. Food value.
4. Study of batters—pancakes and muffins.
5. Making biscuits, yeast bread.
6. Use of left-over bread (bread pudding).
7. Cake—kinds, preparation of pans, etc.
8. Make loaf and layer cake.
9. Pastry—apple and lemon pies and cheese straws.

Meats
1. Kinds.
2. Composition.
3. Food value.
4. Uses of parts.
5. Preparation of meat—stock soup, broiled steak, left-over meat (pie), and different ways of cooking pork.

Salads
1. Kinds.
2. Food value.
3. General directions for making salads.
4. Make potato salad with dressing.

FIRST AID

Preserves
1. Kinds.
2. Food value.
3. Composition.
4. Methods of cooking—peach and pear preserves.

Canning—Fruits and Vegetables
Pickles—cucumbers and pears.

Beverages
1. Kinds.
2. Food value of each.
3. Preparation of cocoa, tea, and coffee.

Lesson in serving a meal.

NOTE.—This course of study has been used in a one-room cooking-school with the above equipment.

SEWING

1. Work-bags—illustrating the basting, running, and hemming stitches.
2. Cooking aprons and caps.
3. Stove-lifters.
4. Table-cloth and napkins—illustrating the overhand stitch.
5. A simple sewing-apron.
6. Underwaists—learning how to make buttonholes.
7. Underskirts—application of different stitches learned.
8. Tailor-made shirtwaists.
9. Kimonos—long and short.
10. Hemstitching handkerchiefs.
11. Fancy stitches—applied on bureau-scarf.
12. Embroidery—centerpieces.
13. Stenciling—sofa-cushions, bureau-scarfs, and curtains.

NOTE.—All of this work has actually been done in one, two, and three room schools of this county. In order to make sewing popular the course of study must be tentative. The children are often given their preference as to what problem they shall undertake.

Some one said of a farm-demonstration agent that he made the biggest track of any man in the state, since big crops of corn and grass sprang up in every field over which he walked. In the tracks of most of the supervising teachers and inspectors spring up large crops of improved school conditions. What do they accomplish? They do the next thing, no matter how seemingly insignificant. Here is the report of one state supervisor on a visit he made to a country-school district with the county superintendent:

In company with Superintendent B—— I recently spent an entire week visiting the schools of —— District, —— County. It was no pleasure trip; nor was it taken simply for the purpose of dropping into a school, complimenting the teacher and pupils, and passing on to the next place.

Our general plan was to visit each school, ascertain its physical needs, test the pupils, confer with the patrons, and close the week with a meeting of teachers and trustees for the purpose of deciding upon certain definite things for the improvement of school conditions.

This district is country "sure enough," as they say. There is one small town in the district. It is a poor agricultural section, the homes are small and far removed from the public roads, the people are just good, plain farmers. There are the usual number of churches and a few illicit stills. At intervals of about three miles we found six one-room and three two-room school-buildings.

The school levies in this district are at the maximum. Two of the trustees are engaged in commercial pursuits, the third is a farmer; all are good, capable citizens, devoting as much time to the school as they can spare from their private affairs.

School No. 1.—One-room school; about thirty-five pupils. Teacher graduate of a good high school; her second year in the work, but first at this school. We tested the highest class (average age about twelve years) on arithmetic and spelling. In arithmetic the test was a simple example in long division, such as 846,750 divided by 34. Out of twelve pupils five obtained the correct answers. In spelling, the results were very good, there being four perfect papers and only twelve mistakes. There were seven patrons out at this school, and they listened very attentively to our talks. This school has raised the necessary funds to obtain a library.

School No. 2.—Two-room school; about fifty pupils. Tested pupils in writing; results fair. Pupils backward in arithmetic. Fine entertainment here by pupils, who gave evidence of being carefully trained. Pretty blackboard calendar. Room was ventilated by means of windows. Seventeen patrons at the meeting, about one-third of whom were mothers with small children. After talks one of the patrons promised to act as a committee to get covered water-coolers. The teachers and three mothers were appointed a committee to raise funds for a library. Some of the older pupils were designated to see that pictures were obtained for schoolroom decoration. A school league was organized.

School No. 5. — One - room school; about twenty pupils. Teacher attended summer normal. Some pictures and pretty maps on the wall. Teacher tests pupils each month.

School No. 7. — One - room school; about twenty pupils. Teacher graduate of high school with normal-training department. Some pretty pictures on walls; attention paid to ventilation. Twelve patrons were out at this school. Money has been raised for a library.

School No. 9.—One-room school; about twenty pupils; new teacher. The superintendent tells me that this has been a troublesome school, with annual change of teachers. Pupils backward in arithmetic, geography, grammar, and several other things. The same story in all the schools. Great problem with the teacher was to reduce the number of classes. I tried to figure it out for her on the following basis: Five classes in reading, total recitation-time one hundred minutes; five classes in arithmetic, total recitation-time seventy-five minutes; spelling, geography, history, and grammar classes—thirty minutes to each subject. Teacher said she would try to work it out and let me know results.

On Saturday we held a meeting of all the teachers and trustees just to talk matters over. All teachers were present except four who could procure no conveyances; one trustee was absent through failure to receive notice. We met in the home of Mrs. W——, one of the teachers, who resides near the center of the district.

Each teacher made a report for her school, setting forth her difficulties and the needs of the school from the physical side.

During the following summer every school in the district was painted and equipped with patent desks and good stoves.

The trustees ordered floor-oil for all of the schools, and requested the teachers to hold entertainments to raise funds for the following things, in the order mentioned: Covered water-coolers, window-shades, libraries, and pictures.

Pupils' monthly report-blanks were also ordered by the trustees, and the teachers were requested to do more drill work and give out monthly reports to the pupils.

The teachers subscribed to a school paper and made definite arrangements to circulate among themselves two copies of a book dealing with some of the technical questions that were suggested by the conference. It was unanimously decided to meet again on the second Saturday in January, to hear reports as to how the work was progressing. The teachers will be entertained by the school league.

Now this is the record of just one trip made to one country-school district by one state supervisor in the company of the county superintendent, which resulted not only in a knowledge of what each school was doing and a criticism of its work, but also in a meeting of the teachers of the district with the trustees, in plans for coöperation among them, and in a whole list of concrete improvements.

This more intimate and intensive cultivation of the teacher is working transformations everywhere. A supervisor says of one school:

With a little effort on the part of the teacher in charge, the following improvements have been made in a one-room school since it came under our supervision. The building has been painted inside by the children and patrons; shades have been put up at the windows; sanitary water-cooler and individual drinking-cups have been provided; lock has been put on the door; oil has been furnished for the floor; waste-paper basket has been furnished; and the most valuable improvement has been the seventeen-dollar equipment for a cooking-school.

All this was done from the proceeds of two entertainments given at the school. The total improvements made in the last three months have cost thirty-three dollars and fifty cents.

The school board appreciated the services of this teacher so much that after one month they raised her salary seven dollars per month and gave her lumber enough to put up a wood-house. The wood-house has been built by the patrons.

It is because there are many concrete instances like these that this special work of teaching the teacher on the job is spreading. State after state has put demonstrators into the field to supplement the inadequate professional equipment of its country teachers, to knit the school more closely into the community, and to continue the real work of education outside the schoolroom and extend it over twelve months in the year.

The West Virginia plan of district supervision, authorized by law in 1907, has attracted wide attention. The "district" in West Virginia is the magisterial district. In 1911–12 there were thirty-seven "district" superintendents, working in nineteen counties the minimum number of schools to one superintendent being fourteen, the maximum sixty-seven, with one hundred and twenty-six teachers. In 1912–13 the number of district superintendents was increased to fifty-eight in twenty-seven counties.

Although West Virginia has a compulsory school-attendance law, it has been found that since the appointment of district supervisors the average daily attendance in thirty-seven districts has increased from 68.7 to 85.8 per cent. The state superintendent argues that if the same rate of increase develops throughout the state, as he has reason to believe it will, it will so add to the daily attendance that the cost per pupil will drop from $23.92

to $18.40. His argument is a good one. If the teacher and the equipment are provided for thirty pupils and only twenty attend, there is an immense loss to the state not only in money, but also in citizenship. The work of the district superintendents has resulted in better daily programs and courses of study, better equipment and buildings, more school-libraries, a deeper interest among the patrons. And, most important of all, the quality of the teaching has greatly improved.

In 1911 Oregon enacted a law which provides that in each county having more than sixty school districts the county school board shall arrange all the school districts in the county, except the first-class districts, into supervisory districts. Each supervisory district must contain not less than twenty nor more than fifty school districts. A district supervisor is placed in charge of each such supervisory district, and must devote his entire time, for at least ten months in the year, to the supervision of his schools. His salary is fixed at not less than $100 nor more than $120 per month. The State Department of Education makes a very favorable report of the effect of this law.

In 1912 Kentucky authorized the appointment, by any county board of education, of county supervisors, to supervise the schools under the direction of the county superintendent.

North Dakota, by law, provides for one or more assistants to county superintendents having fifty or more schools.

Maryland has enacted a provision similar to that of North Dakota.

In Pennsylvania the school law of 1911 provides that every county superintendent with more than two hundred teachers under his charge shall have one assistant; with more than four hundred teachers, two assistants; with more than six hundred and less than eight hundred, three assistants; and for every additional four hundred teachers, or fraction thereof, shall have an additional assistant. The minimum salary for each assistant is $1,200 a year.

The work of the supervising industrial teachers in a few counties in Virginia, South Carolina, Alabama, Mississippi, and Louisiana is similar to that of these district superintendents, except that more emphasis has been placed by them on simple industrial work. Many of them also, after supervising the schools during the session, organize garden clubs in the spring and act as demonstration agents in gardening, poultry-raising, and domestic science for the girls and their mothers during the vacation months. They are thus employed from nine to twelve months during the year. They do anything and everything that will improve the school and community life. They insist on painted or whitewashed schoolhouses, on clean school-yards, clean windows, clean rooms, clean floors, fresh air in the schoolroom, clean outhouses, and clean children. They help the teachers to arrange their daily programs; often teach classes; introduce cooking, sewing, manual training; show the teachers how to correlate work; visit the homes of the people; organize school leagues; hold patrons' meetings and talk improved home conditions; raise money for school improvements, and in every way possible relate the work of the school to the life of the community. They help the teacher do the next thing, usually by showing her how to get the pupils and parents to do it.

To aid them in systematizing their work the supervising teachers are required to submit a monthly accounting of their time.

In April, 1911, the state supervisors of rural schools from ten states met in Jacksonville, Florida, organized, and worked out a program of coöperation. The constructive plans adopted by this conference are so full of promise for the development of a coherent program common to all the states that they deserve wide publicity.

A. *Rural School Survey*

As its first action the conference agreed upon plans for an educational survey in each of the ten states represented. The purpose of this survey is to collect and tabulate the facts that will set forth the status of the rural schools in each county. This survey has been started in four counties in nearly all the states represented. The plan is to add a few counties each quarter until each state is covered.

The result will be a collection of facts concerning:

I. The Rural Schoolhouse and its Equipment:
   The bare, cheerless one-room frame, on through the various types to the modern house, showing the dreary, forbidding surroundings of the farmers' children at school.

II. The Teacher, setting forth:
   A. What her training has been.
   B. What has been her career as a teacher.
   C. How she is doing her work.
   D. Her salary, with cost of living.
   E. The difficulties that beset her.
   F. How her efficiency can be increased.

III. The School, exhibiting:
   A. Attendance:
      1. The children's ages, health, etc.
      2. What per cent. are in school:
         (a) the entire term;
         (b) part of the term;
         (c) not at all.
   B. Instruction:
      1. What is taught, with lists of subjects.
      2. Number of grades and classes; number and length of recitation periods, etc.
      3. The methods of teaching:
         (a) Traditional and fruitless.
         (b) Semi-effective.
         (c) Effective.
      4. The training each child gets.

IV. Conditions that Determine the School:
  A. The multiplicity of schools in the district and county, and the causes that produce this.
  B. Small amount for maintenance of each school.
  C. System of administration and its influence on the school.
  D. Result.
  E. Is it possible for such conditions to command the services of a trained teacher?
  F. How can favorable conditions be brought about?
V. The People:
  1. Their conception of the function of the school and their attitude toward it.

The county superintendents and teachers are taking a zealous interest in the investigations, hence the supervisors expect to gather the fundamental data needful in working out the problem of rural-school development.

B. *Constructive Plans*

The members of the conference agreed that:

1. The fundamental necessity is a content for the rural school. What exists is traditional and well-nigh worthless. It was further agreed that this content is to be worked out through experimental and demonstration schools.
2. To create conditions that will make it possible for trained teachers to work in the country, existing schools must be consolidated, wherever consolidation is feasible.
3. As it is impossible even then for the existing institutions to train a sufficient number of teachers for the schools, the teachers must be trained in the schools. This demands a system of expert supervision.

It is believed that taxation will become an easy matter when the schools are made vital and effective. The question now is the best system of taxation. Shall the burden rest upon the local district, upon the county, or upon the state?

The general working-plan can be summarized as: 1. Content; 2. Consolidation; 3. Supervision; 4. Taxation. Exceptional conditions in one state impel the supervisor to put taxation first. In other states the supervisors deem concurring efforts advisable.

I. The Content of the Rural School:

To get at the bottom facts the supervisors are investigating the causes of the impotency of the traditional school, the results of which will be duly submitted. Various constructive plans are under way; the most notable of these is the experimental effort at Rock Hill, South Carolina, the purpose of which is to work out a germinal school which will transplant itself.

II. Consolidation:

The conference agreed upon plans for collecting data concerning consolidation possibilities, plans, and prospects. Each county superintendent will be furnished with blank forms for:

A. A statement showing—revenues of the district for school purposes; expenditures; number of schools, etc.

B. A statement of the cost of maintenance for the existing schools and of the cost of the new central building with equipment, along with estimate of maintenance for the consolidated school.

C. A pen-sketch showing:

1. The central school toward which weaker schools are gravitating, or the new center, with the surrounding schools.

2. Distances between schools.

3. Number of children in each school, with estimated number in the consolidated school.

4. Number of school-wagons.

D. A map of the county showing consolidation possibilities.

E. A statement setting forth:

1. The causes that are working for consolidation. Why are some schools gravitating toward a central point?

2. What keeps consolidation from tak-

ing place? What hindrances and influences are holding it back?

3. What is needed to remove these hindrances? What must be done to bring the consolidation about at once? This will show what supplement may be needed for local resources or efforts.

III. Supervision:

The state supervisors are formulating plans to show:

A. The waste of public funds due to the lack of efficient supervision.

B. The present status of supervision in each county; area, number of teachers and schools nominally under supervision; salary and efficiency of the county superintendent, etc.

C. The necessity for the immediate introduction of expert supervision seen in:

1. The untrained teachers that fill the country schools. Inexperienced young women and young men selected from the brighter pupils of the schools, often children of trustees or of parents who have influence with trustees.

2. The fruitless methods of teaching handed down from past generations. The training of the teacher in modern methods is the next task.

3. The perpetual changing of teachers from school to school. A teacher seldom remains in a school two successive sessions. The school thus develops no individuality. Children four months with a teacher, eight months out of school, and then comes a stranger. Continuing intellectual effort unknown.

D. The supervisors are therefore working out plans for:

1. Organizing the school system so as to make supervision possible.

2. Training the teachers now at work
in the schools.

Beginning next fall, when the survey is under way the quarterly reports of the state supervisors will exhibit:

1. The results of the investigation, with the present status of the rural schools, ending with a collection of data for the entire state.
2. The consolidation plans and prospects, with statement of what has been accomplished.
3. Supervision plans and prospects, with a statement of what has been accomplished.
4. Progress in legislation and taxation.

These reports will contain the data needful in any effort for the development of our rural schools.

To collect data and to focus it on the vital problems, the conference created the following permanent committees:

1. Legislation and taxation.
2. Course of study.
3. Community activities of the school.
4. Consolidation.
5. Supervision.
6. Experimental schools.

The reports of these committees, to be submitted a year hence, will set forth the year's achievement and recommend the next thing to be done, along with ways and means.

It is a big work—that of carrying first aid to the citizen-maker. It consists in holding up the hands of ill-trained, inexperienced teachers, struggling alone in the little one-room schoolhouses at the thousands of dim crossroads all through the land. Sometimes the supervising teacher must show some discouraged Miss Hopkins or Miss Briggs how to teach some particular little thick-head his lessons; sometimes she must persuade a reluctant school board to call for a larger tax levy, even if they can't see the object of the extra month of school it is to pay for; sometimes she must show by personal use of the broom what a schoolroom free from cobwebs and with a garnished floor looks like—she must do the next thing, whatever it is. It is her job to make the work of the teacher effective, to fill in the gaps between the teacher's training and efficiency. It will be many a long year before all the teachers in our rural schools will be able to attend the normal schools and training classes; the only hope of securing efficient teaching in the rural schools within the near future is to send first aid to the inexperienced teachers on the job.

XIII

THROUGHOUT the United States the county is the unit of rural-school supervision, except in New England and Ohio, where the unit is the township; New York, where the unit is the district, which may be a county or only part of a county; Virginia, where the unit is the division made up of one or more counties; and Nevada, where the unit is the district made up of from one to six counties. In thirty-eight states the rural schools have no supervision except that given by the county superintendent. In twenty-eight states the county superintendent is elected by the people in the same manner as other county officers. In Maryland, Louisiana, North Carolina and Georgia he is appointed by the county board of education, and Iowa has recently passed a similar law; in Tennessee he is appointed by the county court; in Indiana by a county board composed of trustees, one from each township; in Pennsylvania by a county board composed of township school directors; in Delaware by the Governor; and in New Jersey by the State Board of Education. The district superintendents of New York are elected for five years by district boards of directors; and the division superintendents of Virginia and of Nevada are appointed by the state boards of education for a term of four years. In other states the term varies from four to two years. In nineteen states the county superintendent is elected biennially by the people; changes are frequent; and in only seven of these nineteen states is he required to have teaching experience. In some states the county superintendents are expected to be administrators; in some, supervisors; in some, both; and in still others, neither. As a supervisory unit the average county is too large and contains too many schools for efficient supervision by the county superintendent. To meet this difficulty the office of assistant county superintendent has been created in certain states for the supervision of school programs and methods of instruction. In some states some of the excessive burden of the county superintendent's work has been shifted to district superintendents, supervising teachers, state inspectors and supervisors. But this movement toward efficient supervision is progressing very slowly. In some states the county superintendent is still overworked and underpaid; the office, therefore, fails to attract the best-trained men, and as a result the rural schools and the rural communities suffer for want of intelligent leadership.

But here and there the very difficulties of the situation have made an especial appeal to the patriotism of men and women capable of seeing the relation of the rural-school problem to community and national prosperity, and they have done work of far-reaching and permanent value.

If it is asked what the county superintendent can do for the good of his community, the answer is, What can he not do? His real difficulty lies in an excess of opportunity. To begin with, there are his routine duties—the administration of the county school funds, the examination and certification of teachers, the keeping of statistical records and making reports to the county board and the state superintendent of public instruction, conducting teachers' institutes, and visiting schools for general supervisory purposes. But as the rural school becomes the center of community life—the training-ground for citizenship in the widest sense of the word—and as assistants are provided to relieve him of the details of supervision, the county superintendent faces unrivaled opportunities for developing and rebuilding his county socially and economically.

We know a county superintendent of schools who, upon assuming office in 1903, faced a school situation that had not advanced six months in twenty years. The county was thinly settled and financially poor; the schoolhouses were wretched; the taxes were utterly inadequate; the teachers poorly paid; the term short; the people had ceased to hope for good schools. The former superintendent had "visited" the schools regularly, giving as many as two hours to each school in the year; he had sent in monthly and annual reports to the state superintendent; had held a one to three day funereal affair called a "teachers' institute"—all this for twenty years! And yet in 1903 there was not a sanitary school-building in the county, not a library or a debating club, not so much as a thought of making the school a meeting-place for the community, or in any way relating its work to the community life. When the new superintendent—with the extravagant salary of four hundred dollars a year—took hold he first made a survey of actual conditions and then asked himself: "What is the matter here? What is back of this sterile educational condition?" And he saw several things that answered his questions. The roads were very bad, thus keeping people from the markets, from the churches, and from the schools, from social visits and gatherings. He hunted out the few people who were interested in good roads, joined with them, and helped to organize a good-roads movement.

There was only one telephone line in the county, and only two telephones on that. He saw at once that the isolation of the people could be overcome first by telephone lines and then by roads. He saw that with telephones throughout the county, people would be able to get to market by voice if not by body, could talk with one another, could save hours and even days of time in innumerable ways, and could thus enlarge their community life. What particularly appealed to him was the isolation of the country *women* during the winter months. He talked the matter over with three or four—one of them an active good-roads man—and a telephone company was organized. He became general manager, and, though laughed at by many, he talked telephones all over the county while visiting schools. And while talking telephones he talked good roads and good schools. In a year's time the entire county and five or six adjoining counties were networked with telephone lines, and he could talk with most of his school trustees and to many of his teachers at any hour of the day, wherever he happened to be.

The building of telephone lines was his first step toward improving the schools, because it was the first step in breaking up the terrible isolation of country life. While building telephone lines and visiting schools he came into contact with all classes of people, stayed in their homes, and talked better conditions in season and out. When he left the superintendency in 1905, after two years of agitation, the school and road questions were getting warm, indifference had given place to earnest advocacy or violent opposition, and when that stage is reached the battle is practically won. The good-roads advocates and the good-school advocates have kept together—they need each other—and in the past six years there has been more improvement in roads and schools than in the previous thirty-five years combined!

This is rural leadership: To inventory actual conditions; to diagnose the underlying trouble or community disease; to show the people how to organize the forces that produce a cure; to "stay by the job" with a persistent, unconquerable, fearless determination. This is rural leadership as one county superintendent of schools understands it.

Four years ago a vacancy occurred in a county superintendency. A young preacher who had formerly taught applied for the place and was elected. Asked why he had decided to leave the ministry for school-work, he replied that he was leaving the pulpit only for a time: "The greatest need of these people right now is education," said he. "There are several preachers in this county, but nobody is working for better schools. When this county has adequate schools I may resume my work in the pulpit." With a zeal not surpassed by Paul, with tact and great energy, with absolute fearlessness, with definite policies, he is transforming the schools of his county. From a place near the foot of the list his county system has climbed to a position among the half-dozen best school systems in the state. Working on a salary of about seventeen hundred dollars, he spends probably half of it in pushing his work and in helping ambitious girls to attend one of the state normal schools. The county has been there for generations; the schools for more than forty years. When he took hold the school system was where it had been for decades. What caused the change? This superintendent put his great energy and heart and brain into his work. He temporarily left the ministry to place educational opportunities in reach of all the children of his county. He has linked himself with every forward movement in the county. He is not uneasy about his "job." He is not thinking about that side of his work. He long ago placed that matter in the hands of God, and is giving every ounce of brain and heart and energy to finance adequate and beautiful buildings; to make the school the community center; to get the best of teachers and pay them good salaries. He has a vision—an intelligent sympathy with every movement that makes for the improvement of life—economic, social, moral, mental, physical—in his community. That is leadership. That is the opportunity of the county superintendent of schools.

Three years ago a board of education deliberately refused to re-elect a university graduate as superintendent in a county, and selected in his place a man who had only a high-school education. The man selected had previously taught a year or two, and then had gone to work on a railroad; when elected he was farming. He was a school trustee—the most active trustee in his county. It seemed very unwise to turn down a scholar for a man with limited education. Why was it done? Because the scholar did not get anywhere. All his motion was up and down, and never forward. The other man had an enthusiasm for schools that amounted to a passion. He is now revolutionizing educational conditions in his county. In two years he has done more than was done in the previous thirty-eight years. What was the difference between these men?

The scholar made his round of "visits"; shook hands with the teachers; talked platitudes to the children; made out his reports; talked about the importance of education; deplored the indifference of the people; and folded his hands in pious resignation over the sad condition of affairs. The other man made his round of visits, too, and saw things and told the people about these things. He shook hands with the teachers, and then he turned in and shook the people and shook them hard. He did not stop at deploring the indifference of the people; he began to wake them up. And to-day he has the whole county aroused—those in favor of better schools stirred because the schools are not better, and those opposed to taxation stirred because they see the school tax going up to a figure that will get results.

One night this superintendent, while on one of his visits to country schools, stopped at a modest home in a remote rural community. An old ramshackle school which had been locked upon with contempt for many years had been displaced, and under his aggressive leadership a nice new building had taken its place and had just opened. He spent the night at this little home, and learned that the little boy and girl in the home had never gone to school and that their parents were not sending them to the new school. Neither of the parents could read or write.

He talked with them very seriously about the importance of educating these children, and soon persuaded them to let him take the two children to school the next morning. He took them in his buggy, drove the short distance to the school, and had them enrolled. A few months later he had occasion to visit this school again, and stopped at the same home to spend the night. After tea, when the supper-table was cleared, the children and both parents took their seats around the table, and in a few minutes the children were teaching their father and mother how to read and write. He learned that they were being given lessons regularly by the children.

This superintendent has enthusiasm; he thoroughly believes in what he is doing; he has definite policies; he is determined to have a good school in reach of every child in his county; and he has every opponent of school progress on the defensive. He has a heart that reaches out through his hand to every child in his county. He believes that the children should have a square deal. That is rural leadership—the opportunity of the county superintendent of schools.

Do not misunderstand! We are not decrying scholarship. Scholarship is a good thing to have on one's person if one has common sense enough to control it. But if it makes one a Pharisee, woe be to his soul and to his enthusiasm! If it short-circuits one's energy, wherein is every-day life benefited? Scholarship is a great thing if well used. Like money, it should be put to good use and not hoarded or selfishly used. We have plenty of mere scholars in the world! Oh, how many of them we have! But the thing that moves this world is enthusiasm, and when well directed it is the power that makes the wheels of the world go round. The need is for scholarship that is consecrated to human betterment.

Two years ago a new superintendent took hold of a large county that was in a very bad way educationally. There was that dreary expanse seen in so many country districts: wretched school-buildings; poorly paid, disheartened teachers; indifferent attendance; no interest in the schools among the masses of the people. This condition had existed for thirty-five years. After working at the problem a year this county superintendent concluded he would kill two birds with one stone—improve the school-buildings and grounds and at the same time arouse the interest of the people in their schools. How did he go about it? He sent out a circular asking the patrons to come to the schoolhouse on Washington's Birthday. He stated that the children would have appropriate exercises, and that he wished the people to bring hoes, axes, brooms, paint, and other materials to clean up and improve the schools and school-grounds. He got the teachers and pupils stirred up, and they in turn stirred up the patrons.

What was the result? There was never before such a celebration of the birthday of the Father of his Country! The people turned out by the hundreds. They came with their dinners and stayed all day. They cleaned up the schoolhouses and school-yards; they painted and whitewashed school-buildings; they built fences; they formed school leagues—one of the most potent factors in rural-school work; they contributed money for school libraries, and maps, and flags. They did in one day for their own schools what probably could not have been done otherwise at an expense of several thousand dollars. And, better than all this, they got an idea and an example of the good of community effort—of coöperation—and became interested in their schools by putting their own hearts and time and energy into school improvement.

Washington's Birthday was never celebrated more appropriately anywhere. To clean up a schoolhouse and its environment is more patriotic than raising a flag over a dirty shack! Is it not clear that it is much easier to get the school levy increased; much easier to talk improved school conditions; much easier to interest the people in consolidated schools; much easier to get things done for schools in that county than ever before? That superintendent touched a chord that awakened other chords. He saw a strategic opening. He skilfully used it. And that is leadership.

The following incident occurred in a mountain county: A stream and gorge separated two communities that would otherwise have been only one community. There were two small schools to serve these communities. The new county superintendent believed it would be a good idea to make the two communities one community by building a good foot-bridge and building one nice, central school. But he found that for years the county supervisors had refused to build a foot-bridge for this purpose, claiming that it was up to the school trustees, while the school trustees declared they would build schoolhouses, but not bridges. And through this kind of pig-headedness that exists in so many communities the children had for years been deprived of a graded and high school. But the new superintendent went at the matter quietly. He told the trustees that the children, not the supervisors, were being hurt, and he got their agreement to furnish the materials if the supervisors would do the work. Then he approached the supervisors and told them in turn that their refusal thus far had hurt the children, not the trustees. He asked the supervisors if they would agree

CELEBRATING WASHINGTON'S BIRTHDAY

"THE PEOPLE TURNED OUT BY THE HUNDREDS. THEY CLEANED THE SCHOOLHOUSE AND THE SCHOOL-YARD."

to build the bridge if he could get the trustees to furnish the material. They consented. Whereupon he informed them that the deal was closed. The bridge was built; the new central school was built; these two communities have now been fused into one community, and they have a modern consolidated school.

"That is a very small thing," some one may say. Yes, but all big things are made up of many small things. It is the power to fuse many small things into one great whole that spells success and means the capacity to lead. And it is because so many school-people sit down and wait for some big opportunity to come along, and refuse to take hold of the first thing and the next thing, that we do not have better schools and better coöperation and better conditions in our rural communities. The school superintendent or principal or teacher who "despises the day of small things" will never go far along the road to success. There is not any small thing when that thing is an effort to improve life. And if a worker for better social conditions, whether through schools or otherwise, thinks that anything is too small for his great mind and his transcendent dignity to notice, the smallness is in him, not in the thing that waits to be done.

The greatest work for the regeneration of society is not being done in the high places. The kindergarten is but a little thing—just a little group of children spending two or three hours a day with a teacher who is planting in their hearts the ideals of a social democracy. The United States Senate is a big thing; and yet the kindergarten has probably done more in the last twenty years to regenerate human society than the United States Senate.

Leadership is needed everywhere, and nowhere is there more crying need for it than in our rural communities. What kind of leadership? Not a leadership that successfully organizes one group to prey upon another group; not a leadership that successfully organizes one business to beat down another business; not a leadership whose success means the destruction of a rival. Such leadership is degrading in purpose and in result. We need a leadership that spells better social conditions, better citizenship; a leadership that succeeds, not through competition and not through combination for selfish purposes, but through coöperation for the benefit of humanity. That kind of leadership bruises no hearts, taints no character, begets no human despair. If it destroys, it destroys only that which obstructs social progress.

The task of the schoolman of to-day is to organize Life itself through the school. That school alone completely justifies itself which consciously, constantly, and sympathetically reaches out, touches, and improves every social and economic interest that concerns its community.

If this is the proper conception of a school; if education is not merely the learning of books, but the development of power for service; if it is not merely the development of power for service, but the development of interest in and the desire to serve every phase of life in a community, it follows that a superintendent of schools or a principal or a teacher may make himself the instrument for the proper organization of life in his county.

What has been the reason for the haphazard growth of our communities, whether city, town, or county? Why is it that in the great majority of our communities those things which touch the civic life have, like Topsy, "just growed," unorganized, unthought-out, unbalanced, temporary, unsatisfactory, leading usually into a blind alley? Has it not been because we have had so few leaders with a vision?

Not in the history of this country have there ever been such opportunities for leadership as are offered to-day to rural-school superintendents. There is so much to do, and they have such a splendid vantage-ground, that it is almost impossible to overstate the opportunities that lie in their grasp to transform the communities in which they live.

Now, we have all had tons of advice from every conceivable source as to what a superintendent should do: He should visit the schools, and he has done so; he should advise with the teachers, and the poor things have certainly been dosed with advice; he should talk with the pupils, and most of the children can repeat in their sleep the platitudes they have heard from his lips; he should make reports, showing how many visits he has made to the schools, and the state departments are filled with his records; he should hold teachers' institutes, and they have been held throughout this country, year in and year out, where the teachers have met and discussed such thrilling topics as "How to Maintain Discipline," "How to Teach Grammar," "The Value of Latin," "Is Corporal Punishment Necessary?" etc. And yet 60 per cent. of the country schoolhouses in the United States are unfit, from the standpoint of health and sanitation, for the use of children. Tens of thousands of schoolhouses are not schoolhouses, but shambles. In tens of thousands of them the work is purely and absolutely formal, and in these the schoolroom, instead of being a place of life, is a place of death to youth and hope and enthusiasm. What is the matter? A lack of aggressive leadership; a lack of a vision as to what the school is, and what its possibilities are.

In every community will be found one or more persons who would like to do something for the improvement of the roads; another group is interested in public health; another group, in better schools; another group, in more scientific methods of farming; another group, in community libraries; another group, in providing lectures and other entertainments for the community; another group, in athletics and play.

The county superintendent better than any one else

can and should interest each of these groups in the work of all the other groups, and cause each group to see that by "joining hands all 'round" a complete transformation of the community can be accomplished. He should link himself sympathetically and actively with the state boards of health, agriculture, and public highways, and try to get each of them severally and in a body to coöperate with him in the improvement of his community. It is not necessary that the county superintendent should be an expert in road-building, or in public health and sanitation, or in scientific farming, or in athletics, but he should be expert enough to know the difference between a good road and a mud-puddle, to detect the superiority of brain-farming over elbow-farming, to know the difference between the teacher who arouses the enthusiasm of the children and one who casts the shadow of death wherever she goes.

It is a rare thing to find a man or woman who combines the vision, the patience, the aggressive will, and the administrative talent to bring together into one organized whole the various groups that may be found in almost every community, so that there may be a coöperation that will bring great results. Why are they rare? Why should not every county, why should not every rural community, have leaders of this type? All of these activities lie within the domain of education. Education is the development of all life, not of one section or of one compartment of life. If this is true, think of the various things that may very properly occupy the attention of a county superintendent —proper health conditions in and around the school, including ventilation, lighting, proper school-hours, and play; attractive school buildings and grounds; consolidation and transportation; community and school libraries at the school; community entertainments at the school; public sanitation and hygiene; good roads leading to and from the school; better conditions on the farm, including better gardens, better farming, better water-supplies, and better sanitary conditions in and around the homes. Do not all these things tend toward the improvement of life, and do they not properly come within the domain of education? Think for a moment what would be the result in this country if next spring and summer every child who left the schoolroom, from the sixth grade up, should have an intelligent conception of all these necessities and an enthusiastic desire to secure them for their communities!

The schoolroom should give the children these civic ideals. It can be done, it should be done, it must be done, if we are to conserve our natural resources; if we are to cure national inefficiency and conserve national efficiency; if we are to prevent national decay; if we are to solve the human problem. A superintendent may say that his community is not interested in any of these things, but he is mistaken. Some person or persons can be found who will be interested in at least one of these activities, and that is all that is really necessary. Starting at Nowhere with Nothing and getting Somewhere with Something is, after all, the real test of useful leadership. This nation would be transformed if every school-worker would do his or her *usual* work in so *unusual* a manner that the *unusual* would become the *usual!*

It is not necessary to wait to perfect a scheme or plan. It is, of course, all-important to have a definite and wise plan, but there are, alas, so many people who are not willing to undertake anything unless every obstacle has been met and overcome *before the plan is even started!* Such people are vanity and vexation of spirit. They are moral cowards who always see a lion in the path. They desire to wait until somebody else has worked out the plan. Suppose everybody sat back and waited?

Others are afraid that they will make a mistake or do a new thing awkwardly. Better make several mistakes and do things very awkwardly than to sit still and do nothing. It has been wisely said that "many of our fairest schemes fail because of their very perfectness."

"This is the King's business and requires haste," and the county superintendent needs to take hold, and to take hold *now*—to take hold of something definite for the improvement of the rural community through the schools; to assume an aggressive attitude; to take his official life in his hands, or rather to place his official life in the hands of the Lord God, and go to work; if necessary, to fight, and to let it be known once for all that he is enlisted not for a battle, but for the whole war.

A county superintendent who is not fearless should have the "recall" applied to him. He should understand that if not fearless and aggressive in behalf of the children, he will be marked for slaughter, and that if he does his duty he will be protected by the school authorities at any cost. If he does his duty faithfully he has a hard time; it is then that he most needs the active support and protection of his superior officers.

And is it not high time superintendents were letting it be known that they propose to champion the cause of the country children and help them come into their long-withheld heritage of opportunity; their long-denied right to a healthy body, a trained capacity, and a desire to serve the state? Who can doubt the issue of battle? In a fight for children's rights there can be but one outcome. And if superintendents are afraid of the fight they should get out of school-work. A school superintendency, whether state, county, or city, is the last place on earth for a moral coward, or a place-seeker, or an unconsecrated man or woman.

We speak of the "fundamentals" in education—what are the fundamentals? A sound body, a trained capacity, and an unselfish outlook on life. And yet year in and year out we permit the children to go to school and to

THE COUNTY SUPERINTENDENT

acquire arithmetic and adenoids; history and hookworm; algebra and astigmatism; cube root and consumption; Caesar and spinal curvature. And then they go forth to serve—themselves! Now what doth it profit a state if its children gain the whole world of knowledge and lose both health and the soul of good citizenship?

Superintendents and teachers are engaged in one great work. They fight ignorance and inefficiency, which know no state lines. An illiterate child in Virginia is a matter of grave concern to Iowa; a diseased child in Iowa should awaken grave concern in Vermont. If ignorance and disease scorn state boundaries, surely all school-workers can take a national outlook and consecrate their manhood and womanhood to the regeneration of human society through the twenty million children of our public schools. It is not money that is most needed, but that which money cannot buy—a consecrated leadership that not only preaches a crusade, but lives a crusade in behalf of American childhood.

XIV

THE STATE SUPERINTENDENT OF PUBLIC INSTRUCTION

IN some of our states the state superintendent of public instruction is an administrator; in others he is a supervisor; in others he is both; in some he is neither.

In nearly every state in the Union he is elected by vote of the people, and in nearly every state the people vote for a party name, not for a man or a woman who has a definite educational program and the experience and ability to carry that program out. In one or two states he is appointed and removable at will by the successful gubernatorial candidate of one or another party machine. Depending for his position upon the good will of a party or its momentary leaders, he is not likely to be too definite in advocating educational reforms that depend for their success upon the tedious process of educating the people to their importance. Definiteness and the courage of convictions are exceedingly dangerous things in a close state or in one in which the political leaders, and not the superintendent, control the educational department, and, what is more to the point, control the party machinery. Not only is his tenure of office nearly everywhere uncertain, but in several states is made short by enactment, and in a few states crass stupidity not only makes his tenure short, but makes it impossible for him to succeed himself.

The head of the extension work in one of the state universities says: "The boys' and girls' club work, which was started by the state superintendent, has been turned over entirely to this department. The change in state superintendents (every two years) made it almost impossible for a permanent policy to be developed."

Here is a revel of rotation that should make every political hack hopeful! The application of the pork-barrel philosophy of government to the office of state superintendent of public instruction has brought into contempt a position that should be one of the most responsible in public life. Dutton and Snedden in their epoch-making book on school administration have hardly one word to say for or about the state superintendent. Why should they? His local habitation is but temporary. His name to-day may refer to one who is addressing ten thousand teachers with authority; to-morrow to a peddler of encyclopedias or subscription books desperately struggling to keep his family alive, for his tenure of office, like his salary, is in almost all the states disgracefully short.

But here and there he is slowly rising above the miasma of partisan politics and pork-barrel philosophy. A few states have begun to recognize that the state superintendent of public instruction should be a man or woman with a vision of the true function of public education in a democracy, with a passion for public service, and a grasp of the possibilities of developing an efficient citizenship through the schools. In these states he is a permanent officer, appointed because of his special qualifications at an adequate salary, and removable only on public proof of incompetence or malfeasance in office. When this condition becomes universal the state superintendent will be administrator or supervisor according to the needs of the moment, but always helper, inspirer, organizer, and leader. He will be the central educational dynamo in his state, sending his power of sympathy, inspiration, and courage into every school.

Massachusetts looks over the United States and picks any one she thinks worthy of this great office, pays an adequate salary, and offers a life tenure for efficiency of administration and supervision. New York State does likewise. And New Jersey has shown a tendency to do the same thing, though the experiment is still too young there to show whether the office will be made, as it is in some other states, a part of the perquisites of the Governor, or will be regarded as above the changes and spoils of office.

This is not on the face of it an encouraging outlook. Such conditions and limitations do not invite the best talent to offer itself for educational leadership in the public-school systems of the states unless there happens to arise, as there sometimes does, a man or woman who is willing to make a personal sacrifice for a great cause; and this has often occurred, as the history of this office in many states will show. But it is not merely pathetic—it is tragic—that men and women of great capacity for leadership in this important office must make a large personal sacrifice or refuse to apply for the position. For of all offices in the state it is the one that should by permanency of tenure and by salary invite and demand the ablest leadership that can be found. Of all places it is the very last one that should be sought by the demagogue or the moral coward or the unconsecrated man. A traffic in the opportunities of hundreds of thousands of children is a sin so heinous that language halts in attempting to describe it.

The limitations attached to the office of state superintendent of public instruction in most of our states, the restrictions placed upon that officer in any attempt to administer and supervise the school laws for the purpose of making efficient citizens, are not unique to that particular office. It has been the history of all our public offices to a greater or less degree.

Indeed, it seems difficult for a people who attempt to govern themselves to see the folly of trying to administer public business by scattering and dividing responsibility. The folly of shifting administrations in great commercial organizations is a lesson our people have gradually learned through bitter experience. To invest large sums of money in a commercial enterprise and then to intrust that enterprise to amateurs, or to make the administrative position in that enterprise the prey of spoils politics, would be regarded by the smallest investor as recklessly unbusinesslike, and yet in our greatest business of all—the federal, state, and local government—that is precisely what we do. Our national government is run without a program and without any regard for business principles. In January, 1912, the Federal Commission on Economy and Efficiency completed a survey of the national government. In transmitting this survey to Congress the President said:

Never before have the foundations been laid for a thorough consideration of the relation of all the government's parts. No comprehensive effort has hitherto been made to list its multifarious activities or group them in such a way as to present a clear picture of what the government is doing. Never has a complete description been given of the agencies through which these activities are performed. At no time has the attempt been made to study all these activities and agencies with a view to the assignment of each activity to the agency best fitted for its performance, to the avoidance of duplication of work and plant, to the integration of all administrative agencies of the government into a unified organization for the most effective and economical despatch of public business. Administrative officials have been called upon to discharge their duties without that full knowledge of the machinery under their direction which is so necessary to effective control, much less have they had information regarding agencies in other services that might be made use of. Under such circumstances, each service has been compelled to rely upon itself, to build up

its own organization, and to provide its own facilities regardless
of those in existence elsewhere.

After a hundred years of self-government it required a
special investigation of a special commission to reveal
even to the officers of government precisely what the
federal government was. While our schools and colleges
learnedly expounded the Declaration of Independence and
the tri-partite division of federal authority under the
Constitution, while our newspapers entertained their
readers with cock-pit gossip of interdepartmental scandals
and the personal foibles of candidates and bosses, the
complacent voter went to the polls and took merit to himself for dropping a scratched paper into the slit of a box,
that, for all he knew, might just as well have been the lid
of an oven. If our government is in confusion, our public
business shot through and overgrown with inefficiency,
corruption, and graft, who is responsible but the complacent, self-satisfied citizen and his public-school system, and
his newspaper and magazine press, which, in response
to his demand, purveys rumor and gossip instead of
facts?

We are a business people. We glory in our commercial
triumphs. We make no secret of the fact that we regard
ourselves as resourceful at a business transaction as the
Connecticut Yankee at King Arthur's court. The phrase
"a billion-dollar Congress" we like to roll upon our
tongues, and our complacency purrs when foreign observers
declare that such lavishness in public expenditure would
bankrupt a less opulent nation. We are a business
people; but how far do we apply our business intelligence
to that most vast of all our business establishments, the
federal government? In May, 1912, the Subcommittee
of the House Committee on Appropriations held public
hearings to ascertain the wisdom of continuing public
support to the President's Commission on Economy and

Efficiency. What follows is a characteristic fragment of the evidence:

MR. CLEVELAND (Chairman of the Commission on Economy and Efficiency): The only information that can be obtained about the current liabilities of the United States Government is the amount of Treasury drafts and checks on depositories outstanding and short-term loans and the matured debt. There are millions of dollars of obligations outstanding that nobody knows anything about, and as to whether the amount is $100,-000,000 or $50,000,000, no one can even guess. With this situation in mind we claim it is impossible for the Secretary of the Treasury to inform himself, or the President, or Congress, or anybody else about what is the current financial condition of the government of the United States. . . .

MR. FITZGERALD (Chairman of House Subcommittee): How does it happen that these are not rendered in the Treasury?

MR. CLEVELAND: The account in the Treasury is for money advanced to disbursing agents. These accounts do not show what obligations are paid until after vouchers are audited; that is, the record of payments is from three months to a year and a half behind. There are from $300,000,000 to $700,000,000 of unaudited payments not on the books. That is as close as you can get to the obligations of the government of the United States from the books of the Treasury.

What a commentary upon the civic purblindness of the American people! In May, 1912, not even the Secretary of the Treasury could come within fifty millions of guessing the actual financial condition of the federal government.

And as for business methods, the federal government still remains an almost unexplored kitchen-midden of obsolete practices. In a vague way we have known that the government employed in the neighborhood of four hundred thousand men and women, that it transacted a business as varied as that of the entire commercial world, and that it spent more than a billion dollars annually, and yet an investigation reveals that the government is neither coherent as a business organization nor efficient as an instrument of public welfare. On a magnified scale it possesses all the characteristics of a sprawling mushroom town. Through lack of coördination and planning its services are in a perennial state of partial demoralization; departments, divisions, bureaus that should be bound together by a common intelligence, a common purpose, and a conscious spirit of coöperation in the public interest are scattered, mutually ignorant of one another's activities and equipment, often hostile therefore, and at cross purposes. And because of this vast planlessness millions of public money run to waste.

This reckless folly runs through the administration of all our governmental activities—state, city, county, and district. Why does such a condition of affairs exist? It arises from two things: First, from the ingrained belief among the rank and file of our citizens that the public treasury is a general pork-barrel; that, national, state, city, county, and district governments being of, for, and by the people, their treasuries should be the common spoil of the people; and, second, from the hoary tradition that, since public offices and jobs are few in comparison to the total number of the people, there should be rotation and duplication in office so that as many faithful servants of the triumphant machine as possible may have their turn at the public trencher. For generations the public appointments have been determined not by the fitness of the candidate or by the wisdom of his program, but by his loyalty to the party machine and the lobbies back of the machine.

But the bitter fruitage of the belief that public business is for private ends and that public affairs can be efficiently administered with divided responsibility and by men inexperienced in the special business of their offices has caused a general awakening, a nation-wide revolt against the misuse of public office and public funds. In the reckless scramble for special privilege some of the people have gotten ahead, the majority have been "disinherited." It should have been manifest at the start that this result was inevitable. Our democracy cannot be successful until public office is regarded as a public trust to be administered in the common interest, and until public appropriations are voted, not as a reward for service to a lobby or machine, but for the execution of an intelligently considered program openly proposed by technical experts in the permanent civil service.

In the fundamentally important business of education— the making of efficient citizens from the raw material of childhood—the essential division of administration and supervision have been crippled and demoralized by the pervasiveness of this pork-barrel philosophy of government. Public education can never be successful in the best sense until the rank and file of our citizens understand, and until they compel our legislators to understand—and indeed refuse to send to the halls of legislation those who do not understand—that the function of the state superintendent of public instruction as the administrator in the public-school system is to see that every dollar voted in the educational budget goes for educational purposes, and that his function as supervisor is to see that the work for which money is spent is well done and done in compliance with the educational demands of district, county, city, and state. The welfare of our public-school system requires an educational program, an educational budget based upon that program, an administrative staff to look after the business management of educational funds, and a supervisory staff to look after the efficiency of the teaching force.

While, therefore, the outlook for a larger and more extended field of usefulness in this important office has been very discouraging, there is another side to it that is very encouraging. The opportunities for constructive statesmanship in educational policies are greater than ever before because of this awakening of the people everywhere in this country; because the people seem determined to take possession of their own governmental affairs—federal, state, county, and city—and to have these affairs administered and supervised intelligently and sanely for the general welfare. This awakening of the people promises a just and proper appreciation of intelligent and unselfish leadership and service—an appreciation that will not permit it to be hampered and endangered by partisanship and by the use of public office for private ends.

The state superintendency has never been the place for the man who, while using it as a stepping-stone to something "better," has himself proven a stumbling-block to educational progress. And to-day, when public education has taken on a new meaning; when that meaning has broadened from academic scholarship to include also a training in all the activities of life; when the demand is made that education shall have as its conscious purpose the making of an efficient citizenship; when the business of education has grown to such enormous proportions that it reaches into and has much to do with the affairs of every county and district and community and home; when, in fact, it influences to an increasing extent every individual in the state and nation, and affects his mental, physical, industrial, and social welfare—a type of leadership is demanded that calls for initiative with a clear outlook and a broad comprehension, for training of the highest order, for moral courage that will not compromise the rights of the children; for a consecration that not only believes in the sublime work of making citizens, but lives that belief.

Initiative, training, courage, consecration—all are essential, but in importance the last is first, for without consecration the other qualities will not have the "staying" quality necessary, while with it they will be permeated with enthusiasm—with a passion for service.

THE STATE SUPERINTENDENT

In the organization of country life it is necessary to go into "the very heart of the people's every-day experiences"; and this is the work of the rural schools. The state superintendent, then, must have, first, an educational program. To have a sound educational program that will be of lasting benefit to the people whom he represents he must be intimately acquainted with the history of his people, with their customs, their traditions, their ways of living, their aspirations, their limitations, their industrial and social conditions, their capacities. He must be intimately acquainted with the educational programs of every other state in the Union, else he will, as has been so often done, mistake his impulses and those of others for educational principles and policies, and will thus dissipate or misdirect the opportunities of generations of children who are to be future citizens of his commonwealth. This lack of knowledge, this provincial conceit, has been disastrous in nearly every line of governmental effort in this country.

For the same reason he must be intimately acquainted with the educational program of the United States Bureau of Education and with the information which the Bureau so gladly furnishes to seekers after knowledge. He must be acquainted with the educational programs of other countries in so far as they relate to the problems, present or future, of his own state. All of this requires hard study and extended research and comparison. It requires a proper perspective, and this in turn requires a constructive imagination.

But a knowledge of these problems and programs, and a definite program of his own, are of no value unless they are made of service to others. This knowledge and this educational program must be disseminated in bulletins and circulars and articles, and in addresses informing and educating the people to the support of this program. There is no greater field for effective service to-day by a state superintendent of public instruction than in a continuous and state-wide campaign on every phase of public education. To conduct such a campaign on an intelligent basis and in a manner to impress the hearts and convince the minds of the people he must understand the legitimate function of public education—to produce efficient citizenship.

He must understand that an efficient citizen is one who has health of body, a trained mind and hand, and a desire to serve the state. He must appreciate, therefore, that public education has to do with the health of the individual child and with the public health; and he must understand and be able to discuss questions of lighting, ventilation, sanitation, recreation, fatigue, in their relation to the school program. He must have both the desire and the intelligence to coöperate with the state board of health and with the local health officers in bringing about the highest efficiency in the enforcement of sanitary regulations in the school and in the community.

He must understand clearly the close relations between good roads and good schools, between bad roads and poor schools; he must be able to discuss intelligently and interestingly the effect of good roads in encouraging the consolidation of schools and the effect of consolidation in encouraging the building of good roads. He must be able to show the tremendous increase in power for public service that can be secured by the advocates of good roads and the advocates of good schools through coöperative organization for the benefit of both.

He must understand clearly what is meant by linking up the life of the school with the life of the community; what is meant by life-fitting schools; what is meant by organizing and directing the normal activities of the children and by concentrating these activities upon the every-day activities of the community; what is meant by evolving, from the experiences of the children in their

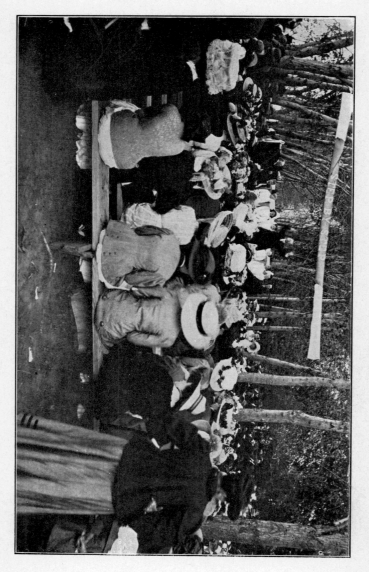

A Lecture on Farm Sanitation in Iowa

relation to the experiences of the community, a course of study; what is meant by taking the experiences of the children—their fund of knowledge with which they come to the school—and capitalizing these experiences by directing them through the channels of arithmetic, language, grammar, reading, geography, history, spelling, botany, drawing, music, literature, upon the community activities. He must understand clearly and must be able to convince the people at large that the educational process is just as good out of the schoolhouse as it is in it, if it is good at all; that education is education whether it is in a home, in a garden, out on the farm, under a tree, in a schoolyard, or in a schoolhouse.

He will understand and be able to make it clear to his constituency that education is a matter of life for life, beginning with life and ending with life, and not a matter of childhood for childhood, beginning with childhood and ending with childhood. He will convince the people, therefore, that the child should not be in school five or six or eight or ten months in the year for a term of years and then stop being educated, but that he should be undergoing the educative process in school and out of school all the time. He will understand and he will convince the people that if anything in life is worth doing it is worth doing well, and whether it be work or play, whether it be plowing a row of corn or reading Greek, whether it be studying music or studying tomatoes, whether it be digging a ditch or performing an operation in surgery, it is best done when he who does it has been trained to do it with efficiency and with a passion to do it better than it has ever been done before. With this view of education for efficient citizenship he will plead for an organization of all the people to educate all the people for the benefit of all the people; that every man may find his place, may know his work, and may do it in coöperation with his neighbors.

The state superintendent must understand clearly and

profoundly that the fundamental business of the country people is production on and out of the land; that agriculture is the basis on which all other businesses rely. He must see that the time is now at hand when the rural public school controls the food supply of the nation. He must understand that this is the era of education in agriculture; that agriculture must no longer be, in the words of Seaman A. Knapp, "a series of motions inherited from Adam," but must be one of the "learned professions." He must not only see that the boy and the man who desire to make a living out of the land shall be trained for that profession as carefully as the doctor and the lawyer must be trained for their professions, but he must understand, and be able to make his constituency understand, that the present courses of study do not permit this, that they are lopsided, and that the country boy and girl are entitled to an education that functions in living on the land and dealing with the soil. He must arouse the people to insist upon a school program that provides not only for the training of the children in the school and on the school-garden and school-farm, but also for the training of these children in their homes, in their home-gardens, and on their home-farms.

He will understand clearly that much of the home has gone into the factory; he will understand the importance of educating boys and girls in the economics of the home, in a home efficiency that will get the maximum of results for every mental and physical effort put forth. He will be able to explain the relation of these things to legitimate school-work and the illegitimacy of any school-work that does not function in home efficiency.

In shaping a school program for the rural schools the state superintendent will see the necessity of extension and demonstration work done by and through the school. He will understand and he will be able to convince the adult communities that it is the business of the school to give a practical instruction in all phases of agriculture to the boys and girls, not merely at school, but at their homes. With power he will plead for a course of instruction that will reach the thousands of boys and girls, young men and young women, middle-aged men and middle-aged women, who work inefficiently because untrained, but who desire a training that is not only adapted to their needs but is adjusted to their hours of labor; and he will use all of his influence to see that every school program shall be so shaped that it will reach old and young—men and women, boys and girls—wherever a human being desires instruction.

But unless he is superficial in his knowledge and vision and purpose he will see that the school program shall not only include extension and demonstration work that trains the boy and his father how to double and quadruple production on the farm, and that will train the girl and her mother how to double and quadruple production in the garden and in the poultry yard, but shall also include the vital study of the proper marketing of these products. He will understand definitely that increased production directly affects the price of land and the rental value of land. He will know that increased production by a boy or man, girl or woman, does not always mean the increased prosperity of the producer, and he will see the relation that exists between the owner of the land and the increased production, whether the owner increases the production or not. He will believe that it is legitimate work for the rural school to teach its students, young and old, how to organize purchasing and selling agencies for the benefit of its members; how to coöperate in all matters of marketing. He will make a study of rural credits and the value of coöperative credits.

He will understand, and will say to his constituency, that the training of Johnny and his father, and of Mary and her mother, to double or quadruple production will be of no benefit to them if they are to be the victims for just that much more exploitation by the land-speculator, the commission-merchant, the middleman, the corporation, or the individual whose purpose is to make money out of the labors and the increased efficiency of Johnny and his father, of Mary and her mother. If Johnny and Mary and their parents do not own the land, there in not a state in the Union that protects them from exploitation by land-owners who are not land-users, and there is not a state in the Union that does not tax the industry of these parents and their children for the sake of the man who owns the land but does not himself use it. The state superintendent will understand that the man who owns the land owns the man on the land, and he will in his campaigns of education ask the citizens of his state what it profits the state or Johnny to train Johnny to get more corn on an acre, of which he is not the owner, if the owner of that land or of similar land at once raises the price or the rent so as to realize a fat interest or return on Johnny's increased efficiency.

These are issues which the state superintendent should have no inclination to avoid, because they are inextricably interwoven with the work of the rural school, if that school is to make efficient citizens, and if that school is to secure to these citizens the reward of their increased efficiency.

For the state superintendent to say that these are matters of politics or of legislation or of governmental policy outside the domain of education is for him to confess either that he has not the courage to face the issues involved or that he does not believe that the function of public education is to produce efficient citizens. Either the land question must be considered in connection with extension and demonstration work by and through the schools, or that work must be stopped. Now that Uncle Sam is no longer giving away land, now that free land is not increasing in area while people are increasing in number, the question of the exploitation of Johnny and Mary is becoming more and more acute.

There are tens of thousands of Johnnys and Marys who desire to make a living on the land. Their attention is being called to the possibilities of a good living on the land by the extension and demonstration work that is being done throughout the United States. They are learning scientific agriculture and gardening, and as soon as they become of age they will seek land on which to make a living based on their scientific knowledge taught them by and through the schools; but most of these tens of thousands of Johnnys and Marys do not own any land, and Uncle Sam has no more to give them. How are they to get it? While there are tens of thousands of Johnnys and Marys without land and wishing to get it in order to make a living, there are millions upon millions of acres of vacant land on which these Johnnys and Marys are not permitted to go, because these acres are held off the market by speculators who refuse to use the land for any purposes except to farm the profits out of these Johnnys and Marys; and so these land-seekers who desire to use the land are debarred from that use by landowners who themselves refuse to use the land and who refuse to permit its use unless Johnny and Mary consent to produce, not for themselves, but for these landowners.

And if Johnny and Mary, in their eagerness to make a living out of the land by becoming producers on that land, rent the land and cause its acres to produce two or three times as much as they ever did before—which they have been taught to do by this extension and demonstration work—what will be the result so far as Johnny and Mary are concerned? In his book on *Land and Labor—Lessons from Belgium*, Rowntree says, "Every improvement in agricultural methods, every fresh discovery which goes to increase the yield from the land, every economy of labor, whether by means of machinery or of coöperation, has two results—the immediate raising of the small holder's profits and the ultimate raising of his rents." And again he says, "It has been shown that the advantages arising from the development of transport facilities, good agricultural education, the wise employment of chemical manure, coöperation for the economical purchase of feed-stuffs and seeds, and the energy spent on improving the live stock, ultimately go past the tenants to the owner of the land."

The state superintendent will realize that this is a question of to-day, and that wisdom demands a campaign of education among the people to bring about a just treatment of the tens of thousands of young men and young women whose attention is being directed to a living on the land. He will see the injustice and the folly of using the public school—which is the greatest organization on earth for the making of efficient citizens, and to which organization the nation must look for its food-supply— he will see the folly of using this organization to arouse the interest of tens of thousands of young men and women in agricultural production and to teach them how to double and quadruple the production per acre, and then supinely permit the continuance of a land policy that puts a premium on the ownership of land without using it, and puts a heavy tax on the use of land without owning it. It will be hard for him or any one else to explain to Johnny and Mary why the man who owns the land but does not use it is lightly taxed, while the man who uses the land but does not own it is heavily taxed. It will be hard for him to explain to Johnny and Mary why the man who uses land is heavily taxed on his industry, while the man who owns land but does not use it is lightly taxed on his idleness. The state superintendent will educate the people at large to see that, while America has been called the land of opportunity, there is no opportunity except in land, and that this has been the land of opportunity only because in the past it has given every seeker an opportunity on the land.

Closely allied to the extension and demonstration work through which alone is there any escape from national hunger, and inextricably interwoven with which is the land question, is the matter of taxation and finance. Everywhere the schools are suffering for lack of money, everywhere the opportunities of the children are thwarted, because the money that should go to the schools is withheld. Large sums are wasted in the public business that might well be used for educational purposes, but large sums also never reach the public treasury that in common justice belong to the public. The public is daily creating values, and is then permitting private interests to gather these values instead of insisting by law that these values created by the public shall be collected by the public for the public use. Were this done, the children's opportunities would not be hampered, their development would not be limited, and there would no longer be a lack of funds for the purpose of educating the seventeen million children and youth of our land for efficient citizenship. The state superintendent will see, and in his campaigns of education will instruct the people in, the close relationship existing between the rural-school work, the land question, and the question of taxation.

A county superintendent of schools said to a state superintendent of public instruction: "My county runs right up to the city of W——. Our tax rate is at the maximum allowed by law, and yet our schools are suffering for lack of money. What can I do?" "How about your assessments?" asked the state superintendent. "Oh," said the county superintendent, "the assessments are very low." "Is that because the land is without value?" "Oh no, the land is very valuable. Land speculators are selling the land in lots at a much higher price for each lot than an entire acre is assessed for taxation." "Well," said the state superintendent, "what makes that land valuable enough to sell in lots?" "Why, it is because people wish to get out of the city and build on them." "Well, what makes the land valuable, then—the fact that it is owned by somebody who has not improved it, or the fact that the people living near it have made it valuable?" "The fact that large numbers of people live near it," said the county superintendent. "Then if the people have made it valuable why do they permit private individuals to reap the value? Why don't the people reach out and take for the common welfare the values made by the people? My suggestion to you is to go back home and preach justice in taxation and to urge upon the people to quit fining industry by taxation and to get rid of the parasites."

The state superintendent of public instruction will be able to present both to the people at large and to their representatives in the state legislature the best principles and methods of financial aid by the state for the promotion of education in the local communities. Realizing that the work of the rural school is to produce efficient citizenship, he will advocate state aid that will not pauperize or pensionize the local communities, but will stimulate them to the largest degree of self-help; that will give the greatest amount of aid where it is most needed; that will distribute the financial aid of the state according to the needs of the communities, and not according to the dictates of political expediency. He will, of course, from his study of the experiences of other states, understand that the mere giving of money by the state without attaching legitimate conditions is fatuous. He will see the folly of a statement recently made by one educational leader that the rural-school problem in his state had been solved because the state had given one thousand dollars to each rural school. He will know that problems are not solved in this way. He will fully understand that the nearer he gets to a definite educational program the nearer he gets to the solution of the problem of finance. He will understand that a financial budget does not precede, but follows, an educational program, and that the lack and the waste of public-school funds arises mainly from a lack of understanding and appreciation of this stern fact.

The states which have gotten the most satisfactory results from the expenditure of school funds are those which have both local and state school taxes and which give state aid only for specific purposes and follow up the gifts with close inspection. It is everywhere recognized now that unconditional gifts from the state are largely wasted and probably do more harm than good. Funds for specific purposes given by the state with certain conditions attached have been exceedingly fruitful in results; as, for example, a state high-school fund, a graded-school fund, a daily-attendance fund, an agricultural-education fund, a manual-training fund, a transportation fund, etc., followed by close inspection and given on condition that the local communities shall do so much for themselves in the way of finance before receiving this aid. Almost any community will make a special and sometimes extraordinary effort to meet the state conditions by local taxation and local contribution in order to secure the state funds.

A large number of states have one or more of the state school funds mentioned above. North Dakota has an excellent law to encourage the association of rural schools into one group for the introduction of industrial work, and Minnesota has a similar plan. The state superintendent of public instruction, having familiarized himself not only with the laws in the various states in regard to state aid, but also with the results which have been obtained from the workings of these laws, will inform the people, and will prevent much of the half-baked legislation with which so many of the states have been afflicted in the past, because of the ignorance of legislators who regard their impulses as thoughts.

The state superintendent, realizing that the sole purpose of public education is to produce an efficient citizenship and that this efficient citizenship must be based upon a healthy body, a trained capacity, and a desire to serve the state, will advocate before the people plans for the proper training of those who are to be the citizen-makers—the teachers—so that these citizen-makers may go to their work with the highest degree of trained efficiency and with a full knowledge of the purpose for which they are sent. He must be able to argue, to debate, to plead, to convince, for he will need to break through the crust of custom and the thickness of tradition, which have accumulated about our courses of study and which have done so much to perpetuate class education, which has no place in a democracy.

Gathering about him and consulting with progressive leaders in education, in agriculture, and in all the other activities that touch rural life, he will formulate a school program that will encourage the proper functioning of the school-work in terms of citizenship. He will make it clear to his constituency, and especially to all those engaged in school-work, that life is more than raiment, and that the life of the children as shown in their enthusiasms, their interests, their experiences, and their activities must not be wrapped up in the raiment of formalism, of red tape, of statistics.

Having formulated an educational program, and having in his campaigns of education enlightened the people as to this program, he will have little difficulty in presenting an educational budget that will have the sympathy and support of an educated public. He can then show the necessity for expert assistants to act as an administrative staff to look after the business management of educational funds and of a staff of supervisors to look after the efficiency of the teaching force.

THE STATE SUPERINTENDENT

Is this an impossible task for a man occupying the position of leader to thousands of teachers and hundreds of thousands of children? Is it asking too much of a man who has the opportunity and the privilege of actually shaping the character of the citizenship of his state for generations to come? Can anything be too much to ask at the hands of a man or a woman who has or who seeks the most important office in any commonwealth in the Union? Such men and women have been among us, such men and women should be demanded by the peoples of our states, and such men and women should be encouraged to seek this position of leadership, and should be protected in this position as long as they exhibit those qualities that make a great educational leader—initiative, training, courage, and consecration.

INDEX